'This is a welcome addition to an area of growing interest and importance. Not only does the book cover all the major areas of interest, it has valuable mini cases that lend insight and each chapter has useful revision questions to aid student understanding.' – **Professor Paul Burns**, *Professor of Entrepreneurship and Dean, The Business School, University of Bedfordshire, UK*

'This valuable text on social enterprises is well written, clearly structured and informative. It serves as an excellent guide on how to create and maintain sustainability – emphasising the role of the social entrepreneur – and is supported by interesting case studies and examples. It should have considerable appeal to all actual and aspiring social entrepreneurs as well as to students seeking to understand or engage in this emerging field. The authors are to be congratulated on complementing the existing literature.' – **Ken O'Neill**, *Chair in Entrepreneurship and Business Development at the University of Ulster, Northern Ireland*

'An excellent and much needed publication. We can no longer ignore the importance or potential of social enterprise. Increasing worldwide interest in social enterprise recognises that we cannot afford to create wealth through enterprise that is divorced from our social objectives, our common values of equality and justice and our desperate need to preserve a sustainable planet.

Neither can we underestimate the complexity and subtlety of the movement we have started. Social enterprise is not business nor is it community development. It is a new discipline where the rules are being made daily by practitioners, activists and "social entrepreneurs".

The time has come for us to consolidate our knowledge and share our experiences. The time has come for the academic world to value and foster our new methods of management and governance. The time has come for a book such as this.' – **Cliff Southcombe**, *Managing Director, Social Enterprise Europe*

'Provides a comprehensive and well-researched guide for current and aspiring social enterprise leaders alike. It is worth paying attention to the international case study examples, which are particularly illuminating.' – **Matt Jarratt**, *Social Enterprise London, UK*

'A thorough introduction to social enterprise. Highly readable, presenting many of the current debates and dynamics in the sector and exploring pertinent issues for social enterprises on the road to sustainability. A valuable addition to the growing body of knowledge in this area.' – **Ranjit Bansal**, *Social Enterprise West Midlands, UK*

social enterprise
developing sustainable businesses

Frank Martin

and

Marcus Thompson

palgrave
macmillan

© F. Martin and M. Thompson 2010

All rights reserved. No reproduction, copy or transmission of this
publication may be made without written permission.

No portion of this publication may be reproduced, copied or transmitted
save with written permission or in accordance with the provisions of the
Copyright, Designs and Patents Act 1988, or under the terms of any licence
permitting limited copying issued by the Copyright Licensing Agency,
Saffron House, 6–10 Kirby Street, London EC1N 8TS.

Any person who does any unauthorized act in relation to this publication
may be liable to criminal prosecution and civil claims for damages.

The authors have asserted their rights to be identified as the authors
of this work in accordance with the Copyright, Designs and Patents Act 1988.

First published 2010 by
PALGRAVE MACMILLAN

Palgrave Macmillan in the UK is an imprint of Macmillan Publishers Limited,
registered in England, company number 785998, of Houndmills, Basingstoke,
Hampshire RG21 6XS.

Palgrave Macmillan in the US is a division of St Martin's Press LLC,
175 Fifth Avenue, New York, NY 10010.

Palgrave Macmillan is the global academic imprint of the above companies
and has companies and representatives throughout the world.

Palgrave® and Macmillan® are registered trademarks in the United States,
the United Kingdom, Europe and other countries

ISBN 978–0–230–20372–3

This book is printed on paper suitable for recycling and made from fully
managed and sustained forest sources. Logging, pulping and manufacturing
processes are expected to conform to the environmental regulations of the
country of origin.

A catalogue record for this book is available from the British Library.

A catalog record for this book is available from the Library of Congress.

10 9 8 7 6 5 4 3 2 1
19 18 17 16 15 14 13 12 11 10

Printed and bound in Great Britain by
CPI Antony Rowe, Chippenham and Eastbourne

contents

list of figures

list of tables

list of examples

list of minicases

preface

This is a book about social enterprises and how they can be managed so as to be successful in the longer term. Social enterprise is now a much used term and its use has almost matched the use of the words enterprise and entrepreneurship in the economy. However, the main feature of this text is not a discussion or review of social enterprise as an emerging element of the economy. Rather, it is about what it takes for a social enterprise to sustain and develop its activities. Hence the sub-title of this text, 'Developing Sustainable Businesses'.

Essentially we are examining what makes or will make a social enterprise successful and how different social enterprises are from other forms of business. It is argued here that good business practice is needed for a successful social enterprise just as good business practice is needed for the success of any enterprise.

The aim

The aim of this book is to help you understand the essence of the entrepreneurship, management and leadership tasks in a social enterprise, and whether or not this differs from the same elements in any business. We also want to present suggestions for good business practice in a social enterprise setting and to stimulate your thoughts on how a social enterprise should be managed with the longer term in mind.

Who should read this book?

This book is aimed at anyone with an interest in social enterprise but particularly at students studying social enterprise at universities and colleges with perhaps a view to starting or joining a social enterprise at some point in the future. It is also aimed at the staff in social enterprises and at those individuals who are working to support the development of the social enterprise sector especially in the support network. The text has been written in the UK and this obviously provides us with much of the context for the book. We have however consciously sought to relate to social enterprises in many other countries and to connect these examples to the material within the book.

Thank you

The authors would like to thank you for at least looking through this text and we hope it will have met your needs in this area in some small way. We are always acutely conscious of the fact that everyone with a product or service needs customers. This certainly applies to this text and to the social enterprise sector. If you meet the needs of your customer the enterprise should flourish!

acknowledgements

The authors and publishers wish to thank the following for permission to reproduce copyright material:

Virtue Ventures for the extract from 'Operational Models in the US', source: www.virtueventures/setypology (accessed June 2009); and Figure 9.1 'Hybrid Spectrum', source: 'Social Enterprise in Context', Virtue Ventures LLC (2007).

Harvard Business Review for Figure 3.3 'The Five Phases of Growth', L. Greiner, 'Evolution and Revolution as Organisations Grow', *Harvard Business Review*, vol. 50, July–August (1972), pp. 37–46.

The San Francisco Chronicle for an excerpt from '3 of region's brightest win "genius" fellowships', Sabin Russell, *The San Francisco Chronicle*, 19 September 2006, www.sfgate.com.

Pearson Publishing for Figure 4.1 'Spotting Opportunities' from Wickham, P. A. (2006) *Strategic Entrepreneurship*, 4th edition, FT/Prentice Hall; and Figure 5.2, 'Vision, Mission and Strategy' from Wickham (1998) *Strategic Entrepreneurship*, 3rd edition, FT/Prentice Hall. p. 133.

Orion Books for Figure 7.3 'The Ethic/Profit Trade Off' from Goldsmith, W. & Clutterbuck, D. (1984) *The Winning Streak*, Weidenfeld & Nicolson, London.

The Big Give for Minicase 7.1, 'PAYES', excerpted from www.thebiggive.org.uk.

Martin Stead and Gerard Hastings for Figure 7.5 'Social responsibility in marketing', after MacFadyen et al. (1999) and the excerpt from *A Synopsis of Social Marketing* by Lynn MacFadyen, Martine Stead & Gerard Hastings (1999). The Institute of Social Marketing, University of Stirling, www.ism.stir.ac.uk/pdf_docs/social_marketing.pdf.

Social Marketing Quarterly for Figure 7.6 'Social & Ethical Delivery', R. J. Marshall & L. Petrone, 'Positioning Social Marketing', *Social Marketing Quarterly*, Washington, DC, Vol. 10, Issue 3 & 4, 2004, pp. 17–22; and 'An Ethical Checklist for Social Ethical Marketing', Donovan, R. & Henley, N. (2004) 'Social Marketing: Principles and Practice', *Social Marketing Quarterly*.

The Social Audit Network for Figure 8.3, 'The SAN Social Accounting and Audit Process', source: www.socialauditnetwork.org.uk.

Sage Publishers for Table 9.2, 'Managerial Role Change', source: Hood, C. (1995) 'Contemporary Public Management: A New Global Paradigm', *Public Policy and Administration*, 10 (2), p. 271.

Emerald Group for Figure 9.2 'Entrepreneurial Mindsets', source: Thompson, J. (1999) 'A Strategic Perspective of Entrepreneurship', *International Journal of Entrepreneurial Behaviour & Research*, Vol. 5, No. 6, pp. 279–96.

Cengage Publishers for Figure 9.3, 'EVR Congruence', source: Thompson, J. & Martin, F. (2005) *Strategic Management: Awareness & Change*, 5th edition, Thomson Learning, p. 126.

Every effort has been made to trace all copyright holders, but if any have been inadvertently overlooked the publishers will be pleased to make the necessary arrangements at the first opportunity.

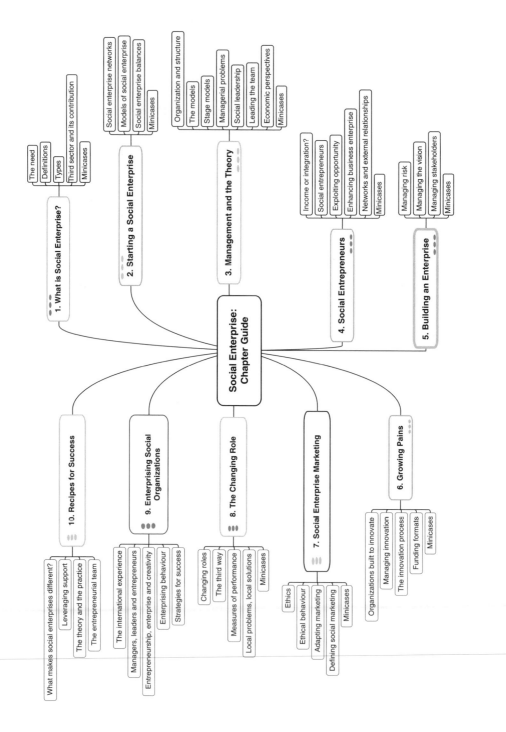

Social Enterprise: Chapter Guide

1. What is Social Enterprise?
- The need
- Definitions
- Types
- Third sector and its contribution
- Minicases

2. Starting a Social Enterprise
- Social enterprise networks
- Models of social enterprise
- Social enterprise balances
- Minicases

3. Management and the Theory
- Organization and structure
- The models
- Stage models
- Managerial problems
- Social leadership
- Leading the team
- Economic perspectives
- Minicases

4. Social Entrepreneurs
- Income or integration?
- Social entrepreneurs
- Exploiting opportunity
- Enhancing business enterprise
- Networks and external relationships
- Minicases

5. Building an Enterprise
- Managing risk
- Managing the vision
- Managing stakeholders
- Minicases

6. Growing Pains
- Organizations built to innovate
- Managing innovation
- The innovation process
- Funding formats
- Minicases

7. Social Enterprise Marketing
- Ethics
- Ethical behaviour
- Adapting marketing
- Defining social marketing
- Minicases

8. The Changing Role
- Changing roles
- The third way
- Measures of performance
- Local problems, local solutions
- Minicases

9. Enterprising Social Organizations
- The international experience
- Managers, leaders and entrepreneurs
- Entrepreneurship, enterprise and creativity
- Enterprising behaviour
- Strategies for success

10. Recipes for Success
- What makes social enterprises different?
- Leveraging support
- The theory and the practice
- The entrepreneurial team

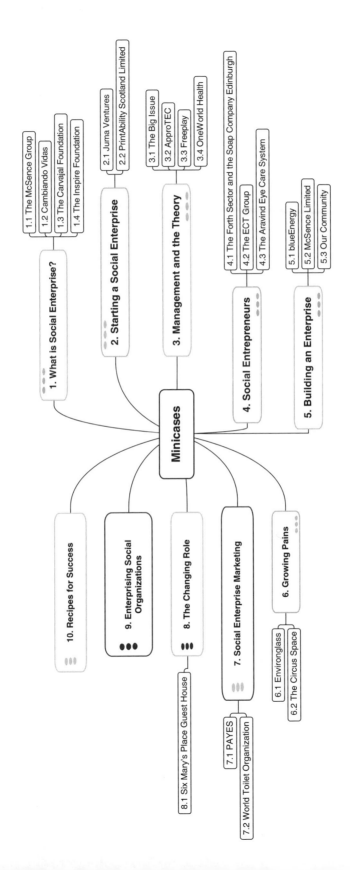

Minicases

1. What is Social Enterprise?
- 1.1 The McSence Group
- 1.2 Cambiando Vidas
- 1.3 The Carvajal Foundation
- 1.4 The Inspire Foundation

2. Starting a Social Enterprise
- 2.1 Juma Ventures
- 2.2 PrintAbility Scotland Limited

3. Management and the Theory
- 3.1 The Big Issue
- 3.2 ApproTEC
- 3.3 Freeplay
- 3.4 OneWorld Health

4. Social Entrepreneurs
- 4.1 The Forth Sector and the Soap Company Edinburgh
- 4.2 The ECT Group
- 4.3 The Aravind Eye Care System

5. Building an Enterprise
- 5.1 blueEnergy
- 5.2 McSence Limited
- 5.3 Our Community

6. Growing Pains
- 6.1 Environglass
- 6.2 The Circus Space

7. Social Enterprise Marketing
- 7.1 PAYES
- 7.2 World Toilet Organization

8. The Changing Role
- 8.1 Six Mary's Place Guest House

9. Enterprising Social Organizations

10. Recipes for Success

1 what is social enterprise?

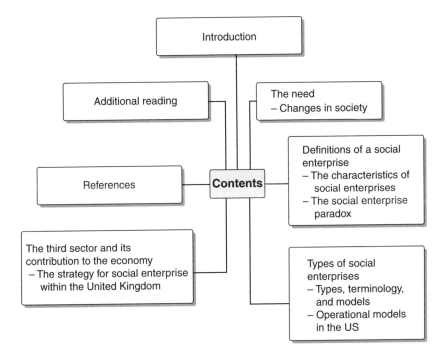

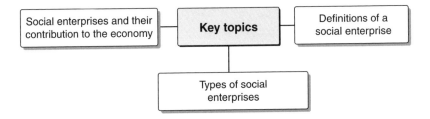

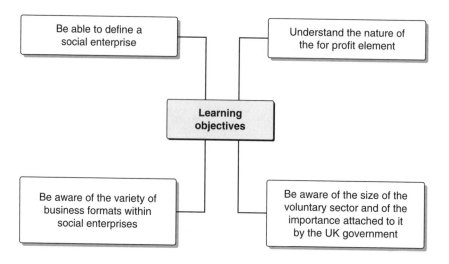

Introduction

Chapter 1 sets the scene for understanding social enterprises within the wider business community. It looks at how policymakers currently view the role of social enterprises in the economy. At this stage, we are looking at the larger and economic issues that drive and affect the formation and performance of social enterprises and why governments and others of influence seek to encourage the 'social economy'. To help understand policy, the former Department of Trade and Industry (DTI) publication entitled *Social Enterprise: A Strategy for Success* has been used as a central plank to define how most socially orientated firms see this issue. The role of the DTI and of the Department of Business, Enterprise and Regulatory Reform (BERR) is now subsumed into the new Department for Business, Industry and Skills (BIS).

From this we will seek to present an overview of the many operational models that could be used to set up and manage a social enterprise. We will also introduce one of the comparator themes within the book: the difference between the US approach to thinking about the overall social enterprise model and the perceived different approach adopted in Europe.

Finally, this chapter will look at the scale of the social enterprise sector in the United Kingdom to highlight the importance of this significant sector within the overall economy. After the first chapter we will look at individual enterprises and how they can be managed successfully.

The aim of this chapter is not simply to define social enterprise but to discuss the changes that are taking place in this new and emerging business format.

The need

It is easy to start any textbook on social enterprise by looking at the definitions of a social enterprise and to list the many different forms that make up our understanding of the concept. Yet what we are really examining is quite often very simple: social entrepreneurs. These are people who are inspired to believe in a social cause and who decide to do something about it. *The classic bias for action.*

To explain, we start with the phrase: 'Poverty robs us of our dignity'. However it is not just poverty that robs people. It is also hunger, disease, and waste (a waste of human life). It is not just the poverty-stricken who are directly the victims of these conditions. Because these conditions are so widespread throughout the world, they undermine all societies. At a recent executive education programme held at Wharton University many problem areas were examined.[1] One of the presentations was based on the present economic conditions in Haiti. The country is described as one of the poorest countries in the Western Hemisphere with 80 per cent of Haiti's nine million citizens living below the poverty line. People in Haiti are so poor they sometimes stave off hunger pains by eating cookies made of mud.[2] Some Haitians do have work in the sweat-shops of multinational companies, working all day in various garment-manufacturing factories for about $1 a day. The conditions in Haiti can rightly be considered to be less than humane. The Haitian government really does not look like it is capable of making a significant impact with respect to the plight of its citizens. So what next?

We can, in terms of Haiti, consider what it means to really live below the poverty line in that country. This is not easy. We can also point to an example of poverty robbing people of their dignity much closer to home. In Glasgow today, 35 per cent of children are in families who are on out-of-work benefit. In the UK as a whole this figure is 20 per cent. These children are considered to be living in poverty based on the criteria of the family being on out-of-work benefit (see www.ecpc.org.uk).

While the Haitian government is likely to be classed as a failed government, would we also classify the UK Government and the Scottish Executive as failed governments? Both Tony Blair and Gordon Brown, really, in this case, do seem to mean it when they set eradicating child poverty as a main goal of government. In June 2009 Prime Minister Gordon Brown introduced into parliament a Child Poverty Bill with the aim of taking 4 million children out of poverty by 2020. But fortunately (perhaps) the government does now seem to realize that it cannot solve things by itself and is actively embracing the idea of 'The Third Sector'.

Changes in society

Someone once said that the poor are always with us. The same could be said for hunger, disease, and waste. Today we are as a society much less likely to think that governments should and can solve these issues. We also have less confidence in institutions to solve these problems. To some extent in parallel with this view, there is more of a desire and belief that as individuals – social entrepreneurs, people within a social enterprise, people who care about others and about society – we can make a difference in what can be done. In the case of Haiti there is a clear need for alternative forms of enterprise based on improving the income and health not only of individuals but of whole communities.

This is particularly the case with Minicase 3.4 OneWorldHeath and in Minicase 4.3 The Aravind Eye Care System. In the case of OneWorld Health, $10 for a course of treatment can stop someone dying from the second most deadly parasitic disease in the world after malaria. The Aravind Eye Care system saves thousands of people from blindness for the cost of a few dollars.

Definitions of a social enterprise

Within the entrepreneurship and small firms' literature definitions are a thorny question. Those familiar with Winnie the Pooh might be familiar with the 'heffalump':

> [A] rather large and important animal. He has been hunted by many individuals using various trapping devices, but no-one so far has succeeded in capturing him. All who claim to have caught sight of him report he is enormous, but disagree on his particularities.
>
> (Kilby, 1979)[3]

The (social) entrepreneur 'heffalump' is discussed in Chapter 4, but the main focus throughout the book is less on the individual entrepreneur and more on the social enterprises that they form. The management question addressed is what would make these ventures succeed and how different are they from other forms of (small) business.

Within the UK there is a basic consensus on what constitutes a social enterprise. The most common definition that appears in texts written about social enterprise is

> [a] social enterprise is a business with primarily social objectives whose surpluses are reinvested for that purpose in the business or in

the community, rather than being driven by the need to maximise profit for shareholders and owners.

(DTI, 2002)[4]

This definition is derived from the DTI's *Social Enterprise: A Strategy for Success* published in July 2002. By this definition a social enterprise is a business that conducts trade in the market in order to fulfil its social aims. This means that it does not exist for the primary purpose of creating a profit for its owners in the way a conventional business would do. Instead it reinvests its surplus to achieve a specified social purpose.

Simply put, a social enterprise is a business venture that brings people and communities together for economic development and social gain.

Because it is considered a business rather than a charity, the social enterprise is expected to generate a surplus and that surplus is to be used for the benefit of the community that it serves. There are however, many forms that social enterprises can adopt in order to define more clearly their purpose for various categories. These categories are as follows: community enterprises, cooperatives, development trusts, charities with trading arms, credit unions, social businesses, mutuals, fair trade organizations, and social firms. Social enterprises are part of the wider social economy. Pearce (2003) adopts a three-system framework to the economy. System 1 covers the private system; System 2 covers the public planned economy; and System 3 being the third system, covering self-help, mutual and social purpose organizations. There is some confusion here over what is meant by the social economy, social enterprises, and the third sector, as these terms are used interchangeably.

We prefer a four system model: government, the private sector, and the voluntary sector, with for-profit social enterprise straddling all the others, seeking at times to be independent through the build up of income streams from a mixture of grants and funding from the other three.

While we are dealing with the wider social enterprise model we are concerned to define one category in particular within social enterprise, namely the social firm. In part this is to prevent confusion between the two – the social enterprise and the social firm. Example 1.1 provides a fuller outline of the role of social firms.

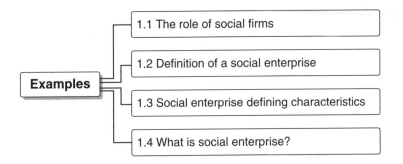

Examples
- 1.1 The role of social firms
- 1.2 Definition of a social enterprise
- 1.3 Social enterprise defining characteristics
- 1.4 What is social enterprise?

Example 1.1   The role of social firms

[A] social firm is a small business that provides employment opportunities for people who are disabled or disadvantaged in the labour market. Social firms have both commercial and social objectives. They operate in the market place generating income through sales of goods or services and they also employ a significant number of employees who have a disability who are fully integrated into the business. Social firms have a focus on developing a flexible, supportive working environment within a commercial operation. (Davister, Defourny & Gregoire, 2004)[5]

A good example of a for-profit social enterprise in action is to be found in the community-based operations of The McSence Group, provided as Minicase 1.1.

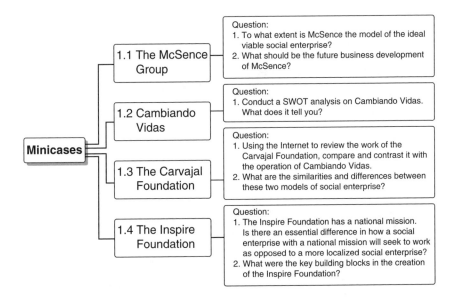

Minicases

1.1 The McSence Group
Question:
1. To what extent is McSence the model of the ideal viable social enterprise?
2. What should be the future business development of McSence?

1.2 Cambiando Vidas
Question:
1. Conduct a SWOT analysis on Cambiando Vidas. What does it tell you?

1.3 The Carvajal Foundation
Question:
1. Using the Internet to review the work of the Carvajal Foundation, compare and contrast it with the operation of Cambiando Vidas.
2. What are the similarities and differences between these two models of social enterprise?

1.4 The Inspire Foundation
Question:
1. The Inspire Foundation has a national mission. Is there an essential difference in how a social enterprise with a national mission will seek to work as opposed to a more localized social enterprise?
2. What were the key building blocks in the creation of the Inspire Foundation?

Minicase 1.1   The McSence Group

It was back in 1984 that Brian Tannerhill, a local resident in Mayfield, Midlothian, first initiated the idea of forming a Community Business that would provide employment and services to his local community. This business was to be called Mayfield Community Self Employed Natural Collective Exercise or, more simply, McSence.

The support of local businesses was crucial to the early development of McSence. At the outset Brian Tannerhill persuaded local traders to commit £5 per week for the first year as a contribution to the start up costs of the community owned business on the condition that it did not compete with any of the contributors. This initiative raised £7500 and resulted in local business people being invited onto the Board to provide invaluable business experience.

Since those early days, McSence has grown into a group of companies that employs over 50 local people and generates an annual turnover of approximately £1.2 million. These companies include McSence Heatwise, McSence Limited, McSence Services, McSence Workspace and McSence CyberCycle that cover insulation, office cleaning, renting of workspaces to local community groups and local businesses and training and employment initiatives for local people.

Profits generated by the companies are ploughed back into the local community with recent examples being the provision of a youth centre and sports equipment for local youngsters.

Source: www.sensscot.net and www.mcsence.co.uk, accessed December 2008.

McSence was set up in response to the devastating effect of the 1984 coal miners' strike to create employment that would pay wages to local people. McSence was started entirely by private funding without any government grant or subsidy and continues to be a business run for the community by the community. Any profits made by the five operating companies are passed back to McSence Limited and this money is used to invest in new ventures for job creation for local people and in the form of community grants.

Chris Shaw, Chairman of the Board of McSence Limited

QUESTION

1. To what extent is McSence the model of the ideal viable social enterprise?
2. What should be the future business development of McSence?

The characteristics of social enterprises

The DTI definition implies a series of characteristics that distinguish this form of enterprise. These characteristics have been referred to as

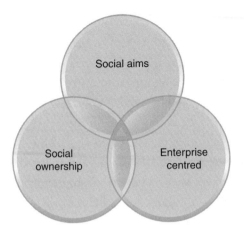

Figure 1.1   **The triple bottom lines**

'triple bottom lines' – aims that have been adopted by the social enterprise community to distinguish them from for-profit small businesses (Social Enterprise London)[6] see Figure 1.1.

Social aims

Social enterprises exist to serve a social purpose and in order to achieve this they conduct some form of trade. These social aims should be explicit and might include job creation, training or the provision of local services. Associated with the social aims social enterprises can be expected to have ethical values that might include local capacity building or addressing social disadvantage. They are accountable to their members and the wider community for their social, environmental and economic impact. They are also independent from public sector ownership and this makes them accountable to community stakeholders.

Social ownership

Unlike a conventional business social enterprises are not constituted to distribute profits to individuals but instead they hold their assets and income sources in trust for use by the community they serve. These are autonomous organizations that have governance and ownership structures based on participation by stakeholder groups (users or clients, and local community groups etc.). Profits are distributed for the benefit of the community or as profit sharing to stakeholders.

Enterprise centred

Social enterprises are directly involved in the production of goods or the provision of services to a market. They seek to be commercially viable trading concerns that make an operating surplus. While social enterprises may earn income from public service contracts and sales, they are not directly managed. It is the combination of these three factors: social aims, social ownership, and enterprise centred that defines the scope of their activities. Social enterprises are *hybrid* organizations that are expected to perform in the market like a small business but which retain the management ethos and values of locally defined charitable organizations. The tag 'triple bottom lines' may explain why this is an emerging term that is becoming used for a range of voluntary organizations that make the transition from a charitable to an enterprise orientation. In other words, a social enterprise does not just exist to create shareholder value through increased profitability, but encompasses a wider community stakeholder value of social awareness and environmental responsibility.

When putting together two words with meanings as broad as 'social' and 'enterprise', it generates confusion, especially at the international level.

This may in part explain the different approaches to supporting social enterprises in the US and Europe. This difference of approach will be covered in Chapter 9 and referred to further in this chapter. It also points to a paradox. A social enterprise can be viewed as a new form of business organization but it is one that is derived from two existing forms of business: small business and not-for-profit organizations. Social enterprises are hybrids and as hybrids they can be expected to inherit both the good and the bad forms of their for-profit and not-for-profit business cousins. They can be seen as being halfway between the two since they have dual objectives: to make a profit for their stakeholders (in their community) and to contribute to the broader social good, while making a surplus.

Because of this paradox, social enterprises can be expected to play down their levels of profit-making in order to emphasize their social and environmental values. In terms of competitiveness, and unlike their small business counterparts, they can be expected to be more co-operative with other social enterprises – working to achieve specified social gains within the community. Given the limitations of access to support and funding, co-operation is often more of an ideal than a reality in the social enterprise economy.

Types of social enterprises

Social enterprises combine the need to be successful businesses with social aims. Unlike profit-orientated SMEs they, ideally, will emphasize the long-term benefits for employees, consumers, and the community. They come in a range of business formats but the most common factor is that they are mostly, but not exclusively, local and community-based organizations. Their format encompasses community enterprises and mutual organizations such as co-operatives, alongside non-governmental organizations. As yet the format does not facilitate working, or co-operating internationally. Even within the European Union levels and opportunities for multi-lateral co-operation between the 27 member countries, remain limited.

Types and terminology

Within the UK, there is no single legal model for social enterprise. Social enterprises can encompass companies limited by guarantee, industrial, and provident societies, and companies limited by shares; some organizations are unincorporated and others are registered charities (DTI, 2002).

The following list is taken from the Development Trusts Association and encompasses the types of firms and terminology often associated with the social economy.[7]

SEL 'social enterprise' definitions

(a) Community business

A trading organization which is set up, owned, and controlled by the local community and which aims to create ultimately self-supporting jobs for local people and to be a focus for local development. The term community business is normally used for social enterprises that have a strong geographical definition and focus on local markets and local services.

(b) Community Development Financial Institution (CDFI)

A financial services provider (possibly a community based bank, community loan fund or a community development venture fund) which has a mission to achieve social objectives. Some CDFI's will focus specifically on financial services for business and social economy organizations rather than on the needs of individuals. They may provide equity, quasi-equity or debt services. While some UK CDFI's are regulated as banks or building societies, most do not have deposit-taking status. The legal forms most often used are the Industrial and Provident Society (IPS) and, in association with charitable status, the company limited by guarantee.

(c) Co-operative

An autonomous association of persons united voluntarily to meet their common economic, social, and cultural needs and aspirations through a jointly owned and democratically controlled enterprise. An Industrial and Provident Society is a body incorporated under the Industrial and Provident Societies Acts, including most Co-operatives, quasi-charitable societies for the benefit of the community, and some development trusts.

(d) Micro-finance

Small savings and loans facilities with no (or very low) minimum deposit; and other financial services like insurance, money transfer or bill payment designed for people on low incomes.

(e) Mutuals

They take many forms: credit unions, co-operatives, building societies, and employee-owned businesses. They are organized by their members who band together with the common purpose of providing a shared service for which they all benefit.

(f) Non-profit or not-for-profit

These terms are commonly used to describe organizations which do not distribute profits, although they seek to make an operating surplus.

(g) Social business

A term sometimes used by social enterprises where there is a small core of members who act in a similar way to trustees. These social businesses often focus on providing an income or employment opportunity for disadvantaged groups, or providing a service to the community.

(h) Social firm

A small business created to provide integrated employment and training to people with a disability or other disadvantage in the labour market. It is a business, which uses the market-orientated production of goods and services to pursue its social mission. A significant number of its employees will be people with a disability or other disadvantage in the labour market. Every worker is paid a market wage or salary appropriate to the job, whatever his/her productive capacity. Work opportunities are distributed equally between disadvantaged and non-disadvantaged employees. All employees have the same employment rights and obligations.

http://www.dta.org.uk/resources/glossary/selsocialenteprisedefinitions. htm (accessed in June 2009)

For the purposes of this book the working definition of a social enterprise is provided as Example 1.2

Example 1.2   Definition of a social enterprise

A social enterprise is a business venture that brings people and communities together for economic development and social gain.
Because it is a business, it is expected to generate a surplus and that surplus is to be used for the benefit of the community that it serves.

The defining characteristics are provided as Example 1.3.

Example 1.3   Social enterprise defining characteristics

Social aims
Social enterprises trade as a means of achieving these.

'Non-profit distributing'
Profits are reserved for reinvestment.
Social enterprise is not about amassing personal wealth.

Exercise some form of 'common ownership'
Usually owned in common by members and/or stakeholders.
Have some form of **democratic involvement** in management/decision making.

Exercise wider accountability
May be answerable to a 'constituency' of users, members, or stakeholders – sometimes a mixture of all three.
Tend to serve local communities.

Operational models in the US

Virtue Ventures, a US-based consulting firm specializing in social enterprise, have produced the following list of social enterprise operational business models:

- Entrepreneur support: The entrepreneur support model of social enterprise sells business support and financial services to its target population or 'clients', self-employed individuals or firms.
- Market intermediary: The market intermediary model of social enterprise provides services to its target population or 'clients', small producers (individuals, firm or cooperatives), to help them access markets.
- Employment: The employment model of social enterprise provides employment opportunities and job training to its target populations or 'clients', people with high barriers to employment such as disabled, homeless, at-risk youth, and ex-offenders.
- Fee-for-Service: The fee-for-service model of social enterprise commercializes its social services, and then sells them directly to the target populations or 'clients', individuals, firms, communities, or to a third party payer.
- Low-income client: The low-income client as Market model of social enterprise is a variation on the Fee-for-Service model, which recognizes the target population or 'clients' a market to sell goods or services.
- Cooperative: The cooperative model of social enterprise provides direct benefit to its target population or 'clients', cooperative members, through member services: market information, technical assistance/extension services, collective bargaining power, economies of bulk purchase, access to products and services, access to external markets for member-produced products and services, etc.
- Market linkage: The market linkage model of social enterprise facilitates trade relationships between the target population or 'clients', small producers, local firms and cooperatives, and the external market.
- Service subsidization: The service subsidization model of social enterprise sells products or services to an external market and uses the income it generates to fund its social programmes. The service subsidization model is usually integrated: business activities and social programmes overlap, sharing costs, assets, operations, income and often programme attributes.

- Organizational support: The organizational support model of social enterprise sells products and services to an external market, businesses or the general public.

Source: www.virtueventures/setypology (accessed in June 2009)

In addition, time and practice and the development of the social enterprise will mean that the very specific operational definitions given above will change and that we will see the combination of models to capture opportunities in both commercial markets and social sectors. Combining is a strategy to maximize social impact as well as diversify income by reaching new markets or creating new enterprises. In practice, most experienced social enterprises combine models, as few social enterprise operational models exist in their pure form. Operational models are like building blocks that can be arranged to best achieve an organization's financial and social objectives.

Model combinations occur within a social enterprise (complex model) or at the level of the parent organization (mixed model). An example of each of the model combinations is shown as Minicase 1.2 Cambiando Vidas (complex model) and Minicase 1.3 The Carvajal Foundation (mixed model).

Minicase 1.2 Cambiando Vidas

Cambiando Vidas (an example of a Complex Model social enterprise)
In 1999 a new paved highway opened along Mexico's formally isolated coastal fishing villages in Nayarit State. This opened up the area to tourists, and consequently, to large developers. The result was a dramatic shift in the local economy from fishing and agriculture to tourism and infrastructure development. The shift displaced local residents, most of whom are poorly educated peasants who lacked the know-how and capital to capture the changing market. In response, Cambiando Vidas – 'Changing Lives', an educational organization – launched a comprehensive, multifaceted rural development programme with complementary enterprise and social service components to preserve the local community and provide new livelihoods for its residents. Cambiando Vidas built a 'tool lending library' where residents could borrow hand and power tools and use them as implements in economic activities tied to tourism and construction. The second social component was a vocational training programme to teach construction skills – masonry, electrics, plumbing, and carpentry – to unemployed youth and adults in the community. On the enterprise side, Cambiando Vidas has initiated a B&B project and built (so far) six comfortable tourist rooms above

residents' homes. Income from room rental is divided between owners as family income, and a revolving loan fund to build more B&B rooms. Apprentices from the vocational training programme provide the labour to build the B&Bs and gain work experience in the process. Cambiando Vidas plan to create local employment by launching a construction business and bidding directly on small building contracts, where it has identified a viable niche, as well as subcontracting to large developers. Profit from the construction business will be used to fund the secondary education and vocational training programme.

http:// www. virueventures.com/setypology/index,accessed in December 2008.

QUESTION

1. Conduct a SWOT analysis on Cambiando Vidas. What does it tell you?

Minicase 1.3   The Carvajal Foundation

Encouraging self-help in Colombia (mixed model)

The Carvajal Foundation, established in 1961, is one of the oldest and best examples of social enterprise in the Latin American region. The foundation was launched through a sizeable donation by the Carvajal Family, which donated 35.54 per cent of its shares in its successful Colombian business operations. For more than four decades, the foundation has engaged in social development, mobilizing volunteers and large donations to catalyse change in the poorest communities across Cali. Carvajal's accomplishments include community-based programmes at the local level as well as national programmes, all of which have developed promising practices and economic development models that have been shared and replicated by other business and community groups in Colombia and elsewhere in Latin America.

As a social enterprise, the Carvajal Foundation has a firm commitment to its social mission to combat poverty on all fronts, and to deliver solutions that address community problems. The foundation's mission to realize the full development of individual potential is achieved mainly through education, entrepreneurial development, health care, housing, culture and arts, and environmental programmes, and incorporates business criteria into its activities, seeking to maximize operational efficiency and effectiveness.

Source: http://www.virtueventures.com/setypology/index,   accessed   in December 2008.

QUESTION

1. Using the Internet to review the work of the Carvajal Foundation, compare and contrast it with the operation of Cambiando Vidas.
2. What are the similarities and differences between these two models of social enterprise?

Based on the cases above, it becomes evident that social enterprises:

1. Facilitate enterprise or social programme growth.
2. Increase revenues by entering new markets or businesses.
3. Augment breath or depth of social impact by reaching more people in need or new target populations.

In this sense a social enterprise is an amalgam of different types of not-for-profit organizations. Each of the formats listed have specific structural differences in how they are organized. But, it is not appropriate to classify them according to a legal definition, based on articles of associations or taxable status. It is the element of looking outside the legal status of a business, and the elements of community engagement and creating access for the disadvantaged that make the format distinct from those of smaller firms that trade for profit. Instead, the social enterprise can be seen as a value-based marketing organization that ethically addresses failures in the delivery of services to vulnerable groups within its communities. It does this by responding to a commercial imperative – setting up commercial trading operations that allow it to function independently.

For an example of the role of a social enterprise in helping a vulnerable group of people, in this case young Australians with mental health problems, please read Minicase 1.4 on The Inspire Foundation.

Minicase 1.4   The Inspire Foundation

In late 1992, when a young man took his life on an Australian farm in north-eastern Victoria it had a huge impact on the young man's family and friends, – one of them was his cousin Jack Heath. At the time Jack was working in Parliament House Canberra as a Senior Adviser to Prime Minister Keating. In the prime minister's office, Jack was involved in the formulation of the multimedia initiatives detailed in the Government's major arts and communications policy statement, 'Creative Nation'. Daniel Petre, Michael Rennie and David Harrington played a key role with Jack in constructing those initiatives – Daniel was then head of Microsoft Australia and Michael and David were working for management consultants McKinsey & Company. In early 1995 Jack took leave from the Prime Minister's office. During that time he reflected on his own life and aspirations and the increasing number of youth suicides in Australia. When the Microsoft Network was first established, international figures participated in live chat sessions to encourage people to take up the new technology. From his home in Canberra, Jack joined people around the world in a chat session with American mind-body specialist Dr Deepak Chopra in

San Francisco. Dr Chopra responded to a number of questions posed by Jack and, excited by the immediacy of the response and potential power of the technology, Jack called Daniel Petre. Familiar with Jack's concerns about the rising rates of youth suicide in Australia, Daniel suggested that Jack should consider doing something about this pressing social issue by harnessing the power of the Internet.

Microsoft then generously provided some seed funding that enabled the development of a prototype of the Reach Out service. In late 1996 Paul Gilding, who had recently returned to Australia after serving as Head of Greenpeace International, joined Jack, Michael and then Alexandra Yuille in formally establishing what is now the Inspire Foundation.

From this initiative, Reach Out was established to carry out the mission of helping young Australians lead happier lives through improved mental health. Reach Out is a web-based initiative to help the 480,000 Australians aged 18–24 living with an anxiety or substance abuse disorder. Funding for the work of Reach Out comes from public subscription and from community based fundraising.

Source: http://www.inspire.org.au and http://www.reachout.com.au, accessed June 2009.

QUESTION

1. The Inspire Foundation has a national mission. Is there an essential difference in how a social enterprise with a national mission will seek to work as opposed to a more localized social enterprise?
2. What were the key building blocks in the creation of the Inspire Foundation?

The third sector and its contribution to the economy

Regardless of how social enterprises see themselves, government and policymakers see a different picture. The 'third sector' is increasingly referred to by politicians as *the* solution to engaging communities. Third sector organizations can be described as the organizations and groups that occupy the space between the state, the citizens and the private sphere, what is sometimes referred to as nongovernmental organizations, non-profit organizations or simply civil society (Cabinet Office, 2008).[8] Social enterprises are one of the key players within the third sector.

The following is extracted from an HM Treasury report from the United Kingdom *The Future Role of the Third Sector in Social and Economic Integration* (HM, July 2007).[9]

The third sector is a vital component of a fair and enterprising society, where individuals and communities feel empowered and enabled to achieve change and to meet social and environmental needs. The Government recognizes the value of the diversity of organizations in the sector in providing a voice for underrepresented groups, in campaigning for change, in creating strong, active and connected communities, in promoting enterprising solutions to social and environmental challenges and in transforming the delivery and design of public services. The third sector has always been at the heart of social and environmental change and the Government wants to continue to work to create the conditions where organizations can grow and achieve their aims.

The same report notes that

the third sector makes an enormous contribution to our society, economy and environment. Hundreds of thousands of organizations and millions of volunteers make a practical difference in communities, from working with young people to developing new ways of recycling household waste.

(1.10)

The third sector, sometimes referred to as not-for-profit organizations, is the term applied to the wider voluntary sector. It is noted that of the 166,000 registered charities in the UK there are *around 55,000 social enterprises*, according to the Annual Small Business Survey by the DTI (2005).[10] In essence the survey stated that what the UK government seeks is a partnership that ensures that *public services are able to improve further by fully drawing on the understanding and experience of third sector in designing, developing and delivering services*.

[S]ocial enterprise offers radical new ways of operating for public benefit. By combining strong public service ethos with business acumen, we can open up the possibility of entrepreneurial organizations – highly responsive to customers and with the freedom of the private sector – but which are driven by a commitment to public benefit rather than purely maximising profits for shareholders.

From this discussion, it is apparent that the role of social enterprises within the UK economy is changing and changing quickly. The speed of this change may explain the interchangeability of the terminology that applies to social enterprises. With the rapid growth in the sector, it is inevitable that there would be concerns over assessing the impact of social enterprises.

The strategy for social enterprise within the United Kingdom

Within the Cabinet Office is the Office of the Third Sector. The Office of the Third Sector's responsibilities include national policy on social enterprise. The policy view from the Cabinet Office is based on the need to ensure that social enterprise activity is focused on working across government to create an environment in the UK for social enterprises to thrive. 'Our vision is of a dynamic and sustainable social enterprise sector contributing to a stronger economy and a fairer society.'

The government's commitments to supporting social enterprise are set out in the *Social Enterprise Action Plan*, which includes actions to raise awareness of social enterprise, ensure social enterprises have the right support, advice and finance, and enable them to work with government.

In 2007 The Office of the Third Sector commissioned a report into how the impact of the social enterprise sector could be assessed.

> It is the view of the report's authors that it is the very diversity of the sector that will make it difficult to assess its impact. Official research from the DTI (2005) shows that social enterprises employ more than 775,000 people in the UK and are operating in a diverse range of trades. The research also shows that UK social enterprises have an annual turnover of £18 billion. While they are found across the country, 22% are in London. Only half of all social enterprises operate in areas of high deprivation, with about 49% working in more affluent wards.
>
> (Hart and Houghton, 2007)

The question is whether the public-private partnership within a social economy is particular to the UK. Young (2000) identified five inter-related trends within the developed economies.[11]

Young argues that non-profit organizations are adjusting their business models to create earned income and developing their own commercial independence from traditional public sector funding sources. 'Within the US this is generally recognized as having given impetus to social purpose enterprises in which revenue generated businesses are owned and operated by non-profit organization's for the express purpose of employing at risk or disadvantaged individuals' (Young, 2000).

In this context please consider Minicase 1.2 Cambiando Vidas and Minicase 1.3 The Carvajal Foundation.

He also notes that that the relationship between profit and non-profit organization has become closer as they both collaborate in terms of social and environmental projects. In economic terms, the expectations for the social economy remain high. When the UK, the US and even the United Nations embrace the concept, it means that the changes can be expected to accelerate.

> '[S]ocial enterprises' ... offer a solidarity-based model of organization to help their members achieve their socio-economic goals, through the creation of employment, provision of financial services, and promotion of social integration. These organizations also empower community members and encourage social change through responsible citizenship that exercises control over production, consumption, savings, investment, and exchange.
>
> (Ocampo, 2007)[12]

In the next chapter, we look at the support environment that aims to encourage the formation and growth of social enterprises. What is not in doubt, it would seem, is the willingness of governments to support social enterprise, and the question to be addressed is about these support mechanisms. Should they be the same or should they be different to those available to small businesses as a whole?

Example 1.4 provides a summary of the issues covered in this chapter.

Example 1.4   What is social enterprise?

There are a number of different definitions.

This is an emerging area of study. Definitions overlap.

Focus is on the business not the entrepreneurial individual as a means to success.

Triple bottom Line has been adapted to mean Social Aims, Social Ownership & Enterprise.

Paradoxically a social enterprise will play down profit-making to emphasize their social and environmental values.

Legal Models include amalgams of community businesses, co-operatives and social firms.

Government has its own perspective on the role and emphasizes support for disadvantaged groups, regeneration and 'public good'.

Revision questions

- Of the operational models listed in this chapter, can you identify a social enterprise to match each model?
- Which type of social enterprise is (a) McSence and (b) Inspire?
- What might a government hope to gain from a policy of actively supporting social enterprise?
- Is there an essential difference in how financial support should be assessed between small businesses and social enterprises?

References

1. Wharton Business School, University of Pennsylvania, *Eradicating Mud Cookies: Global Executives Try to Connect Profit to Social Good*. From http://knowledge.whartin.upenn.edu/article.cfm?articleid=2277, accessed in July 2009.
2. A video by CNN exists of this happening.
3. P. Kilby, *Entrepreneurship and Economic Development* (New York: Free Press, 1979), p. 40.
4. Department of Trade and Industry (DTI), *Social Enterprise: A Strategy for Success* (London: DTI, 2002).
5. C. Davister, J. Defourny & O. Gregoire (2004) 'Integration of Social enterprises in the European Union: An Overview of Existing Models', International Society for Third Sector Research, Toronto, Canada, 2004.
6. Social Enterprise London, available at http://www.sel.org.uk/knowledge.html, accessed in June 2009.
7. Development Trust Association, see http://www.dta.org.uk/, accessed in June 2009.
8. Cabinet Office, 'Better Together, Improving Consultation in the Third sector', 2008. Available as a download at http://www.cabinetoffice.gov.uk/media/99612/better%20together.pdf, accessed in June 2009.
9. HM Treasury, *The Future Role of the Third Sector in Social and Economic Regeneration*, July 2007, Cabinet Office Cm7189.
10. Annual Small Business Survey, 2005, DTI available, from http://www.berr.gov.uk/files/file38237.pdf, accessed in June 2009.
11. D. R. Young, *Alternative Models of Government-Nonprofit Relations. Nonprofit and Voluntary Sector Quarterly*, vol. 29 no.1 (2000), pp. 149–72.
12. Statement by Mr. José Antonio Ocampo, Under-Secretary-General for Economic and Social Affairs to the Civil Society Forum on 'Employment Working for All: Partners in Innovation', New York, 3 February 2007. Available at http://www.un.org/esa/desa/ousg/statements/2007/20070203_civil_society_forum.html.

Additional reading

Bridge, S., Murtagh, B. and O'Neill, K., *Understanding the Social Economy and the Third Sector* (Basingstoke: Palgrave Macmillan, 2009).

Dees, J., Emerson, J. and Economy, P., *Strategic Tools for Social Entrepreneurs* (New York: Wiley, 2002).

Hart, T. and Houghton, G., *Assessing the Economic and Social Impacts of Social Enterprise: Feasibility Report*, Office of the Third Sector, 2007. See www.cabinetoffice.gov.uk/third_sector and www.hull.ac.uk/ccrs.

Pearce, J., *Social Enterprise in Anytown* (London: Gulbenkian Foundation, 2003), p. 25. http://www.virtueventures.com/setypology/index.

2 starting a social enterprise

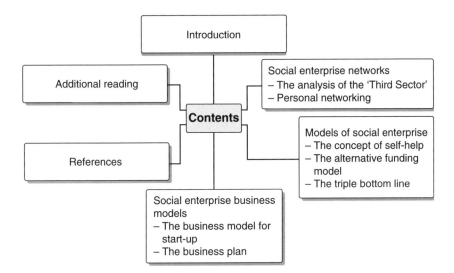

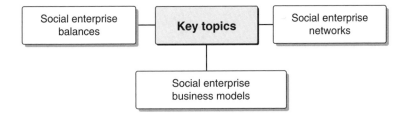

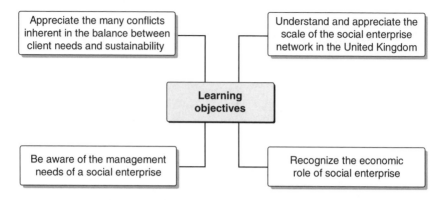

Introduction

Here we examine the support structures that exist for social enterprises within the UK and align these with the role of the 'social entrepreneur' as a leader and driving force in bringing new projects to fruition. The chapter is designed to help those thinking about launching a new social enterprise. Rather than a list of who you should approach, the chapter discusses how an approach can best be made. It illustrates the importance of using informal social networks to set up and run a new business as well as advocating a hybrid approach to launching a new venture using the best practices from the small business community. Suggestions on funding options are provided in a supplemental topic.

This chapter builds upon the argument made in Chapter 1 that there is no single definition of social enterprise, and while there are a number of formats employed in the third sector, social enterprises are being seen by government as bridging the gap between the public and private sector in terms of service delivery to vulnerable groups.

Social enterprise networks

In policy terms the UK government believes in the following four economic roles:

1. fostering a culture of social enterprise, embedding the change that is already underway, especially through inspiring the next generation to start thinking about the social impact of business;
2. improving business advice, information and support available to social enterprises;
3. tackling the barriers to access to finance that restrict the growth of social enterprises;
4. enabling social enterprises to work effectively with government to develop policy in their areas of expertise.

Given the UK governmental commitment to supporting and promoting social enterprise, the question remains: what elements of the existing support network can best be deployed to assist the development of social enterprise? The first point to understanding how this network is expected to deliver its objectives is to recognize the scale of activity that social enterprises engage in.

The analysis of the third sector

Any analysis of the size and scope of the 'Third Sector' clearly indicates the reasons for the importance given by governments and policymakers to encouraging the formation of organizations such as social enterprises.

"The UK government now estimates that there are around 55,000 social enterprises across the UK. These companies have a combined turnover of £27 bn per year and account for 5 per cent of all businesses and contribute £8.4 bn every year to the UK economy equal to nearly 1 per cent of annual GDP. The average social enterprise employs 10 people. Location wise, the vast majority of social enterprises (86%) are located in urban areas and operate mainly within the health and social care sector. They commonly derive their main income from 'community or social services' (21%). However, a big growth area for trading social enterprises has been the rising popularity of Fair Trade products – the biggest example of which being, Cafe Direct.

www.startups.co.uk (accessed December 2009)

Assuming the United Kingdom figures are correct, an extensive support network exists of people who have set up social enterprises. This networking is the very first place to start when launching a new enterprise. Social networking is recognized as a strategic marketing tool for small businesses. This concept, which has been extensively studied, (Birley, 1985;[1] Gilmore and Carson, 1999[2]) suggests that the owners of small businesses collect market information through personal contact with customers and suppliers, competitors and other knowledgeable market actors. This does not take place in the form of traditional unstructured market-research but instead as an ongoing enquiry and evaluation of options.

The concept implies that small businesses, and this should include social enterprises, do not have perfect knowledge of market opportunities and competitors and the owners selectively seek out the information that they require. The concept of imperfect knowledge is closely related to Penrose who viewed business, large or small, as consisting of both physical and human resources. Penrose went on to propose that business growth is constrained by the availability and quality of the management resource. In many studies on small businesses this link between the ability of the entrepreneur to create a successful business has been linked back to education.

More recent studies have concentrated on social capital. In other words *'the prospects for growth for a new venture depend on the ability of the entrepreneur to capture external resources, including tangibles such as capital, suppliers and intangible resources such as information and knowledge'* (Liao et al., 2003[3]). Social networking refers to the latter. A review of points with respect to social networking are provided as Example 2.1.

Personal networking

The ability to access intangible resources depends upon who you know rather than what you know. It is important to note that the networks can be classed as formal or informal and the research indicates that the more successful smaller firms have larger networks than those that exist within the bigger corporate organizations. The research also confirms that there is a relationship between the intensity, durability and frequency of the social network and the ability to set up a successful new venture. The informal network implied here will not only include those who have already set up social enterprises and business ventures but 'external brokers' – individuals who work for support organizations and who are able to give advice in a formal sense on how best to set up a new business whether it is a social enterprise or not.

This is not to suggest that Networking should not be formally planned with definitive aims in mind such as gathering information about new business. It is to suggest that unplanned and opportunistic approaches to key actors are just as valuable in identifying opportunities and securing new business. The advice therefore is simple: if you wish to raise funds, if you wish to secure new income streams, if you wish to extend a business, make sure you speak to as many people as possible in order to secure the best options. Here, arguably, social enterprises have an advantage over most small businesses in the sense that social networks available at the community level, and the social networks available at the support level, should be accessible and less restrictive. Strategically this resource, namely the willingness of others to help, is a key advantage for this business format.

Models of social enterprise

Within the voluntary sector, social enterprises make up an increasing proportion of business activity. The Office of the Third Sector, located within the United Kingdom government Cabinet Office (2009) indicates (2009) that there are 62,000 social enterprises in the United Kingdom, and that they contribute £24 billion to UK output.

An example of the growth in the sector is the growth of social firms within the UK. A social firm is one type of social enterprise. The specific social purpose of a social firm is to employ people who are disadvantaged in the labour market normally through a disability.

Social Firms UK (2007)[4] claims the British social firm sector grew by 15 per cent in 2006 compared to 2005. In its annual survey, it claims there are now 137 businesses of this kind in the UK, with the majority located in the West Midlands and Scotland. The study also revealed that 'the number of full-time equivalent jobs in the sector rose by a third to 1652, of which 52% are held by disabled and disadvantaged people'. Their analysis indicates that there is almost an equal split between existing social firms and 'emerging social firms'.

Rather than delve into these statistics, it is better to examine the 'drivers' – the economic, social and political factors that are encouraging the emergence of social enterprises within the third sector of the economy. An understanding of the drivers will provide an understanding of what type of support new and existing social enterprises require and from whom. Understand the drivers and you will understand how you can access the formal and possibly the informal support networks. Traditionally, there have been three quite different sectors within the economy: the public sector (government and its various agencies), the private sector (for-profit companies of all sizes) and the non-profit sector. The non-profit sector can be variously defined as the voluntary sector, charities and not-for-profit. These overlap as shown in Figure 2.1.

The Institute for Social Entrepreneurs (2009)[5] argues that the

'boundaries are beginning to merge: Nonprofits are adopting entrepreneurial strategies and starting businesses; for-profits are invading territory previously occupied only by nonprofits and government; and public sector agencies are forming partnerships with the other sectors and developing entrepreneurial strategies of their own.' They state: 'Social enterprises are hybrids mixing social values and goals with commercial practices, operating in the market. They are constitutionally uncomfortable; there is always a tension between their social goals and their commitment to commercial operation. For

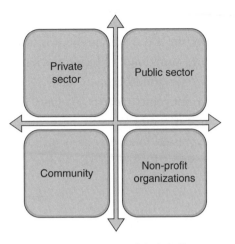

Figure 2.1 **Actors and their influence**

precisely that reason, they have to question how they operate, and that is what makes them innovative. Social enterprises are driven by social goals – to provide education, childcare, family support – but they often deliver most of that through the market by selling services and products.'

The concept of self-help

The early Victorian philosophies were based on the idea that the solution to a community's problems lies in the community's own hands – in their own localities. Essentially this was the concept of 'self help'. This concept is best known from the work of Samuel Smiles in the nineteenth century who wrote 5 textbooks on the subject of self-help. This value is reflected in the localization of social enterprises that are created to have a local impact on a specified part of a community. This can be seen as the antithesis of a public sector or governmental department that delivers social policy through its civil servants. From a policy perspective social firms can therefore be seen as an ideal state; a locally grown and locally controlled business with local stakeholders. The ultimate in community self help that requires the minimum of interference from the public sector. This does tend to accord with some of the thinking on entrepreneurship. Kets de Vries (1977),[6] views the entrepreneur as a non-conformist social deviant. This sociological perspective is consistent with the need to create a not for profit organization that directly addresses a social problem that is not currently being addressed. So, while the public sector may be embracing the social entrepreneur as a hero, the social entrepreneur is often at odds with the public sector – capable, sometimes, of biting the hand that feeds it.

The philosophical association between today's social enterprises and the early co-operative movement partly explains their present role as agents for change when it comes to regenerating urban economies. The agent for change is expressed in an emphasis on social investment such as jobs and training, with the aim of the re-investment being social-economic output.

The alternative funding model

Where the social enterprise can be seen to be different from the voluntary sector in general is on their level of dependency. Boschee (2006)[7] argues that 'the traditional business model for non-profits, depends solely or almost entirely on charitable contributions and public sector subsidies, with earned income either non-existent or minimal'.

In this text we have stated that social enterprises seek to generate surpluses so as to invest these surpluses back into the communities they serve. Without the capacity to do this they will have a high level of external dependency. Social enterprises need to create both social and financial value through obtaining their funding from a mixture of:

1. Charitable contributions
2. Public sector subsidies
3. Earned income

This is shown as Figure 2.2.

Jim Schorr is the executive director of San Francisco-based Juma Ventures. It is his view that

> The first generation of social enterprise have failed to realize its vision of using business models to create both social and financial value. ... The overwhelming majority of social enterprises are small retail businesses – ice cream shops, thrift stores, restaurants, cafes and the like – that have not succeeded and never will succeed on a double bottom basis ... we must find new solutions.
>
> (Schorr, 2006)[8]

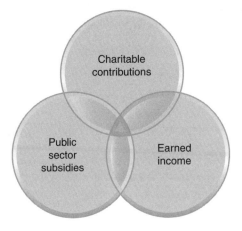

Figure 2.2 **The alternative funding model**
Source: Based on Boschee, 2006

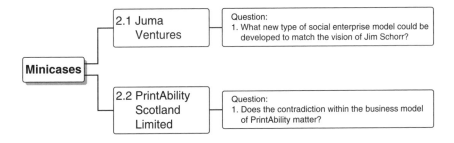

Minicase 2.1   Juma Ventures

Juma Ventures has been at the forefront of the social enterprise move-ment in the nonprofit sector for more than a decade. They launched their first social enterprise in 1994 – at that time, Juma was the first nonprofit in the US to be awarded a corporate business franchise – opening a Ben & Jerry's ice cream shop in San Francisco. Since then, Juma has devel-oped and operated eight social enterprises where youth have received jobs and business skills training, and saved toward college and other pur-poses. For more than a decade now, in partnership with Centerplate, Juma has operated the concessions for ice cream, coffee and nuts at the Giants baseball and 49ers football games in San Francisco, where each year about 100 youth work as vendors at AT&T Park and Monster Park.

In 2006, in a new partnership with Aramark, Juma launched conces-sion operations at the Oakland Coliseum during A's baseball and Raiders football games. In 2007, Juma expanded to Memorial Stadium in Berkeley, and Qualcomm Stadium home of the San Diego Chargers and San Diego State Aztecs football games. They also partnered with Levy Restaurants at the Warriors stadium in Oakland to employ youth as cart employees selling Dryer's ice cream and coffee. In 2008, Juma expanded nationally, employing youth at the Nationals Stadium and RFK Stadium in Washington DC. Juma youth have earned over $1.4 million in wages, while our social enterprises have generated over $9 million in earned revenue.

Source: www.jumaventures.org

Essentially it is the view of Schorr that new solutions are needed:

'The first is to develop new social enterprise business models that can scale to a size where they generate sufficient revenue to cover both direct and indirect business costs, as well as the incremental costs that are a function of the social mission. Secondly to make a compelling case for ongoing funding subsidies to sustain social enterprises'.

QUESTION

1. What new type of social enterprise model could be developed to match the vision of Jim Schorr?

In part what is being argued here is that certain activities – business models carried out by social enterprises – cannot 'wash their face' financially but do provide a service in a cost-effective way so as to be worthy of subsidies from governments, foundations and individual donors.

This concept of mixed revenue sources creates a dilemma in terms of the support structure needed to nurture social enterprises. One side of the argument says that support should be directed within the existing (for-profit) support network since social enterprise compete and trade within laissez faire market places. There is an equally compelling argument that support should be provided by specialist organizations that are dedicated to responding to the special needs of social enterprises that generate revenue from trading and fundraising activities. This argument may be seen as efficiency versus effectiveness and the efficiency argument, centralizing services through social enterprises, is the more prevalent.

The triple bottom line

Conventionally, an organization's 'bottom line' provides shareholders, accountants and auditors with financial measures of performance and accountability. The concept of the Triple Bottom Line was first developed by John Elkington in the early 1990s, to encompass social and environmental, as well as economic, impact. It has travelled a long way and is quoted in almost all texts on social enterprise. By 2001 the

European Commission was recommending a triple bottom line framework for published accounts.

Regardless of whether the support delivery is to come from the existing or a new dedicated support network, there are two issues that need to be addressed in terms of any support infrastructure. The emphasis, for the moment seems to be based around two key concepts.

1. Capacity Building.
   This refers to the ability of staff within a social enterprise to marry commercial and social objectives to create an organization that generates and distributes a surplus.
2. Sustainability
   This refers to the ability of the business to identify long-term and growing areas of revenue generation that do not conflict with ethical considerations in terms of the delivery of services and deployment of resources.

Either of these concepts would be difficult to deploy through a support network but combined, their effect is one of walking on eggs. And, according to the UK's Office of the Third Sector, 'the responsibility for delivery of support services will be through the existing "Regional Development Agencies" who will work with stakeholders, including specialist support agencies, to use the money to meet the support needs of social enterprises in their region'.[9]

The merging of small business support with social enterprise support into the existing national and regional support organizations has advantages and disadvantages for newly formed social enterprises. Positive consequences include the recognition that the management needs of social enterprises are similar to entrepreneurially managed organizations, and that social enterprises are legitimate forms of business, capable of making a contribution to both economic growth and social welfare. A disadvantage is the implication that the formal social network required for both business formats is the same. In other words, there is no requirement for specialist social enterprise business advice in marketing, financial planning and legal areas.

In the UK, at least, this may explain the emergence of local organizations that collectively represent the needs of local social enterprises. It also confirms the case for local social firms to band together, to collectively share resources and learn from their experiences of trading in a competitive marketplace. Just like entrepreneurial organizations the best support networks are going to be informal social networks.

Social enterprise business models

Social enterprises are diverse and the dual and conflicting concepts of capability and sustainability apply in different ways to different organizations. Social enterprises serve client needs and this means that they operate at different stages of integration with mainstream and for-profit businesses and public agencies. It could be argued that it is their level of integration with the local community that provides them with the ability to lever resources. These resources can include market resources, public sector subsidies, private sector sponsorship, public donations and, last but not least, the services of volunteers. This may explain a conundrum – why some social enterprises rely on subsidies while others aim for self-sufficiency in terms of their social output and in terms of their resource funding. For the former, capability could be seen to be of more importance than sustainability. It is this balance between capability and sustainability that most affects the business model and how commercially orientated firms will be.

Business models for start-up

As is the case with a business of any kind, the nature of the potential viability of a social enterprise will be determined by its business model. The traditional themes of a business model are products (or services), customers and competitive logic – the compelling reason for people to buy the product or service. The product of service is the *WHAT* in the business model. In terms of products or services, customers are needed – they are the *WHO* in the business model. In this regard they can be local, regional, national or international. The link between products (or services) and customers represents the *WHY* – the compelling reason to buy. The final element that needs to be covered is the *HOW* element. This covers the structure of the organization, its operations and the activities that are carried out by people. The people and systems need to be in place often as volunteers.

1. WHAT?
2. WHO?

3. WHY?
4. HOW?

The social enterprise when starting-up needs to be able to have an answer for each of the above. It also needs to consider the future. As with business strategies, business models have life cycles based on the traditional view of products and markets. In addition to this there are the concerns over revenues. As we have indicated a social enterprise should seek to be self-sustaining at least to some extent and the business model should address how revenues will be generated. In many small businesses the revenue model is quite simple. The entrepreneur identifies an opportunity, quite often the funding for the business will come directly from the entrepreneur and the income of the business from selling the products or services directly to customers who value the product enough to pay for it themselves. However, it is often the case that this basic model has to be altered to take account of the circumstances that the social enterprise finds itself to be in.

So, it can be postulated that social firms

> share the goal of producing an explicit benefit for the community or at least for a disadvantaged group within it. To achieve this goal, they develop an entrepreneurial logic with a continuous activity producing goods and services, a certain level of paid work, a largely autonomous management and a significant level of economic risk.
>
> Davister et al., 2004[10]

On this classification of activity, Davister et al. (2004) identify criteria that affect the commercial aspects of the business model:

1. An explicit aim to benefit the community
   Social enterprise serves the community at large or a specific group of people within this community while promoting a sense of social responsibility at the local level. The balance here determines the level of cross subsidization between revenue stream and services.
2. Limited profit distribution
   Some social enterprises, such as traditional 'non-profit' organizations spend the revenue raised on community delivery while other re-invest or redistribute the surplus. Social enterprises do not tend to engage in profit-maximizing behaviour, although where income

is to be redistributed profitable revenue streams are all the more important.

3. Decision-making power not based on capital ownership
    Unlike private enterprises, where decision-making power is linked to share capital, social enterprises often apply the '*one member, one vote*' form of decision-making. This means that decisions rest within the community rather than within the individuals who founded the business. Where decision-making is concentrated, a firm can move quickly but where consensus is required decisions can be compromised.

4. A minimum amount of paid work
    Social enterprises combine monetary and non-monetary resources, especially voluntary workers. Unlike voluntary organizations social enterprises will have a core staff of paid workers as part of their fixed cost structure. Where core staff exceed volunteers, there is an imperative to cover overheads before a surplus is generated.

5. A high degree of autonomy
    Even though some social enterprises are financed by public authorities, they are not managed directly by public authorities or other organizations. This autonomy is also evident in their capacity to put pressure on local politicians and to choose their funding sources. Greater independence does however limit access to core funding sources.

6. A significant level of economic risk
    Like any business, a social enterprise needs to be managed efficiently in terms of its services and the financial balance of the organization. The founders of such an enterprise thus assume economic risk linked to commercial activity. The more innovative they are, potentially, the more at risk they are of loosing money.

7. An initiative launched by a group of citizens
    Collectivism is a principal element of service delivery and this means all elements of the community must agree on priorities. On the basis that it is not always possible to keep all the people happy all the time, a schism can appear which damages the reputation of a business within its community.

Given the interaction and balance between capability and sustainability and Davistor's categories, it can be seen that social enterprise is a generic rather than a specific form of business. The original definition by Spreckley (1981)[11] would therefore still apply.

> An enterprise that is owned by those who work in it and/or reside in a given locality, is governed by registered social as well as commercial aims and objectives and run co-operatively may be termed a social enterprise. Traditionally, 'capital hires labour' with the overriding emphasis on making a 'profit' over and above any benefit either to the business itself or the workforce. Contrasted to this is the social enterprise where 'labour hires capital' with the emphasis on personal, environmental and social benefit.

Because social enterprises are hybrids that mix social values with commercial practices, there is always a tension between their social goals, helping people sustain themselves within society and their commitment to commercial operations. An example of this tension is provided as Minicase 2.2.

Minicase 2.2   PrintAbility Scotland Limited

PrintAbility Scotland Limited is a social enterprise for people with or recovering from mental health problems commissioned by Aberdeen City Council Social Work Department. The business commenced trading on 1 May 2001, offering the latest digital printing technology as well as more labour intensive print finishing and collation. PrintAbility Scotland Limited offers work and skills training to people who are disadvantaged from obtaining competitive employment. PrintAbility Scotland Limited aims to provide a long-term place of work for some individuals, while allowing for a 'move on' culture after training for others. It is a fully-fledged supported employment project, yet it is also a commercial enterprise. PrintAbility Scotland Limited believes that working in an active and real workplace increases users' confidence and self-esteem.

Printability Scotland Limited's aim is to be the first true Social Firm in the North East of Scotland whereby subsidies will be reduced so that at least 50% of the workforce with mental health problems will become fully waged. Although Printability requires to be subsidized, it will, like any other business organization, aim to make a profit as the pursuit of profit should be seen as essential to keep the enterprise vibrant and give it direction, it will not be pursued at the expense of any individual's health.

PrintAbility Scotland is aiming for a mix between revenue generation and subsidy and it is these two models that will further refer to within this text as they form the basic models of social enterprise currently in operation. What does need to be carefully considered is whether or not there is a problem in this two directional model. Will the drive towards self-sufficiency affect the subsidy or change the social ownership or social aims of the enterprise?

Source: www.printability.org (accessed December 2008)

QUESTIONS

1. Does the contradiction within the business model of PrintAbility matter?

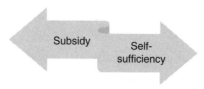

Figure 2.3   ***Conflicting purposes***

This potential conflict is shown as Figure 2.3

The business plan

We have identified above the criteria that can influence and affect the business model adopted by a social enterprise. We have also indicated that starting a social enterprise may be a very different exercise from that of a basic business start-up. The basic business start-up that dominates most very small businesses is concerned with satisfying a very small number of stakeholders, mainly the proposer and their immediate family (who have everything to lose should the business not succeed), and, if there is a need for external finance, the source(s) of that finance. Starting a social enterprise may be a much more varied affair with potentially multiple stakeholders whose needs have to be catered for in the plan. However, few business start-ups of any kind can bring themselves into being without a business plan of some kind. There are essentially two main purposes that a business plan should serve.

1. To assess feasibility especially with respect to the financial side of the proposed business.
2. To communicate to others the nature of your idea.

The structure of a business plan is pretty much a given feature these days and would look pretty much like this:

- The executive summary

This is a 'snap shot' of everything that is in the full plan. In length the summary would be in the region of one to two pages and is the most important part of the document. It must sell you and your idea to anyone whose support you may need. A poor summary could doom your idea.

- The Introduction. What is the nature of the business idea? Who is involved and how will the enterprise be organized and managed.

Here you are expanding on the basic information provided in the executive summary especially trying to clearly state why a social enterprise is needed. What is the need? What is your motivation for wanting to meet that need? It should identify the stakeholders in more detail and should indicate how you plan to develop the enterprise over time.

- What is it that you are proposing to offer?

Here you are expanding on the information given in the introduction. Outline the key features of the product or service being offered. How will it be organized and delivered?

- The nature of the market you are proposing to enter?

Identify the nature of the customers for the product/service you wish to offer. In a social enterprise the customers may be multi-faceted in that they can range from the person or persons you are seeking to help through to charities and governmental agencies. In this section you should seek to indicate the scale of the need and who, if anyone, is already in the market trying to meet that need. Can you provide evidence of demand for what you are proposing?

- Costing and pricing

What is going to be the cost of providing your product/service? In a start-up, financials vary between the costs based on the capital expenditure incurred to set-up the enterprise and the operational costs of delivering the product or service. Here we are concerned with identifying the true cost. This covers the resources invested and consumed by the business in order to be able to trade and deliver the product/service. Normally we are looking at fixed costs and variable costs.

Pricing seems to be a problem for many small businesses. The enterprise does need to be fully aware of all of its costs in any given time period, and from that decide on a pricing structure that covers costs in whole or in part depending on the nature of the enterprise. Unfortunately many small firms essentially under-price their products/services in order to get business and as a result fail to make the returns they need. In a social enterprise a simple pricing model may not apply, depending on the objectives of the enterprise. Pricing may need to reflect social need balanced out by the need to generate some form of trading profit and return on capital invested. We have already indicated that the normal framework for a social enterprise is that it provides a service of some kind to the community it serves while seeking to make a profit that can be used to develop the enterprise.

In a small business the basic features in terms of pricing are

1. The selling price
2. The cost of sale
3. The gross profit (1–2)
4. The gross margin percentage (3 ÷ 1 expressed as a percentage)
5. The fixed costs
6. Net profit (3–5)
7. Net margin percentage (6 ÷ 1 expressed as a percentage)
8. Break even (5 ÷ 4)

In a full cost model the enterprise would seek to achieve both a gross margin and a net margin to meet a set target and would, where possible, charge a price that would allow these targets to be met. The aim is an acceptable rate of return on the money invested in the business and to have funds for further investment. This is the full cost pricing model. In a marginal pricing model the selling price must at least cover the variable costs. The third method of pricing is the rate of return pricing method where managers will set a sales price that provides a pre-determined rate of return on capital employed based on the following formula:

$$\frac{\text{Capital employed}}{\text{Total annual costs}} \times \text{Planned rate of return of capital employed}$$

In a social enterprise the method employed may need to vary depending on the client, the competitive circumstances and the objectives of the enterprise. For example a social enterprise could be offering a range of products or service that sees the adoption of all of the pricing models outlined above. A marginal price for the service is charged to direct clients while fixed costs are covered by other funding streams such as government grants. In essence each social enterprise requires cost and pricing to be carefully examined within the business plan being produced.

- The marketing plan

How will you get your customers to make use of your product/service? How will you promote your enterprise and its product/service offering?

- The manufacturing plan

Who will produce your product or service? How will they do it?

What equipment will be needed? What type of premises/office will be needed?

- Organization and staffing

What people will be needed and how will they be managed?

Will they be a mix of employees and volunteers?

- Financial forecasts and funding sources

The following would be required here: three years of Cash Flow, Profit and Loss and Balance Sheet. The role of the cash flow is to monitor the money in and money out to try and prevent the enterprise running out of working capital. The profit and loss account is to manage the application of the enterprise's resources to achieve whatever value/profit target has been set. The balance sheet seeks to manage the assets and liabilities of the enterprise in terms of the flow of funds in and out of the enterprise.

In a social enterprise start-up the requirement is to identify the scale of the development funding needed, what that funding is needed for, and the potential sources of the funding. In common with most small business start-ups the third sector traditionally has the possibility of commercial funding, (mainly bank funding) and personal funding from the social entrepreneur and others. In addition to this, grant funding can play a part in both types of start-up. However, public sector funding, charities, communities and philanthropic individuals can be additional sources of funding for the social enterprise. The business plan needs to identify both sources of secured funding and potential sources of funding.

We can in essence only cover the basic skeletal framework of a business plan here in this chapter. For a more detailed look at the creation of a business plan please see: 'A Business Planning Guide to Developing a Social Enterprise'. This is to be found at www.forthsector.org.uk/resources.

Example 2.1 provides a summary of the issues covered in this chapter on starting a social enterprise.

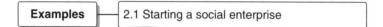

| **Examples** | 2.1 Starting a social enterprise |

Example 2.1   **Starting a social enterprise**

Social enterprises are an established part of the business community.
There is an existing support network in place to help the sector grow.
Social enterprises are more likely to collaborate with each other than SMEs.
Informal contact networks may be more useful than formal (support) networks in setting up and growing a social enterprise
Actors in the public, private and community will see different support priorities.
Capacity building and sustainability are the key goals.
Commercial goals conflicts with social and environment responsibilities.
Conflicts are best resolved through integration with the local community.

Revision questions

1. In an article entitled 'Big Step Forward for Social Enterprise as Scottish Executive Recognises Need for Targeted Support', Senscot made the following observation:

> In Scotland, the needs of social enterprises and emerging social enterprises have largely been confused with the needs of the traditional voluntary sector, with the terms 'social economy' and 'voluntary sector' often being used interchangeably by policy-makers.
>
> The role changed by social enterprises as businesses with double and triple bottom lines has not been recognised or understood.
>
> (Senscot, 2005)[12]

The article went on to state: 'most importantly, and in something of a surprise move, the Scottish Executive supported the Green Party's amendment recognising the distinctiveness of the social enterprise sector and recommending the development of appropriate tailored support for the sector'.

Your task is to compile the arguments for a Regional Development Agency to act as the primary support for the social enterprise sector set against a dedicated national agency specifically for the 'Third Sector'.

The argument must recognize the difference between the different types of firms and identify key sectors or types of social firms for inclusion in the support framework.

References

1. S. Birley 'The Role of Networks in the Entrepreneurial Process', *Journal of Business Venturing*, vol. 1 (1985), pp. 107–17.
2. A. Gilmore and D. Carson, 'Entrepreneurial Marketing by Networking', *New England Journal of Entrepreneurship*, vol. 2, no. 2 (1999), pp. 31–8.
3. J. Liao and H. Welsch, 'Social Capital and Entrepreneurial Growth Aspiration: A Comparison of Technology – and Non-Technology-Based Nascent Entrepreneurs', *Journal of High Technology Management Research*, 14 (2003), pp. 149–70.
4. Social Firms UK (2007), see http://www.socialfirms.co.uk/index/php/Section163.html, accessed on 20 November 2008.
5. Social enterprise terminology, Institute for Social Entrepreneurs (2009), see http://www.socialent.org/Social_Enterprise_Terminology.htm, accessed December 2009.
6. M. Kets de Vries, 'The Entrepreneurial Personality: A Person at the Crossroads', *Journal of Management Studies*, vol. 14 (1977), pp. 34–57.
7. J. Boschee, *Migrating from Innovation to Entrepreneurship: How Nonprofits are Moving Toward Sustainability and Self-Sufficiency* (The Institute for Social Entrepreneurs: Dallas, TX, 2006). See www.socialent.org, accessed December 2009.
8. J. Schorr *Social Enterprise 2.0: Moving Toward a Sustainable Model, Stanford Social Innovation Review*, Summer (2006). pp. 12–13.
9. Social Enterprise Action Plan (2006), DTI, p. 8.
10. C. Davister, J. Defourny and O. Gregoire, 'Integration of Social Enterprises in the European Union: An Overview of Existing Models', International Conference of the ISTR (International Society for Third Sector Research), Toronto, Canada, 2004. See htpp://www.ces-ulg.be/fieladmin/ces-files/pdfs/ Publications/2004/Davister et al., accessed on 20 November 2008.
11. F. Spreckley, *Social Audit: A Management Tool for Co-operative Working*, Leeds: Beechwood College Ltd (1981). www.locallivelihoods.com/documents, accessed December 2009.
12. Senscot, 'Big step foreward for social enterprise as Scottish Executive recognises need for targeted support', Articles 26.05.05 p 1. www.senscot.net/view_art.php?viewed=2561, accessed December 2008.

Additional reading

A list of documents and articles on social enterprise can be found at http://www.unltd.org.uk/useful_links.

Use these as background reading to the subject.

Bridge, S., Murtagh, B. & O'Neil, K., *Understanding the Social Economy and the Third Sector* (Basingstoke: Palgrave Macmillan, 2009), Chapter 6.

Cantillon, B. and Bosch, K. V., 'Social Policy Strategies to Combat Income Poverty of Children and Families in Europe', Luxembourg Income Study Working Paper Series, 2002. Available at www.lisproject.org/publications/liswps/336.pdf, accessed on 11 April 2005.

For Charity Watch, see http://www.charitywatch.org/criteria.html.

Dees, J. G. 'Enterprising Non-Profits', *Harvard Business Review*, January–February, Vol. 76, Issue 1. 1998. pp. 54–67.

McGregor, A., Clark. S., Ferguson, Z. and Scullion, J., *Valuing the Social Economy: The Social Economy and Economic Inclusion in Lowland Scotland* (Glasgow: Community Enterprise in Strathclyde, 1997).

Mouzas, S. , 'Efficiency Versus Effectiveness in Business Networks', *Journal of Business Research*, 59 (10–11) (2006), pp. 1124–32.

Paton, R., *Managing and Measuring Social Enterprises* (London: Sage Publications, 2002).

Penrose, E. T., *The Theory of the Growth of the Firm* (Oxford: Basil Blackwell, 1959).

3. the management and the theory

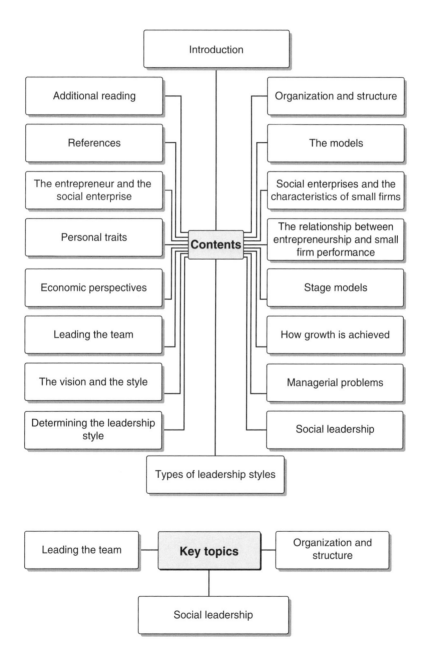

47

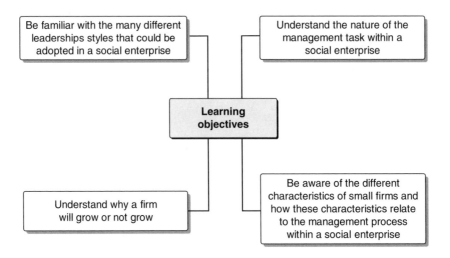

Introduction

This chapter examines the value of selective management theories and concepts that can affect the running of a social enterprise.

In terms of business management, social enterprises are not substantively different from small businesses – even though they trade for a social purpose. Like any for-profit business they operate in a competitive environment and they aim to succeed by establishing market penetration and making a profit through the value-added services they provide. The fact that the profit is not distributed to shareholders but is re-invested or distributed within the stakeholder community is the defining characteristic of the social enterprise. So, while the external trading environment may be different, the way in which the firm needs to allocate and manage its resources can be seen to be similar to with-profit businesses.

This means that the existing management thinking on organization and leadership should still apply, albeit with some modification, to the running of a social enterprise. The question is: what is the extent of this modification?

Organization and structure

According to Prabhu (1999)[1] three types of social organizations can be identified:

1. Charitable organizations that provide relief to the needy and deprived. They are individual-oriented and often based around a moral code. Their approach arises from a feeling of empathy and a belief in sacrifice, which may be derived from religious or philosophical beliefs.
2. Social action organizations are campaigning organizations that actively take up issues of politics and social injustice and attempt to change society.
3. Developmental organizations initiate economic activities among deprived or vulnerable communities by introducing technological and organizational innovation with considerable experimentation, but rarely believe in making core social or political changes. It is

argued that the difference among the three is primarily ideological. Prabhu notes that

> [t]he nature of involvement of members may vary depending on the nature of the task. Some are completely voluntary, with no compensation for services rendered, while others are semi-voluntary, with token or subsistence compensation for full time services. Non-voluntary members, with market compensation for services rendered, form a third type.
>
> (pp. 140–5)

He goes on to argue that this element of voluntary contribution and the fact that social enterprises may not be paying full market rates to employees or members means that 'building and motivating employee motivation and commitment to the organization's mission is important for social entrepreneurial organizations'. Without a high level of motivation, staff turnover can be expected to be high, and volunteers, the lifeblood of many social enterprises, will be difficult to recruit. There are many different ways to instil motivation and team building within organizations; the point being raised here is that motivation is even more important in a social enterprise than it is in a for-profit SME.

This analysis points to a difference between a social enterprise and a for-profit business; namely the relationship between ideology and membership, both of which impact upon decision making within a firm. Delving deeper into the different ideologies, Virtue Ventures[2] distinguishes between the social values and economic values that a social enterprise may seek to create. This emphasis on output rather than function gives an insight into the priorities and drivers and it allows for better classification of a social enterprise in terms of what it is set up to achieve. This is based on the nature of the business model that the social enterprise wishes to adopt.

Virtue Ventures[3] goes on to argue that most social enterprises are set up to combine different aspects of these models and few of them can be expected to exist in a pure form. What is useful about these models is that they differentiate one social enterprise from another in terms of the use of resources, service delivery, fund raising and revenue models. These may be variations on a theme but it is the variations that help to explain the different business models that are available. It is interesting

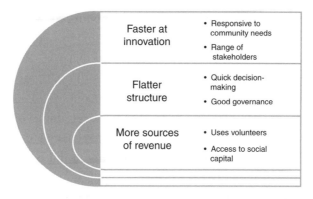

Figure 3.1 *The social enterprise 'entrepreneurial organization'*

to speculate that the 'purest' and earliest forms of social enterprises were orientated toward the employment and self-help model of creating income for vulnerable members of the community. Increasingly it would seem that more complex models are appearing and these are orientated towards the market intermediary model. These are firms that provide local groups of producers with access to wider markets by value-adding to products and offering direct access to wider distribution channels, nationally and internationally.

Social enterprises and the characteristics of small firms

Regardless of their ideological configuration, social enterprises still share many of the characteristics of small firms that are acting in an entrepreneurial manner. Figure 3.1 defines their characteristics in the context of a social enterprise.

This provides a useful reference point. For example, SMEs can also be classified according to their growth ambitions. Social enterprises, like the majority of SMEs, fall into three categories (Birch, 1981)[4]:

1. Mice. Their primary motivation is to create a job for themselves using their existing skills. In the United States, these are often referred to as 'Mom & Pop' businesses and they are also referred to as 'lifestyle businesses'. Mice businesses can be described as not being overtly focused on the commercial imperative of creating a sustainable and highly profitable enterprise. Within the small firms sector they are more likely to be associated with craft businesses or technical and product centred businesses where the emphasis is on creating a 'perfect mouse trap' rather than making a huge profit.

Social enterprise mice are likely to be associated with addressing location-specific and social needs. This means that there is no overt intention to grow outside the community's needs. Storey defines this group as 'trundlers' – those businesses that although surviving remain small in terms of their growth ambitions.

2. Elephants. In comparison, these are the large stable organizations unable to change direction quickly or react to changing circumstances. Elephants can encompass forms of corporate not-for profit businesses and can also include those associated with public sector initiatives. It is these inflexible and larger public sector-managed operations that are increasingly being replaced by community-owned enterprises.

3. Gazelles. They are the third category and are the most aspirational form of business. They are the young or vibrant fast growth businesses that are organized to react swiftly to changing market conditions. They are entrepreneurially managed and are attributed with job and wealth creation within the SME sector. These are also known as the 'fliers' and they can be described as opportunistic. Gazelles do not emerge out of thin air. There is evidence that they often emerge from large companies where individuals develop the management skills to run a fast growing business. They may also only emerge after being in business for many years and showing little or no growth until a trigger point occurs to set them on the growth path. These are individuals that have detailed knowledge of the industry in which they work. They will also have an established network of contacts in the industry, suppliers, customers, etc. (Storey, 1998).[5] Gazelles are the exception for growth is not always a primary objective for all small businesses.

A high proportion of small firms are more interested in maintaining their current level of profit than in expansion. One reason for firms wishing to stay small is that the ownership and the management reside in the same person, or persons; so future company goals are determined not only by commercial considerations but by personal life-styles and family factors.

(O'Farrell and Hitchens, 1988, pp. 399–415)[6]

The majority of small firms do not fit the category of gazelles. In the same way the majority of social enterprises do not seek to become gazelles; they are not necessarily intent on restricting their future growth but nor are they intent in growing outside their community of stakeholders. This is the point at which the discussion on growth gets interesting. A number of authors propose that it is not always possible to restrict growth – even if an enterprise wishes to. There is after all a maxim in business that suggests that if you try to stand still, you will die. In others words we cannot manage inertia.

So, why grow a business? Birley and Westhead (1994)[7] have identified the following reasons:

- To increase their independence.
- To increase their locus of control.
- To satisfy a need for achievement.
- To generate a store of wealth for the owner and his family.
- To provide employment positions for family members; and to ensure the survival of an independent business that can be transferred to the next generation of family members.
- To survive.
- To grow rather than to allow the business to stagnate.
- To make a contribution to the development of the local community where the owner-manager lives.
- To increase the status and legitimacy of the owner(s) and the business in social and business networks.

The relationship between entrepreneurship and small firm performance

What this analysis suggests is that growth depends not just on the ambitions of the entrepreneurial founders, it is also influenced by market conditions. In other words external market factors and internal resource consideration can determine whether a business grows or not. We would also like to add the concept of luck and circumstance. Often growth happens due to factors that have a life of their own. However, the best kind of entrepreneur is the 'lucky' entrepreneur who can make things happen. Research into the relationship between entrepreneurship and small firm performance has used a range of explanatory variables. These include

Opportunity (external)

> This involves the study of characteristics such as industry fragmentation, market trends, entry barriers, and access to finance. This

approach is exemplified by Porter's Competitive Strategy which proposes three generic strategies for coping with competitive forces: overall cost leadership, differentiation and focus.

Ability (internal)

Here studies look at the influence of education, various types of experience, breadth of education and experience, management and team building.

These approaches rely on measures of ability, need, and opportunity to explain a substantial share in the variation in actual (historical) growth rates. Need-related issues appear more important than ability and opportunity and the entrepreneur is presented as a 'local hero'. The view here is that the satiation of need is the major reason why small firms stop growing.

Resource Allocation (internal)

A common problem for fast growth companies is obtaining enough resources to accommodate that growth. A typical entrepreneur often wants to pursue a detected opportunity but lacks the necessary resources to make it happen. Again, gaining access to these resources becomes the 'first' entrepreneurial problem. The ability to exploit resources that are outside the entrepreneur's control is a constant of entrepreneurial high-growth management. This is why entrepreneurs have been defined as being primarily motivated by the pursuit of opportunities, as opposed to managers exclusively concerned with the proper management of resources already controlled by their firm. One way of obtaining more external resources than competitors is by effective networking. So, growth can be threatening because it may mean a dilution in ownership and lack of control especially when external management or external funding is introduced into a new and growing business. Growth may also be a necessity – an imperative that cannot be avoided because of market opportunities.

Stage models

There are several different 'stage models' of growth including Greiner's (1972) five-phase model, Churchill and Lewis's (1983) five-stage model, and Scott and Bruce's (1987) five-stage model. Additionally Flamholtz's[8] (1986) stages of development model highlights the following four-stage process:

Adaptation:
  Getting the resources and finding a niche in the market place.

Resource allocation:
  Assigning resources appropriately.

Co-ordination:
  Getting everyone to pull together.

Integration:
  Getting individual commitment to the firm's success.

While a range of criticisms (Deakins & Freel, 2009) can be levied at stage models in general, about their descriptive nature and the fact that firms do not follow linear paths and often skip stages, the model outlined by Flamholtz does seem to work well for the creation and development of a social enterprise. In various chapters of this book, including the concluding chapter (Chapter 10), the recommendations for a successful social enterprise start-up do connect directly, often in sequence, with the stages in the Flamholtz model.

Greiner, on the other hand, outlines the linear growth of a firm over time with periods of incremental trouble-free growth (that is, evolution) punctuated by crisis points (that is, revolution).[9] Each growth phase is associated with attributes, as shown in Figure 3.2. Deakins and Freel (2009)[10] summarized Greiner's model as follows.

Crisis of leadership
The shift from a Phase 1 firm to a Phase 2 firm is triggered by a crisis of leadership. More sophisticated knowledge and competencies are required to operate larger production runs and manage an increasing workforce. Capital must be secured to underpin further growth and financial control must be put in place. The business must hire additional executive resources and restructure to meet these challenges. Growth is achieved through creativity.

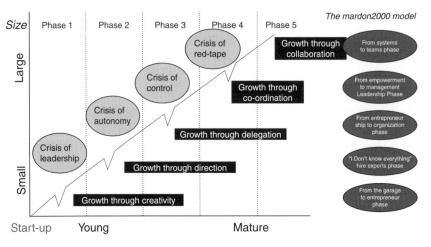

Figure 3.2 **The five phases of growth**
Source: Greiner (1972)

Crisis of autonomy

The control mechanisms implemented as a result of the first crisis become less appropriate as the physical size of the business increases. Line employees and managers become frustrated with the bureaucracy attendant upon a centralized hierarchy. Further, line staff are more familiar with markets and machinery than executives and become torn between following procedures and taking initiatives. It becomes necessary for the owners of the business to delegate to allow sufficient discretion in operating decision making. Growth is achieved through direction.

Crisis of control

Top executives begin to perceive a loss of control as a consequence of excessive discretion resting with middle and lower managers. Problems of co-ordination may be exhibited across divisions, plants or functions. Top management regain control by using (undefined) special co-ordination techniques. Growth is achieved through delegation.

Crisis of red tape

The 'watchdog' approach adopted by senior management and the proliferation of systems and programmes leads to a crisis of confidence and red tape. Further, the business is too large and complex to be managed through an extensive framework of formal procedures and controls. Movement to the next phase is only achieved through a shift towards 'interpersonal collaboration'. Growth is achieved through co-ordination.

The next crisis! No consistently identified crisis in Phase 5 was identified by Greiner. He suggests the crisis will revolve around the psychological saturation of employees. Growth is achieved through collaboration.

While there is criticism of these linear growth models where firms proceed through stages in a systematic way, they are still useful in suggesting that growth is often achieved through a series of steps, disjointed or otherwise, rather than by a steady progression. When growth does occur it requires professionalizing the management – an issue often associated with succession management in the family business sector. This is consistent with Penrose's view of the firm that growth is more often inhibited by management's ability. Rosa (2005) summarizes the literature about why small *family* firms do not grow by identifying:

Managerial problems

- Failure to manage the business competently, failure to plan ahead, failure to react quickly to change, failure to manage growth, especially when the business gets so large that outside corporate managers need to be brought in.
- Not managing the (family) members – How the business is split, personality conflicts, the founding entrepreneur is unwilling to let go.
- Not managing the succession – Founders normally wish to see their children continue it but the main problems are that they leave the succession planning until it is often too late, or fail to resolve conflicts surrounding the succession.

What this does seem to suggest is that social enterprises and family businesses share a number of similarities in terms of making decisions. Failure to plan ahead as the business grows, not managing members and not having a successor in place for the founder of the business apply to whatever business format you examine. There is however a qualification to this proposition. Unlike small firms and family businesses, social enterprises are not individually owned but community owned. Furthermore they are often community managed. This means that ownership and control is executed in a different manner.

Housing Associations are an example of joint (social) ownership. When housing stock is transferred from a public agency into a social enterprise, the stock is not individually owned – it is collectively owned by the house-holding community. Rules govern both the transfer and the management of the stock although that is not the issue. No one individual owns the stock. What this means, at least in theory, is that ownership, or the fear of loosing ownership, is not the same for social enterprises as it is for small firms.

A small business will seek to maintain the maximum amount of ownership, in the form of shares and voting rights, while a social enterprise will, from the outset, have dispersed its ownership to a range of stakeholders. This is the difference between a property management company and a housing association. If ownership and control does not explain the gazelle verses the mice situation, there must be other factors at play which determine why not all social enterprises are growth-orientated. Here is the critical difference: in an entrepreneurially managed firm, the lead entrepreneur individually makes all the decisions – often without referral to others. In a membership organization, decision making is collectively made. In theory, a small firm can make quick decisions but a social enterprise makes slower collective decisions. This decision making process may explain why such a lot of interest is placed on the 'social' entrepreneur as someone who has the moral, rather than the legal, authority to make decisions about the future.

Assuming that a social enterprise competes within a market economy, it must have the means for making decisions about its growth prospects. For community stakeholders and board members, decisions need to be collectively agreed but need to be agreed expediently. Not making decisions will reduce social impact and lead to financial failure. This question of leadership is one that social enterprises share with family businesses but which separates them from entrepreneurially run small firms. It can be both an advantage and a disadvantage, and leadership is one factor that will distinguish a successful social enterprise from a failing one.

Social leadership

Leadership can be described as 'a relationship through which one person influences the behaviour of others' (Mullins, 1999).[11]

Leadership styles

There are a range of leadership styles through which this influence can be achieved. It is important to recognize that no one style is better than others and that, most importantly, different people will use different styles.

- **Inventors** are noted for their creativity. They may be innovative people yet many of their ideas may never become reality because they lack the management and business skills to put a new idea into practice.
- **Promoters** on the other hand are the creative people but these are typically short-term business propositions with a bias towards getting things done quickly rather than improving performance. Because promoters lack good general management skills they are not always the ones that people follow.
- **Custodians** will often look for cost savings and efficiency in business systems. They act as managers with their administrative skills attuned to the efficient management of a business. They would argue that inventiveness and creative thinking are all very well in an uncompetitive or stable business environment, but these are not the skill sets required for a social enterprise that is striving to grow.

Few individuals have all these skills but within any organization, a combination of all three is an asset. A leader does need to possess all the skills sets. Entrepreneurs often express that they lack the skill sets of professional managers. That is why they are entrepreneurs. The role of the leader is to engage the different skills within a team and to use these skills constructively. A team leader in a social enterprise is someone who creates *balance* within a team, with members and with the wider community. To understand how this balance can be created, a leader needs to recognize the different leadership styles that exist and consider which one best fits the needs of the situation at a particular time. Three examples of leadership styles are outlined below.

1. Authoritarian (directive)

   Here a person tells others what they want done and how they want it done – and without always seeking the advice of others. This style can work when management tasks are routine, when time is short and when the team already works well together. It is often employed during crisis management and may be applied during times of staff shortage or equipment failure. The authoritarian style is different from the abusive leader who yells, uses demeaning language, and leads by threats of power. This is not the authoritarian style; it is simply the most unprofessional style of leadership.

2. Participative (democratic)

   This involves the leader involving one or more team members in the decision-making process. Of course team members retain the final decision-making authority. It could be that this style is seen as a sign of weakness. It actually should be seen as a sign of strength since, for participative leadership to take place, the team has to respect the leader. This style is best employed when collective responsibility is called for – when more than one person has the answer to a problem. The participative approach allows the leader to involve the team in order to make better decisions about scheduling, response and the allocation of time. It is a key approach to achieving motivation and commitment.

3. Delegative (free reign)

   In this style, the leader allows the team member to make the decision. However, the leader is still responsible for the decision that is made. This is used when teams consist of specialists who are able to analyse a situation and determine what needs to be done and how to do it. For this style to work you must set priorities and delegate certain tasks. It lends itself to higher-level customer relation management and service quality and may be employed when dealing with complaints or difficult customers.

Different styles should be applied in different circumstances. For example, authoritarian leadership may be the only way to deal with an unexpected crisis, but participative leadership is more fruitful where teamwork is required. A leader needs to balance directive leadership with supportive leadership – depending on the circumstances and this is known as 'situational leadership'. Two things are important in determining which style will work best in a given situation: the impact the decision or leadership action will have on a team and the extent to which team members are competent to complete the task set.

Social organizations trade within a free market economy which means that leaders must necessarily take risks. The risk is evident in the

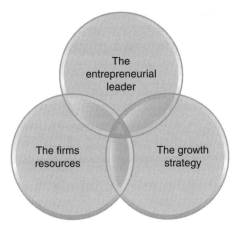

Figure 3.3   **Achieving growth**

concept of free choice – the idea that the consumer has a choice, they are not a captive market and can chose whether or not to purchase a service. This is why leadership is more important than management. Social enterprise leadership is not proscribed or reduced to a series of tasks. Nor is entrepreneurial leadership the only factor to consider.

According to Scott (2002),[12] 'much of the modern leadership literature concentrates on the larger organization'. Leadership looms large in learning organization literature also (e.g. Senge, 1990, p. 9).[13] This introduces the concept of 'entrepreneurial leadership', a style of leadership that is linked to creativity vision and opportunity seeking. Entrepreneurial leaders exhibit less task orientation in the way they exploit opportunities and that is why they are normally attracted to smaller organizations. Figure 3.3 highlights the three factors that are required to be interconnected if growth is to be achieved.

For an example of a particular type of leadership style as exhibited by the co-founder of The Big Issue, John Bird, please see Minicase 3.1. In the context of this case please review the questions on this case at the end of this chapter.

Determining the leadership style

What is clear is that different styles can be applied in different circumstances. For example, authoritarian leadership may be the best way to deal with an unexpected crisis, but participative leadership is more fruitful where teamwork is required. In effect, a leader needs to balance directive leadership with supportive leadership – depending on the circumstances. This is known as 'situational leadership'.

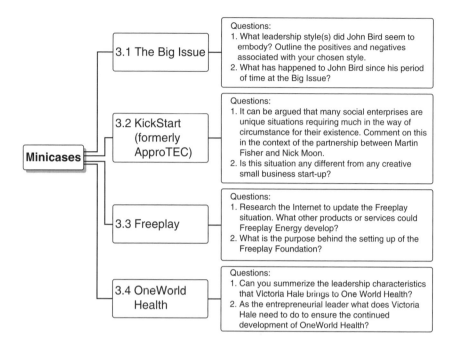

Minicases

3.1 The Big Issue

Questions:
1. What leadership style(s) did John Bird seem to embody? Outline the positives and negatives associated with your chosen style.
2. What has happened to John Bird since his period of time at the Big Issue?

3.2 KickStart (formerly ApproTEC)

Questions:
1. It can be argued that many social enterprises are unique situations requiring much in the way of circumstance for their existence. Comment on this in the context of the partnership between Martin Fisher and Nick Moon.
2. Is this situation any different from any creative small business start-up?

3.3 Freeplay

Questions:
1. Research the Internet to update the Freeplay situation. What other products or services could Freeplay Energy develop?
2. What is the purpose behind the setting up of the Freeplay Foundation?

3.4 OneWorld Health

Questions:
1. Can you summarize the leadership characteristics that Victoria Hale brings to One World Health?
2. As the entrepreneurial leader what does Victoria Hale need to do to ensure the continued development of OneWorld Health?

Minicase 3.1   The Big Issue

The Big Issue was founded in 1991 to address the growing problem of homeless people on the street begging. The Big Issue was established by John Bird with the help of Gordon Roddick of the Body Shop. The concept was simple: create a street newspaper compiled by professionals and then have it sold at a profit by homeless people who keep a proportion of the cover price thus creating a legitimate source of income for which the homeless were actively involved.

The Big Issue works by 'badging up' vendors who have to complete a training period and sign a vendor code of conduct in order to receive an official badge. They are normally given 10 free magazines. When they have sold these they are able to buy copies of the magazine upfront at a cost of 40–50 per cent of the cover price and from these sales the difference obtained represents the profit to the vendor.

The Big Issue was set up as a business response to a social crisis, not as a charity, and it never had statutory funding. The only start-up funding it received was from the Body Shop Foundation. It is financed through cover price sales and advertising, with any surplus going to The Big Issue Foundation. In an interview in 2007, Nigel Kershaw the CEO of the foundation pointed out that the advantage of not having set up as a charity was that there was no board of trustees to consult before taking decisions, allowing boardroom decision making to be unusually quick and effective. In 1993 The Big Issue went regional to cover the whole of the

UK as a weekly magazine with the cover price in each region varied to suit the local market. The goals of the Big Issue are

1. Enable homeless people to earn a legal income through opportunities to help themselves.
2. Invest profits in services to help homeless people and Big Issue vendors tackle obstacles to helping them help themselves.
3. Provide people with a voice in the media.
4. Produce a quality magazine which engages readers with issues that affect their lives but are overlooked by other media.
5. Provide an example of a socially responsible business and an alternative to conventional charity as a response to homelessness.

The role of the founder
Much of the magazine's initial success can be attributed to the founder, John Bird. His entrepreneurial spirit, character and flair, combined with the business acumen of Gordon Roddick, made for a powerful team. However, John Bird, although providing the original drive behind The Big Issue was also seen as the magazine's biggest liability. His combative management style often alienated staff. As a former staff journalist stated: 'John could be a complete nightmare – he would walk in 10 minutes before press time and demand that the cover be changed. He is also a bit of a bully, though he is immensely charismatic.'

Overseas expansion
The magazine unsuccessfully tried to expand overseas and it was only after a period of years that success was achieved, this time in Australia followed by Japan, South Africa, Namibia and Kenya.

Source: www.bigissue.com, www.nesta.org.uk/social-innovation, accessed December 2008

QUESTIONS
1. What leadership style(s) did John Bird seem to embody? Outline the positives and negatives associated with your chosen style(s).
2. What has happened to John Bird since his period of time at the Big Issue?

Two things are important in determining which style will work best in a given situation:

1. the impact the decision or leadership action will have on team members;
2. the extent to which team members are competent to complete the task set.

In this way it is helpful to distinguish between different task needs.

Leadership has become synonymous with good management behaviour. It is almost always linked to the individual at the top. However we need to distinguish between the role of a leader and the role of the manager. Leadership has been described as what individuals do under conditions of change. When organizations are dynamic and undergoing transformation, people exhibit leadership. Management on the other hand is associated with the status quo. Managers focus on stability, controlling performance and managing policies. Leaders are dynamic, responding to change; they are seen as charismatic (Whetten, 2005).[14] The role of the leader is therefore more important when things are changing.

According to Hartigan (2005),[15] social entrepreneurs share many of the characteristics of business entrepreneurs. She states:

> 'Entrepreneurs' of both types share common traits including an innovative, risk-taking approach to a challenge, the ability to seize opportunities, transforming 'business as usual' and mobilizing scarce resources toward that end. Schumpeter called business entrepreneurs the 'change agents in the economy. By serving new markets or creating new ways of doing things, they move the economy forward'. ... Social entrepreneurs are the change agents in the social sector. But in contrast to business entrepreneurs, their best measure of success is not how much profit they make, but the extent to which they generate social value. Their continuous energy to imagine, innovate, implement, improve on innovation, scale up, diversify, defy the usual, break the patterns and move in a new direction, all characteristics that define social entrepreneur. ... The distinction between business and social entrepreneurs doesn't stop there. Business entrepreneurs are subject to market discipline. For them, the profit that their venture generates is a fairly good indicator of the value they have created. Social entrepreneurs enter the scene precisely where markets have failed to deliver critical public goods, particularly to those who cannot pay.

It defies the traditional organizational boundaries that separate the 'social' and the 'business' worlds. Some social enterprises such as KickStart (Minicase 3.2) have generated social value through innovative not-for-profits, others through for-profit micro-lending institutions or community development banks, and still others, such as Freeplay, (Minicase 3.3) by combining not-for-profit and for-profit components.

Minicases 3.2 and 3.3 respectively outline the basic details of Kickstart-ApproTEC and Freeplay.

Minicase 3.2   KickStart (formerly ApproTEC)

KickStart's mission is to help millions of people out of poverty. They promote sustainable economic growth and employment creation in Kenya and other African countries through developing and promoting technologies that can be used by local entrepreneurs to establish and run profitable small-scale enterprises.

In addition to promoting small enterprise development, KickStart's technologies, expertise, and methods are widely applied throughout Africa to support programs in agriculture, shelter, water, sanitation, health, and relief.

The history

In 1991, Martin Fisher and Nick Moon founded ApproTEC, which in 2005 became KickStart. Their model was based on to develop, launch a 5 step process to promote simple money-making tools that poor entrepreneurs could use to create their own profitable businesses.

In Africa, 80% of the poor are small-scale farmers. They depend on unreliable rain to grow their crops and have, at most, two harvests per year. With two valuable assets, a small plot of land and basic farming skills, KickStart in 1998, developed a line of manually operated irrigation pumps that allow farmers to easily pull water from a river, pond or shallow well (as deep as 25 feet deep), pressurize it through a hose pipe (even up a hill) and irrigate up to two acres of land. Our pumps are easy to transport and install and retail between $35 and $95. They are easy to operate and, because they are pressurized, they allow farmers to direct water where it is needed. It is a very efficient use of water, and unlike flood irrigation, does not lead to the build up of salts in the soil.

In 2000, KickStart expanded into Tanzania, and in 2004, they expanded into Mali. They were successful in both countries and today thousands of pumps are in use in Uganda, Malawi, Zambia, Sudan and Rwanda.

The founders

Martin Fisher, PhD and Nick Moon took different paths to Africa, but both went with altruistic visions of using their skills to make a difference.

Nick, born and raised in the far corners of the British Empire, first came to Africa after answering an advert in a London paper looking for a French-speaking carpenter to build a music studio in Togo! He went to Kenya as part of the VSO, the British equivalent of the Peace Corps. After many years of wandering the globe, in Kenya he found his home.

Martin, born in London and raised in Ithaca, NY, went to Kenya on a Fulbright Fellowship to study the Appropriate Technology Movement. His friendships with fellow graduate students from developing countries and his own experience travelling in the remote Andes, started him thinking about the role technology plays in increasing wealth. He was supposed to stay in Kenya for 10 months. He stayed for 17 years.

The two met while working for a large British aid organization and over a period of five years, they worked on just about every kind of development 'intervention', from building rural water systems, to building schools, and creating job training programs.

Source: http://www.kickstart.org

QUESTIONS

1. It can be argued that many social enterprises are unique situations requiring much in the way of circumstance for their existence. Comment on this in the context of the partnership between Martin Fisher and Nick Moon.
2. Is this situation any different from any creative small business start-up?

Minicase 3.3   Freeplay

For many people living in poverty, radio is their lifeline, providing information that can mean the difference between life and death. Clean, safe lighting can make study possible, extend the working day for increased income and improve the quality of health care. Until recently, radios and lights were out of reach for most people in poverty – usually defined as living on less than US$1 per day. Disposable batteries are prohibitively expensive, especially for children living on their own. Kerosene, candles and firewood use more than 15% of already meagre household incomes. They cause respiratory problems and fires that destroy lives and property.

The Freeplay solution
The Freeplay Foundation sought to change all that. Their wind-up and solar-powered Freeplay Lifeline radios provide sustainable access to information and education. Since 2003, more than 160,000 Lifeline radios have been distributed, conservatively reaching six million listeners.

To help meet the need and demand for portable clean energy sources, they expanded into the renewable lighting sector. After conducting lighting needs assessments of vulnerable households in rural and peri-urban areas of South Africa, Freeplay Energy's engineers set out to create clean energy lights called 'Lifelights'. Like the Lifeline radio, they will be powered by patented Freeplay wind-up technology or by solar power.

In addition, we have launched two pilot projects with the Weza foot-powered generator. The Weza, developed by Freeplay Energy, can power cell phones and other low energy devices. Using the Weza, we are working with communities in Rwanda and Zambia to establish self-financing small energy businesses. These entrepreneurs – mainly women – provide fee-based energy services, including cell phone charging and LED light charging and rental.

Our mission
Our mission is to transform lives through dependable, self-sufficient and environmentally friendly technologies. We work primarily in sub-Saharan

Africa with a special focus on the needs of orphans and other vulnerable children, women, refugees and people who are ill.

Freeplay Energy

In 1998, Freeplay Energy (formerly Freeplay Energy Group) established the non-profit Freeplay Foundation as an extension of its social commitment. Although other companies manufactured versions of wind-up and solar-powered radios, only Freeplay had developed patented technology within its products. Freeplay is the world leader in transferring wind-up technology to the poorest of the poor, the people least able to access the information and education that could help lift them out of poverty.

The Foundation is a wholly separate organization from Freeplay Energy with a board of trustees and staff of development sector experts led by Chief Executive Kristine Pearson. The Foundation was registered as a charity in England and Wales in 1998. In 2001, Freeplay became recognized as a 501 (c) (3) charitable organization in the USA, as well as a Section 21 non-profit in South Africa. Headquarters are in London, with a regional office in Johannesburg and satellite offices in the US.

Source: http://www.freeplayfoundation.org

QUESTIONS

1. Research the Internet to update the Freeplay situation. What other products or services could Freeplay Energy develop?
2. What is the purpose behind the setting up of the Freeplay Foundation?

The vision and the style

While a social entrepreneur (see Schwab Foundation)[16] shares many of the leadership characteristics of an SME entrepreneur, they are of a different kind from other social leaders. The social entrepreneur uses commercial skills to identify and apply practical solutions to social problems by combining innovation, resourcefulness and opportunity. Innovation occurs through the finding of a new product, a new service, or a new approach to a social problem. The aim is to focus first and foremost on social value creation and in that spirit to be willing to share openly the innovations and insights of the initiative with a view to its wider replication. The social entrepreneur, just like the entrepreneur, does not wait to secure the resources before undertaking the catalytic innovation. S/he is however fully accountable to the constituencies s/he serves and will need not only a vision, but also a well-thought out roadmap as to how to attain the goal. The social entrepreneur is under pressure to create value in terms of meeting the needs of the community.

The entrepreneur in a for-profit situation is also under pressure to create value and profit but at risk here is their own investment.

The social entrepreneur is therefore the equivalent of the SME founder – someone with vision and who needs to build a team around them to execute that vision. For an example of this please see Minicase 3.4 on Victoria Hale and her role in the creation of OneWorld Health.

Leading the team

Theories go through stages. They are simplifications that shed light into any situation. It should be clear that there cannot be a single theory or business model that explains all social enterprises. The categories of social enterprises such as social firms are used interchangeably within social enterprise and with the social entrepreneur. This in turn is interchangeable with not-for-profit charitable and public enterprises. It's a mess and it makes study difficult especially in a new and emerging area. Theories or ideas such as the classic relations or systems theory can become inflexible, distorting, or causing denial of observable reality. They can also be taken out of context and applied to a time, subject, problem or place for which they are not appropriate. In other words theories can be misunderstood, deliberately or accidentally.

So what is needed is an appreciation of a range of theories and an ability to use them appropriately. This means adapting existing theories, and in this case theories relating to entrepreneurship and the growth of small firms to see where they fit and where they do not. The key is the disassembly and reassembly of ideas – in this case looking at the role of the lead entrepreneur. There is a lack of common language on the subject of what constitutes a 'Lead Entrepreneur'. This is an interdisciplinary subject that encompasses social, economic and psychological perspectives. In the media, entrepreneurship is often associated with innovation, SMEs and business start-ups. Rightly or wrongly the same entrepreneurial characteristics have become associated with social entrepreneurs. The lead entrepreneur can, and often should be, the most experienced. In looking at the literature relating to habitual entrepreneurship, the lead entrepreneur will often be someone who is either a serial or portfolio entrepreneur with a successful track record of social enterprise creation. Here is the notion of the entrepreneur as a 'hero' – the saviour that is so much in evidence in policy approaches outlined in the previous two chapters.

Timmons (1989)[17] has attempted to summarize the personality characteristics of successful entrepreneurs. While he does admit that many of these characteristics can be acquired through learning or from experience, he also considers that there are some attributes which cannot be acquired, that are innate, that perhaps mark out 'born entrepreneurs' from 'made entrepreneurs'. Timmons considers that both the need for achievement and locus of control can be acquired along with other leadership abilities and competencies such as the ability to take responsibility for actions/decisions. Many of these characteristics are management skills. That is, entrepreneurs obviously need to be ambitious but need to be satisfied that they have achieved personal goals and ambitions.

The entrepreneur and the social enterprise

The key characteristic that can be derived from the discussion is that profit or monetary reward is not the sole driving force behind entrepreneurs. There is also the need to build and achieve personally set goals, implying that entrepreneurs have a high need for achievement in order to establish a growing business or an 'entrepreneurial' firm. Similarly, the internal locus of control characteristic has been identified as an important characteristic of potential entrepreneurs. A high internal locus of control means that the person needs to be in control of their own environment, to be their own boss. It is perhaps interesting that Timmons considers that these characteristics can be acquired. It is also interesting that Timmons considers that dealing with failure can be an important attribute of entrepreneurs. However, the ability to tolerate failure depends on the culture. If this argument holds, then social entrepreneurs share many similarities with the founders of growth businesses. They are variations on a theme – with more in common than with professional managers in corporate organizations. One of the biggest challenges both variants face is how to build and motivate a team – in other words how to instil vision and confidence into an organization so that it 'flies' rather than 'trundles'. The value and the leadership style are highly influential in creating a responsive organization – one that is fit for purpose.

Focusing this argument, entrepreneurship has elements of economic activity, personal characteristics and management traits. The social entrepreneurs bring these same characteristics to bear. And, if Timmons (1989) is to be believed, it is not who they are but what they do, in terms of management, that determines their success.

For an example of the difference that can be made by a social entrepreneur and the impact such an individual can have on the lives of people please see Minicase 3.4 OneWorld Health.

The Institute for OneWorld Health is a US-based non-profit pharmaceutical company that develops drugs for people with neglected infectious diseases in the developing world. The founder of OneWorld Health is Victoria Hale. The success of the world's first non-profit drug company has led to Victoria Hale being named, in September 2006, a MacArthur Fellow.

The John D. and Catherine T. MacArthur Foundation has named Victoria Hale, Ph.D., founder and chief executive officer of the Institute for OneWorld Health (iOWH), a 2006 MacArthur Fellow today. These prestigious Fellowships are awarded to individuals who have developed original and creative ideas that have the potential to make important contributions in the future. Dr. Hale is being honored as a Pharmaceutical Entrepreneur for creating a nonprofit model of drug development that is driven by the neglected health needs of people in the developing world.

Source: www.oneworldhealth.org/victoria_hale

For the 45-year-old Hale, the timing of her grant is especially delicious. Her nonprofit pharmaceutical company, the Institute for OneWorld Health, had won clearance a week earlier to sell its first drug in India. It can cure leishmaniasis (Leash-man-eye-a-sis), a parasitic disease that infects 500,000 people a year. Left untreated, it almost always leads to a protracted and painful death. Also known as black fever, it is second only to malaria as the deadliest parasitic infection on Earth. But Hale knew of an old, injectable antibiotic, paromomycin, that had been dropped as obsolete by drug companies 30 years ago that had shown effectiveness against it.

OneWorld arranged a partnership with an Indian drugmaker to reformulate the drug and ran expensive clinical trials that proved the treatment worked. The drug should be available in the impoverished Indian state of Bihar by year-end. A course of treatment requiring a shot a day for three weeks will cost $10. Hale, trained as a pharmaceutical chemist at UCSF, envisioned a nonprofit drug company after stints at the Food and Drug Administration and Genentech, the South San Francisco biotechnology company. The idea caught the attention of the Bill & Melinda Gates Foundation, which has given OneWorld grants totaling $140 million to develop several drugs for the Third World.

Source: Sabin Russell, *San Francisco Chronicle*, medical writer.
(19/09/2006) www.sfgate.com

Minicase 3.4   OneWorld Health

An excellent example of a talented individual with a clear idea that could benefit poor disadvantaged people worldwide for a very small amount of money is the social enterprise founded by social entrepreneur Dr Victoria Hale. The concept of OneWorld Health was actually quite simple. To get round the need for the normal situation where funding of new drugs was part of a cycle involving huge development costs connected to low success rates, pharmaceutical companies had to charge a great deal for the drugs they have successfully developed and taken to market. Other drugs never reached the market place because of the high cost of development by a single pharmaceutical business. This business model meant that people in the Third World who needed basic drugs for eye disease and other common problems or disorders such as diarrheal disease did not receive them, and this led to the death of 1.5 million children under the age of five each year. This unacceptable loss of life was caused by a lack of affordable medicine and it was the vision of Victoria Hale that this could and should be stopped. To this end Dr Hale founded The Institute for OneWorld Health, the first non-profit pharmaceutical company in the United States.

Dr Hale established her expertise in all stages of biopharmaceutical drug development at the US Food and Drug Administration (FDA), Center for Drug Evaluation and Research, and at Genentech, Inc. Using her expertise gained in these organizations she was able to set about establishing OneWorld Health as a social enterprise founded to develop safe, effective, and affordable new medicines for those in developing countries who needed them the most.

As indicated in Chapter 7 of this book, many social enterprises, especially in the US, are supported by donations from wealthy individuals who have made their money through building up large corporations and have decided to use that wealth for the common good. In this regard it is very much a clear example of enlightened self-interest. It is this philanthropic funding that is a major breakthrough for many US based social enterprises. In the case of OneWorld Health it was the Bill & Melinda Gates Foundation who gave, in 2002, two new grants totaling more than $4.6 million to the Institute for OneWorld Health (iOWH) to fund drug development that would treat two parasitic, neglected diseases – Chagas and visceral leishmaniasis.

As outlined above in the business model for iOWH the grant from the Gates Foundation was to allow final testing of paromomycin, a promising new therapy to cure visceral leishmaniasis, a deadly parasitic disease threatening more than 350 million people worldwide.

From these beginnings OneWorld Health has gone on to develop into a major social enterprise and gain for Victoria Hale a range of major awards such as being selected in 2004 as one of 10 of the world's most 'Outstanding Social Entrepreneurs' by the Schwab Foundation for Social Entrepreneurship.

To access OneWorld Health, please visit www.oneworldhealth.org.

To access *Diarrhoea: Why Children Are Still Dying and What Can Be Done*, please visit: http://www.unicef.org/media/files/Final_Diarrhoea_ Report_October_2009_final.pdf.

More on Hale and OneWorld Health may be found at http://www. schwabfound.org/schwabentrepreneurs.htm?schwabid=915.

Additionally, the social enterprise Victoria Hale helped found was honoured as social enterprise of the year by Fast Company magazine in December 2008. This non-profit pharmaceutical company was chosen as one of the top 10 social enterprises in the US. OneWorld Health and nine other groundbreaking social enterprises were singled out for their bold and timely ideas, and for innovative thinking that can transform lives and change the world.

As Storey (1994)[18] points out:

the three components – the entrepreneur, the firm and strategy – all need to combine appropriately in order that the firm achieve rapid growth.

Minicase 3.4 is a good example of the three components all coming together to create a major non-profit organization that as a result of the merging of these components has the capacity to help people in poor countries change their lives for the better.

Example 3.1 provides a summary of the material in this chapter.

Examples ── 3.1 The management and the theory

Example 3.1   The management and the theory

Social enterprises have more in common with SMEs than larger corporation and are closely linked with family businesses.

The literature on small firms, entrepreneurship and family business can be adapted to illustrate growth options for social enterprises.

Not all social enterprises want to be or are capable of being 'gazelles'.

A mouse business is seen by some policymakers as being an inferior business format.

When growth does occur it requires 'professionalizing the management'.

Leadership takes a different form in membership organizations.

Like for-profit organizations leaders in social enterprises need to adapt their styles.

An entrepreneurial leader is the best form of leadership to create a sustainable business at least in the first instance.

Revision questions

Conduct your own research to identify the following:

1. What does 'social entrepreneurship' really mean in my environment?
2. Identify at least one local social entrepreneur. What are the distinguishing characteristics of this social entrepreneur?
3. Why did The Big Issue fail to succeed in the US market? Why was it successful in Australia?
4. At what point in the growth of a social enterprise does the entrepreneurial leader need to consider their position?

References

1. G. N. Prabhu, 'Social Entrepreneurial Leadership', *Career Development International*, 4/3 (1999), pp. 140–5.
2. Available at Virtue Ventures http://www.virtueventures.com/setypology/index.php?id=PROLOG&lm=1, accessed June 2008.
3. See http://www.virtueventures.com/setypology/index.php?id=COMBINING_MODELS&lm=1, accessed June 2008.
4. David L. Birch, 'Who Creates Jobs?' *The Public Interest*, 65 (1981), pp. 3–14.
5. D. Storey, *Understanding the Small Firm Sector* (London: Thomson Business Press (1998), Chapter 5, pp. 112–59 for a discussion on these issues.
6. P. O'Farrell and M. Hitchens, 'The Relative Competitiveness and Performance of Small Manufacturing Firms in Scotland and the Mid-West of Ireland: An Analysis of Matched Pairs', *Regional Studies*, vol. 22, issue 5 (1988), pp. 399–415.
7. S. Birley and P. Westhead, 'A Taxonomy of Business Start-Up Reasons and their Impact on Firm Growth and Size', *Journal of Business Venturing*, 9 (1994), pp. 7–31.
8. E. G. Flamholtz, *How to make the Transition from an Entrepreneurial to a Professionally Managed Firm* (San Francisco: Josey-Bass, 1986).
9. L. Greiner 'Evolution and Revolution as Organizations Grow', *Harvard Business Review*, vol. 50, July–August (1972), pp. 37–46.

10. M. Deakins and M. Freel, *Entrepreneurship and Small Firms*, 5th edn (London: McGraw-Hill, 2009), pp. 177–84.
11. L. Mullins, *Management and Organizational Behaviour*, 5th edn (Harlow: Financial Times-Pitman Publishing, 1999).
12. D. Scott, 'Do You Need to be Creative to Start a Successful Business?' *Management Research News*, vol. 22, no. 9 (1999), pp. 26–41.
13. P. Senge, *The Fifth Discipline: The Art and Practice of The Learning Organisation* (London: Random House, 1990).
14. D. A. Whetten and K. S. Cameron, *Developing Management Skills* (London: Prentice Hall, 2006).
15. P. Hartigan, *Innovating in Response to Market Failure: The Art of Social Entrepreneurship, Examples from Africa* (Geneva, Switzerland: Schwab Foundation, 2005).
16. Schwab Foundation, see http://www.schwabfound.org/whatis.htm, accessed December 2009.
17. J. A. Timmons, *The Entrepreneurial Mind* (Andover: Brick House, 1989).
18. D. J. Storey, *Understanding the Small Business Sector* (London: Routledge, 1994).

Additional reading

Dees, G., 'The Meaning of Social Innovation', Stanford Business School, 2003. See http://www.gsb.stanford.edu/csi/SEDefinition.html.

Dees, J. G., Economy, P. and Emerson, J., *Enterprising Nonprofits, A Handbook for Social Entrepreneurs* San Francisco, Harvard Business Review on Nonprofits. (Cambridge, MA: Harvard Business School Press, 1999).

Doherty, B., Foster, G., Mason, C., Meehan, J., Meehan, K., Rotheroe, N. and Royce, M. *Management for Social Enterprise* (London: Sage, 2009).

Emerson, J. and Twersky, F., '*New Social Entrepreneurs: The Success, Challenge, and Lessons of Non-Profit Enterprise Creation*' (San Francisco: The Roberts Foundation, 1996).

Leadbeater, C., 'The Rise of the Social Entrepreneur', *Demos*, January (1997), pp. 12–21 and 77–83.

McGregor, A., Clark, S., Ferguson, Z. and Scullion, J., 'Valuing the Social Economy: The Social Economy and Economic Inclusion in Lowland Scotland', Community Enterprise Strathclyde (CEiS), 1997, www.ceis.org.uk/resourses-and-publication.html, accessed December 2009. (Contact CEiS direct for access to McGregor, et al.)

OECD, Social Enterprises, Paris, 1999.

Rosa, P., 'Governance in SMEs', *Family Business Review*, vol. 18, issue 4 (2005), pp. 350–3.

Thake, S. and Zadek, S., 'Practical People, Noble Causes: How to Support Community-Based Social Entrepreneurs', *New Economics Foundation* (1997), pp. 11–14 and 17–21.

Schwab Foundation for Social Entrepreneurs, see http://www.schwab foundation.org.

Srikumar, S. Rao, 'The Emperor of Peace Lives Again!' September 7, 1998, www.forbes.com, accessed December 2009.

4 social entrepreneurs

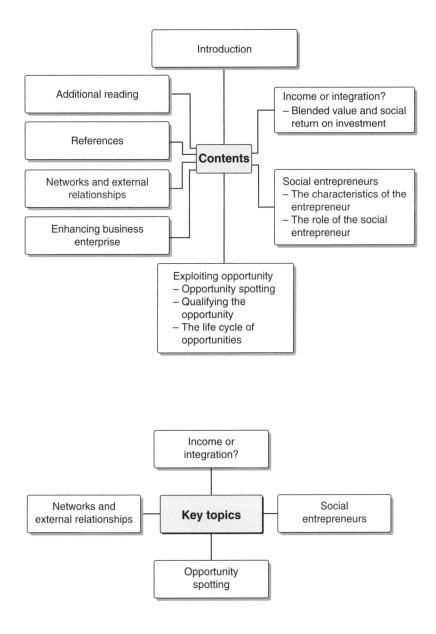

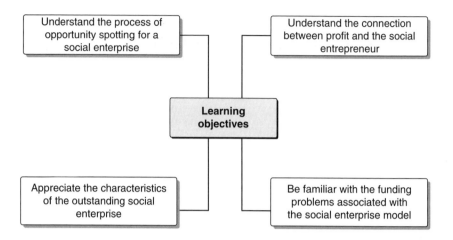

Introduction

This chapter develops the theme of the social entrepreneur and looks more closely at his or her role in creating and managing a successful enterprise. Social entrepreneurship describes a business approach to addressing a social issue. This is an approach that cuts across disciplines such as medicine, engineering, law, education, agronomy and the environment. Nor is it confined to sectors of the economy, and it can be seen in health, transportation, finance, labour, trade, and the like (The Schwab Foundation).[1] Hence, social entrepreneurship is more related to leadership than to management.

It builds upon the idea that 'social' is a variant on the entrepreneurship theme and that existing research and ideas on entrepreneurship and SME business growth can still be used to explain some of the characteristics of successful social enterprises. This success depends in part on the relationship between internal and external resources and this, in turn, influences whether or how far an organization can grow.

To investigate the relationship between the entrepreneur, the firm and the firm's strategy, this chapter looks into the influence of the founding entrepreneur – how they reconcile the need to generate income, their attitudes towards risk and how these are exhibited in the values of the organizations they create. A critical perspective is taken on how a founding entrepreneur may be, initially, an asset and how s/he may later become a disadvantage to the growth of a business.

Income or integration?

To examine the nature of the funding dilemma we can look at one specific category within the broader social enterprise model, that of the social firm.

As we have already indicated in Chapter 1, the classic definition of a social firm is of a business that provides employment opportunities for people who are in some way disabled or severely disadvantaged in the labour market. It is in effect a type of social enterprise that focuses on work integration for severely disadvantaged people. The key characteristics of a social firm are

- Income Generation – At least 50 per cent of the income generated will come through sales of goods or services in the market.

- Integration – A significant number of the employees (at least 25 per cent) will be people with a disability who are integrated into the staff of the business and employed on the same terms and conditions as other non-disabled staff, having the same rights and responsibilities. (Social Firms Scotland)

The challenge with these two characteristics is that they are not complementary. The distinction infers that unless a not-for-profit organization is generating earned revenue from its activities, it is not acting in an entrepreneurial manner. It may be doing social good, creating new and vibrant programs, but it is innovative, not entrepreneurial. (Boschee, 2003).[2] This distinction is important because we have argued that in order to survive, a social enterprise needs to be sustainable – it has to generate income and from this some form of profit. The social firm may actually sacrifice profit to carry out is mission but will still have to generate income. The question of income or integration is therefore an uncomfortable one. It is a dilemma that is not faced by a for-profit firm.

This inherent conflict means that social firms can exist at different growth stages, in terms of their ability to match income with integration. It is the ability to manage this conflict between integration and income that is one of the main factors that can determine the success of a social enterprise. Minicase 4.1 The Forth Sector outlines the model of a central social enterprise hub creating and supporting a number of social firms. Management expertise comes from the hub and this model helps each of the new social firms. From this can spring the creation of earned income which is crucial to the survival of any of the business within Third Sector.

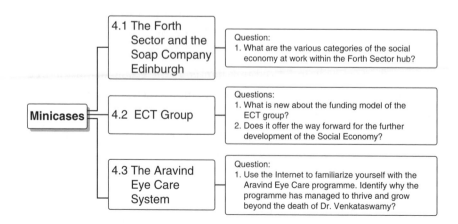

Minicase 4.1   The Forth Sector and the Soap Company Edinburgh

The Forth Sector runs successful social firms (businesses) and develops new business ideas to provide employment for people with mental health problems. The aim of the social firms is to offer real, valued work for staff and trainees while meeting the demands of their diverse customers.

Forth Sector is one of Scotland's leading social enterprises. The aim is to create supportive employment for people with mental health problems through running businesses staffed by them. The opportunities provided within these real working environments support people to

- recover from the impact of their mental ill health
- increase their employability
- regain or retain employment

Forth Sector runs small commercial businesses, trading to high standards. The businesses (social firms) operate in a range of markets, including tourism, catering, laundry and embroidery services and manufacturing/retail. During 2005–6 Forth Sector helped 50 people back into mainstream employment or further education and training. The hub that is Forth Sector has been running small businesses for 15 years so there's a wealth of experience in the management team on how to do it and they operate businesses ranging from manufacturing through services to retail, and company turnover amounts to over £1.5 million. Forth Sector believes in quality and has won national awards including the prestigious Scottish Thistle Award in customer care, the Silver Green Tourism Award, have obtained Investors in People accreditation and the Bronze Scotland's Health at Work Award.

Forth Sector hub
The central support unit provides expertise in finance, human resource, administration, marketing, business development and staff/trainee support to its businesses. This hub structure enables the business managers to concentrate on delivering their business objectives and also provide a supportive working environment. This means they can continue to grow and expand current businesses and seek out new business ideas that will create more jobs for people with mental health problems. The target is to have 85% of our income generated on a commercial basis. One of the Social Enterprises created by The Forth Sector is outlined below.

The Soap Co Edinburgh
The Soap Company was established in 2004 to produce and sell high quality handmade soap and bathroom products. 'We wanted to recreate products that hold on to old fashioned methods and recipes without compromising on quality, and at the same time reflect the contemporary feel of Edinburgh. A small business with a social conscience, we try to source our ingredients locally and are moving to becoming even more environmentally responsible. Everyone at the Soap Co takes pride in being involved in what we do and are knowledgeable about our products. You

only need to look at the visitors book to see the quality service we offer. Our best seller is our hard bar soaps made using the traditional cold-process method. This involves the products being cured for 3–4 weeks on special drying racks, the result is a natural soap that is kind and gentle to your skin. Unlike manufactured soaps this traditional method retains a high content of glycerine which locks moisture into the skin. Our products are made using no sodium tallowate, which is an animal fat and is widely used in the production of commercial soaps.'

Source: http://www.forthsector.org.uk/our_businesses

http://www.thesoapcomedinburgh.co.uk

QUESTIONS

1. What are the various categories of the social economy at work within the Forth Sector hub?

Blended value and social return on investment

Emerson (2000)[3] describes this model of income generation and integration as 'blended value' – the idea that social enterprises are expected to achieve both economic success and maximize social benefits. Such an approach does suggest an unconventional approach is needed to account for success, since the measures of success are both financial and social. Emerson's description can be said to be the very essence of social enterprise in terms of the ability to connect social and community values and at the same time achieve economic outcomes through capital accumulation and wealth creation. This social accounting is distinct from SME accounting because it seeks to quantify social impacts, translating the impacts into monetary values where possible. The 'social pro forma statements' lay out high-level performance goals from which performance metrics and data collection systems could flow logically, and taken together they form a comprehensive social accounting framework. If combined or integrated with financial accounting, such a framework generates a more complete picture of a firm's total creation of value' (Lingane et al., 2004).[4] The authors go on to identify the concept of Social Return on Investment (SROI) to monitor social benefits and costs relative to the company's performance.

They identify four steps to achieving this:

1. collection of ongoing social performance data;
2. prioritization of data important enough to track;

3. incorporation of the data into management decision-making and reporting;
4. valuation to understand what amount of social value is created or destroyed, and by extension where resources should be allocated.

Assuming that ROI is important to a conventional business in attracting investment SROI is likely to be equally important to a social firm, especially when it is seeking external funding support. The Venture Financing Chain is the ability of a business to access outside sources of assistance to fund growth. There are a range of sources available for profit driven SMEs but these are constructed to provide investors with a return on their capital. The most fundamental form of external investment is known as bootstrapping, often in the form of 'family and friends', who invest in a new business. Leaving this aside to be discussed in Chapter 6, the more sophisticated from of equity investment is through the process of business 'angels' and then venture capital firms or even an Initial Public Offering (IPO). As one moves through the different options the potential sums to be raised increase. In other words equity investment is the capital source that allows accelerated growth. Business angel funds and possibly venture capital are equity investments and these are often used by fast growth business to fund the 'second stage of development', that is, the period two or three years after the business start-up. At this point a business will face a new set of operating priorities that might include

- the decision of whether to diversify the product range – either by adapting existing products or by moving into dissimilar marketing situations;
- the need to acquire more professional managerial skills as they face expansion into new markets;
- the need for better Management Information Systems (MIS) to control costs, quality and service delivery.

A lack of financial control can occur in this second phase through poor costing. Once a company moves to multiple trading activities, more attention needs to be given to costing. If an appropriate basis is not devised, pricing errors occur which makes it difficult for new products to survive in a competitive market.

For an example of how a social enterprise can develop please read Minicase 4.2 on ECT Group a major social enterprise founded in 1979 from the initial idea of providing a community transport service to the residents of Ealing. ECT is now growing and developing through selling of some of its businesses to use the capital acquired to develop its other social enterprises.

Minicase 4.2   ECT Group

ECT Group, one of the UK's leading social enterprises, is moving in a new direction it was announced today. The Group, whilst retaining its commitment to the provision of high quality public services for the community and to sustainability and partnership working, is preparing for major changes in direction. ECT Recycling – part of the ECT Group with 1,100 employees – has been acquired by May Gurney, one of the UK's most successful maintenance and support services companies and listed on the London stock market (AIM).

Formed in 1979 as part of Ealing Voluntary Service Council, ECT started life with just four vehicles, providing a transport service to Ealing residents. 28 years later, ECT has grown into a leading not-for-profit organisation with an £55 million turnover, providing a range of high quality services for the community. First and foremost, it's 'business as usual' at ECT Recycling – the current strong management team will remain in place, led by Stephen Sears, and the focus will remain on delivering service quality for its customers and its customers' customers – members of the public.

Stephen Sears, who has led the development of ECT since 1980 said: 'ECT has been looking for a partner for our recycling and waste management business with a good reputation in the local authority market place and with the commercial muscle to help us to secure bigger contracts. This will allow us to deliver our social and environmental objectives as well as the financial results that are essential to continued success.'

The ECT Group (which includes the charity Ealing Community Transport) will continue to operate community transport services in Ealing, Milton Keynes, Cheshire and the 195 bus service. It will maintain its joint venture with Hackney Community Transport (E&HCT), transporting construction workers within the Olympic Park, on behalf of the ODA. The rail businesses – RMS, Weardale and Dartmoor – are in the process of being sold to new owners with the financial firepower and resources to develop them successfully.

Cuckoo Lane Health Care will become an independent organisation. Its association with ECT made Cuckoo Lane one of Britain's most well known nurse-led practices.

Source: http://www.ectgroup.co.uk (News Release 38/08, 3 June 2008)

QUESTIONS

1. What is new about the funding model of the ECT group?
2. Does it offer the way forward for the further development of the Social Economy?

Because of the concept of 'blended values' (see Chapter 6), equity based investments are not a funding source that is readily available to a social enterprise. This is because an investor cannot expect a return on investment through a dividend or sale. Furthermore all forms of equity investment require the current owners to give up part of the ownership and when control of the firm is invested in a community rather than a group of individuals the opportunity for dispersal of shareholder value to outside investors is limited.

A business can grow through retained profits but growth is dependent on always having positive cash-flow. Where capital investment to fund rapid expansion is required, equity investment allows an immediate injection of funds without the requirement to pay back the lender in regular instalments. The question of bank finance is discussed in Chapter 6.

Social entrepreneurs

In Chapter 1 we indicated that there was some difficulty in obtaining a definition of a social entrepreneur. However there are consistent themes that run throughout the mainstream literature on entrepreneurship and these are discussed below.

The characteristics of the entrepreneur

(a) Economic perspectives

The definitions on entrepreneurship go back to c. 1730 when Cantillon defined entrepreneurship and the entrepreneur as someone who buys at a certain price to sell at an uncertain price. Babtiste (1816) saw the entrepreneur as an agent 'who unites all means of production and who finds new value in the products'. A century later, Schumpeter[5] saw the entrepreneur as an innovator who implements change through new combinations. This relates to the entrepreneur as someone who 'creates disruption' and who acts to de-stabilize an economy. In particular, the entrepreneur shifts energy from one part of the economy to another – typified in the move from public social good to community-owned enterprises. A key element of Schumpeter's view is that the entrepreneur is unlikely to find support within the institutional support network. Instead, they seek their own social networks for support and as a result they are part of an exclusive club.

The term 'entrepreneur' originated in French economics in the seventeenth and eighteenth centuries. In French, it means someone who 'undertakes' a significant project or activity. More specifically, it came to be used to identify the venturesome individuals who stimulated economic progress by finding new and better ways of doing things.

Joseph Schumpeter (1943) described entrepreneurs as the innovators who drive the 'creative-destructive' process of capitalism. In his words, 'the function of entrepreneurs is to reform or revolutionize the pattern of production'. They can do this in many ways: 'by exploiting an invention or, more generally, an untried technological possibility for producing a new commodity or producing an old one in a new way, by opening up a new source of supply of materials or a new outlet for products, by reorganizing an industry and so on'. Schumpeter's entrepreneurs are the change agents in the economy. By serving new markets or creating new ways of doing things, they move the economy forward. For a review of the nature of social entrepreneurs please see Example 4.1.

(b) Personality perspectives

McClelland pointed out in his motivation theory that the need for achievement was one of the most important personality traits/motivators for entrepreneurs when they are involved in enterprise. Parental influences are often an important part in the character development of the entrepreneur. Many entrepreneurs have had parents that have encouraged them to be self-reliant at an early age, while remaining supportive and not rejecting their offspring. An entrepreneur's need for achievement manifests itself in a number of ways:

Risk taking
Confidence of success
Desire for independence
Energy in pursuing goals
Measurement of success by wealth
Self-determination

Successful entrepreneurs are convinced that they can control their own destinies. Behavioural scientists describe those who believe they have the ability to control their environment as having an internal locus of control, compared to the others with an external locus of control who believe that their lives are dominated by chance and fate. The commonly held belief is one that sees small business survival and success as being linked to the internal locus of control belief of the owner manager(s) to overcome difficulties that defeated others.

(c) Risk taking

Entrepreneurs are often characterized as risk takers who instinctively know that gains do not accrue to those who always place safety first. However, there is debate over the levels of risk taken, which highlights a distinction between the entrepreneur and the owner manager. At one extreme there is the opportunist entrepreneur who relentlessly pursues every possibility with little regard to the resources available at the time. At the other end of the spectrum is the conservative owner manager, who took some risk to establish his or her enterprise, but whose aim now is to preserve what he or she has achieved.

(d) Desire for independence

A trait which is commonly recognized as prevalent among entrepreneurs and particularly within personal enterprise, is the strong desire for independence; the freedom to create their own futures. This can be linked to their internal locus of control: the belief in their ability to control their own destiny as mentioned previously can lead them to a desire for the necessary independence to make it happen their way.

Following on from the sociological perspective, Drucker (1985)[6] insists that innovation is like entrepreneurship in terms of it being a task that can be organized in a systematic way. In other words they are just simply a part of any manager's job. Drucker (1985) also presents entrepreneurs, not as people who are born with certain traits, but as managers who know where to look for innovation, and how to develop this innovation into useful products or services once they have found it.

Timmons (1999)[7] argues that entrepreneurship is a process that adds value and it is often linked to innovation. The proposition is that through innovation, wealth is created and that this is associated with new employment opportunities within an economy. Schumpeter, in particular supports the idea that entrepreneurship is about the following: the development of new products or services; the development of new methods of production; the identification of new segments and markets; the identification of different sources of supply; and the development of different forms of organization. Therefore, without entrepreneurship, businesses may fail to reach their full potential. They may in fact stagnate and even fail.

As has already been argued, not all businesses, and this includes social enterprises, are entrepreneurial. It is at this point that two divergent approaches begin to appear. On the one side there are those researchers who define entrepreneurship in terms of 'who the entrepreneur is' and then there are those that define them in terms of 'what he/she does'. The former, defining entrepreneurship in terms of the individual, offers only a partial understanding. A 'what he or she does' model is best exhibited by Timmons (1999) who argues that the entrepreneurship process is driven by a set of three integrated forces, all of which can be controlled. These forces are the lead entrepreneur and the entrepreneurial team, 'driven' opportunity, and the creative use of resources that are parsimonious with the venture. The question then remains whether this approach – one that relies upon the entrepreneur as a special manager and leader – helps explain the role of the social entrepreneur in growing a new business.

The role of the social entrepreneur

According to Boschee (2003) a social entrepreneur is any person in any sector who uses earned income strategies to pursue a social objective, and a social entrepreneur differs from a traditional entrepreneur in two important ways. Traditional entrepreneurs, it is argued, are capable of acting in a socially responsible manner and they are not simply dedicated to creating profit at any cost. Traditional entrepreneurs may choose to donate money to charitable organizations and they may, on ethical grounds, be unwilling to engage in certain types of businesses. As Boschee (2003) points out, this is admirable, but their efforts are only indirectly attached to social problems. Social entrepreneurs are different because their vision and revenue streams are directly tied into serving a community need. The traditional entrepreneur is less likely to employ people who are severely disabled, mentally ill or otherwise socially disadvantaged. Social entrepreneurs on the other hand do believe in integration – creating sustainable employment for disadvantaged members of the community.

The second point Boschee (2003) makes is that traditional entrepreneurs judge their ultimate success by financial results. The success or failure of their companies is determined by their ability to generate profits for their directors and shareholders. This driving objective is to offer a decent income for the owner and their family, and secure employment for the workforce. This means that traditional entrepreneurs work for a commercial imperative. For example a firm may choose to replace labour with machinery to make the business more efficient – even if this means reducing staff numbers. This is a commercial imperative to allow it to remain competitive.

Social entrepreneurs have two double bottom lines – a combination of financial and social returns. Creating a surplus is still a goal, but it is not the only goal. Profits are re-invested in the mission rather than being distributed to shareholders. This interpretation means that the term 'social entrepreneurship' refers to the efforts of individuals to create innovative responses to social needs. This 'social' element to innovation is still consistent with a Schumpeterian[8] perspective. This perspective is based on the viewpoint that

Entrepreneurs have a dream – a vision and the will to found a private kingdom.

They have an impulse to compete (unfairly), to succeed for the sake of the venture not for the fruits of success.

Entrepreneurs look for new combinations in the market and creatively combine resources to provide new forms of delivery.

In this way the entrepreneur displaces mature businesses and devalues the old. Entrepreneurs destroy as they create and this is known as Creative Destruction. It may help explain the redeployment and outsourcing of public sector initiatives into more business-orientated and performance-based enterprises. This is encapsulated in terms such as public enterprise, social markets, clients, and community responsibility. The innovation argument supports the notion that social entrepreneurs will be more inclined to experiment in new forms of (social) businesses and that they will be more open and opportunity seeking than a public sector organization. The experimentation and openness further facilitate more 'privatization' and more market-based approaches and business-like methods in the social sector. Hence there is a shift leading to public sector agencies contracting with both for-profit and not-for-profit providers. This shift has brought with it outcomes-based (rather than needs-based) approaches to funding, on the part of both private philanthropies and government agencies, along with more strategic thinking about corporate involvement in social and community issues. Each of these innovations raises questions of ethics, professional preparation, and long-term versus short-term gains.

The process of social innovation blurs the boundaries between charities, government agencies and social enterprises. What all three have in common is the call for more entrepreneurial spirit and innovation within the social enterprise sector.

Social entreprencurship still means different things to different groups, including policymakers. The terms social entrepreneur and social enterprise are often interchangeable. This was described as the entrepreneurial 'heffalump' in Chapter 1. The terms are often applied to not-for-profit organizations (NFP). Others use it to describe anyone who starts a not-for-profit organization. Another application refers to business owners who integrate social responsibility into their operations. It is important to realize that this is an emerging area of study – the definitions are important but the distinction being made is that the enterprise rather than the entrepreneur is much more important for a understanding success.

Exploiting opportunity

Drucker (1985) sees entrepreneurs as exploiting the opportunities that changes in technology, consumer preferences and social norms, create. He says, 'this defines entrepreneur and entrepreneurship – the entrepreneur always searches for change, responds to it, and exploits it as an opportunity'. The notion of 'opportunity' remains central to many current definitions of entrepreneurship. It is the way today's management theorists capture Say's notion of shifting resources to areas of higher yield. An opportunity, presumably, means an opportunity to create value in this way. Entrepreneurs have a mindset that sees the possibilities rather than the problems created by change.

For Drucker, starting a business is neither a necessary nor sufficient condition for entrepreneurship. He explicitly comments that 'not every new small business is entrepreneurial or represents entrepreneurship'. The same would be true of social enterprises – not every new social organization would be entrepreneurial. Drucker also makes it clear that entrepreneurship does not require a profit motive. Early in his book on innovation and entrepreneurship, Drucker asserts, 'no better text for a History of Entrepreneurship could be found than the creation of the modern university, and especially the modern American university'. Later in the book, he devotes a chapter to entrepreneurship in public service institutions.

Although this chapter has only touched on some concepts of entrepreneurship, it does point to a number of ideas.

1. That there are motivational differences, especially in terms of income creation and distribution between a social and traditional entrepreneur.
2. Motivational differences apart, both types of entrepreneurs are creators of wealth and, through the process of innovation, agents of change.
3. Entrepreneurship is not just about starting a business – it is about building a business.
4. It is a process of creative destruction – one in which innovation and opportunity-spotting is central to success.

Taken to its logical conclusion, and following the Timmon's perspective, there is little left to separate the social from the for-profit entrepreneur when it comes to seeking out new opportunities. Opportunity seeking is the key component of the entrepreneurial mindset – regardless of the format of the business: large or small, for-profit or not for profit.

Entrepreneurship brings together creative and innovative ideas and couples these with management and organizational skills in order to combine people, money and resources to meet an identified need and thereby create wealth. Henton, Melville, and Walesh (2003)[9] go on to list the main characteristics of the social entrepreneur as being:

- The ability to see opportunity
- Having an entrepreneurial personality

- The ability to work in teams and provide collaborative leadership
- Having a genuine, long-term, focused commitment to their communities

Dees (1998)[10] supports this idea:

> Traditional theories of entrepreneurship describe a mind-set and a kind of behavior that can be manifest anywhere. We should build our understanding of social entrepreneurship on this strong tradition of entrepreneurship theory and research. Social entrepreneurs are one species in the genus entrepreneur. They are entrepreneurs with a social mission. However, because of this mission, they face some distinctive challenges and any definition ought to reflect this.

Dees was also one of the first to define the social entrepreneur as someone with vision and with energy and that energy is translated into the ability to galvanize a community to address a social or an economic imbalance. He goes on to suggest that social entrepreneurs are not business people but come from a 'civic' background and have a willingness to address social issues. It is this background that Henton, Melville, and Walesh (2003) address.

When selecting the members for its network, the Schwab Foundation[11] identifies the characteristics of an 'outstanding' social entrepreneur. According to the foundation, these are

Innovation. The candidate has brought about social change by transforming traditional practice. Such transformation can have been achieved through an innovative product or service, the development of a different approach, or a more determined or rigorous application of known technologies, ideas and approaches. What is characteristic of a social entrepreneur is coming up with a pattern-changing idea and implementing it successfully.

Reach and scope. The social entrepreneur's initiative has spread beyond its initial context and has been adapted successfully to other settings, either by the entrepreneur him or herself, or through others who have replicated or adapted elements of the initiative.

Replicability. Aspects of the initiative can be transferred to other regions and are scalable. The social entrepreneur is committed to openly sharing with others the tools, approaches and techniques that are critical to the adaptation of the initiative in different settings.

Sustainability. The candidate has generated the social conditions and/or institutions needed to sustain the initiative and is dedicating all of his/her time to it. The organization is achieving some degree of financial self-sustainability through fees or revenues or is engaged in creating mutually beneficial partnerships with business and/or the public sector and where possible economic incentives are embraced. In any case, there is a clear difference from traditional charity and a move towards community-based empowerment and sustainability. There is also a difference with traditional business. The orientation toward social and environmental value creation predominates, with financial return treated as a secondary means to an end, rather than an end in itself.

Direct positive social impact. The candidate has founded, developed and implemented the entrepreneurial initiative directly, together with poor or marginalized beneficiaries and stakeholders. Impact manifests itself in quantifiable results and testimonials and is well documented. There are no significant negative externalities. In very rare instances will the Foundation consider intermediary non-governmental organizations or foundations that seek to create social value through provision of financial and technical support to community-based groups.

Role model. The candidate is an individual who can serve as a role model for future social entrepreneurs and the general public. Reference checks must confirm the unquestionable integrity of the candidate.

Mutual value added. In considering a candidate for acceptance into the Schwab network, the Foundation must see a clear opportunity to provide further legitimacy, networking and resource mobilization opportunities that strengthen and replicate the candidate's initiatives. Candidates must demonstrate an interest in building a network of outstanding social entrepreneurs that stimulates and supports its participants actively to help one another.

For an example of the characteristics of an outstanding social entrepreneur please see Minicase 4.3 on the Aravind Eye Care System founded by Dr. G. Venkataswamy.

Minicase 4.3   The Aravind Eye Care System

Founded in 1976 by Dr. G. Venkataswamy, Aravind Eye Care System today is the largest and most productive eye care facility in the world. From April 2007 to March 2008, about 2.4 million persons have received outpatient eye care and over 285,000 have undergone eye surgeries at the Aravind Eye Hospitals at Madurai, Theni, Tirunelveli, Coimbatore and Puducherry.

Blending traditional hospitality with state-of-the-art ophthalmic care, Aravind offers comprehensive eye care in the most systematic way attracting patients from all around the world. It is a social organisation committed to the goal of elimination of needless blindness through comprehensive eye care services.

Dr. G. Venkataswamy (Dr. V) was born in 1918 in a small village in South India. He received his medical degree from Stanley Medical College, Chennai in 1944. He joined the Indian Army Medical Corps, but had to retire in 1948 after developing severe rheumatoid arthritis – a disease that left his fingers crippled and changed the course of his life. Despite his condition he returned to medical school and earned a Diploma and Masters degree in ophthalmology. With hard work and determination, Dr. V. trained himself to hold a scalpel and to perform cataract surgery. In time, he personally performed over one hundred thousand successful eye surgeries.

He joined the faculty at Madurai Medical College as the head of the department of ophthalmology and later served as the Vice Dean. In these capacities he introduced a number of innovative programmes to attack the problem of blindness in India, including the outreach eye camps, the initiation of a training programme for ophthalmic assistants and the world's first rehabilitation centre for the blind. For much of his life Dr. V. has been a pioneering eye surgeon. In 1976, upon his retirement at age 58, he formed the GOVEL Trust under which the Aravind Eye Hospital was founded. Although he died in 2006, Dr. V. set in motion a 30-year old, and still continuing, crusade against blindness.

Source: www.aravind.org

QUESTION

1. Use the Internet to familiarize yourself with the Aravind Eye Care programme. Identify why the programme has managed to thrive and grow beyond the death of Dr. Venkataswamy?

These characteristics go beyond the capability of one individual and must be reflected in the values and ethos of an organization. The lead 'entrepreneur' must be a manager as well as a leader. The argument points to the ideas that the entrepreneurial ability to spot an opportunity is important but it must be complemented by the ability to (professionally) manage an organization. Mintzberg (1975)[12] sees a manager as the person in charge of an organization or of one of its component parts. He or she has formal authority over that unit, and holds responsibility for its efficient production of goods or services and for the controlled adaptation to changes in its environment. The manager is also concerned with issues of effectiveness, of meeting goals and objectives.

Mintzberg (1975) identifies different interpersonal roles of a manager. Firstly, that person is a figurehead, performing ceremonial duties, for example, receiving visitors. He or she also has a leader role, for example, hiring, training, motivating staff. He also has a liaison role dealing with others outside the organization. A manager's decisional roles can be of four types:

As an entrepreneur – to launch a new idea.
As a disturbance handler – for example, of internal strife and disagreements.
As a resource allocator – he/she decides to allow important decisions and allocates resources of organization.
As a negotiator, for example, drawing up a contract with a supplier.

It is important here to recognize the role that these different management approaches play in the creation and growth of an organization. This is why entrepreneurial skills of innovation and opportunity-spotting must be complemented by traditional people-management skills. To create a successful social enterprise, the lead entrepreneur must have the commercial background to manage growth – or else they must employ people who have that background.

Opportunity spotting

Having discussed the relevance of the entrepreneur and the importance of professional management capability in creating a viable social enterprise, there is on other area that needs to be discussed – the ability to spot opportunities.

Muzyka (2000)[13] states that 'no one should call themselves a successful entrepreneur until they have captured an opportunity'. In essence, entrepreneurs are defined by their ability to spot an opportunity defined as being something that is new and different – and present the possibility for the creation of new value. For a social enterprise, the opportunity needs to be capable of delivering actual valued social and economic outcomes.

Noting that there is a link between innovation and entrepreneurship, opportunity spotting is the way in which individuals and their organization succeed through being creative and innovative. Being alive to opportunities is a key credo for the entrepreneur and over time as the entrepreneur becomes more experienced the ability to spot a viable opportunity is a key learning activity for the entrepreneur. Opportunities are ideas that exploit unmet customer needs and they manifest themselves in the business, or in this case the social enterprise, offering products or services that add value for the enterprise and its stakeholders. Entrepreneurial opportunities offer something new and different to the market and there should be an element of innovation involved and therefore growth potential. For example see Minicase 3.4 OneWorld Health for the combination of innovation and an unsatisfied need.

> Enterprising behaviour is the development of learning skills to enable learning to be personalised, applied to the workplace and continued beyond the education or training programme, with the participants firmly in control of the process.
>
> (Bridge et al. 2003)[14]

Using enterprise as a strategy means being opportunity-focused and, when this is combined with being customer-focused, it means that an organization is pro-active to change rather than reactive.

> Enterprise incorporates those qualities and competencies that enable individuals, organizations, communities, societies and cultures to be flexible, creative and adaptable in light of change. To achieve the above, the individual needs to use his/her imagination, be creative, taking responsibility, organizing, identifying ideas, making decisions and dealing with others in a wide range of contexts.
>
> (Bridge et al. 2003)

The first part of the discussion focuses on the importance of spotting new opportunities in order to keep an enterprise moving forward.

Opportunity spotting is closely linked to enterprise development – the way in which individuals and their organization succeed through being creative and innovative. It is argued that opportunity spotting is a clear constituent of the entrepreneurial leader, in that it is not a process that lends itself to being divided into stages. The degree of opportunity spotting will depend upon the product lifecycle stage and it is critical that there is a knowledge and directional framework for undertaking this process.

Qualifying the opportunity

According to Gibb (1987),[15] the conditions for creating enterprise within an organization are

Motivation – the drive to succeed, generally, or do something in particular.

Ability – the skills and knowledge of business enterprise, such as planning, communicating and presenting.

Ideas – creative imagination to think from different perspectives, and create new ways of working or new products.

Resources – such as finance, knowledge and time.

These four conditions are commonly known as the MAIR model.

While these are skills that some people have and others may not possess, enterprise is not about the individual but about a collective approach of the individuals who make up an organization. There are a number of key components to an organization being enterprising:

Being pro-active – meaning that strategies evolve and are not pre-scriptive. They change a part of the enterprise before the change is necessary.

Focused knowledge – which means that the organization has the resources and especially its people have the knowledge and experience to respond to change positively, especially within the area of enterprise service provision.

Perseverance – referring to the ability to accommodate and learn from mistakes – to continue efforts to make the enterprise succeed, even when the business is not performing as forecasted.

A business strategy should identify the three areas for enterprise development:

Spotting opportunities – creating, identifying and seizing opportunities to survive, grow or make a profit.

Building capability – developing systems, skills, knowledge and attitudes, in order to create, identify and/or seize the opportunity.

Marshalling resources – identifying and obtaining resources such as money, people, and equipment.

Opportunity spotting is a clear constituent of the social entrepreneur and his or her team. It implies that an entrepreneurial leader and the team will continually search for new ideas that can be used for future service developments or income generation. This typically makes the social entrepreneur an agent of change, someone who is linked to creativity, innovation and the search for new product ideas or service ideas (Carson et al. 1995).[16] It is not easy to convert this into process understanding, but the opportunity spotting can be divided into the stages shown in Figure 4.1.

Opportunity construction is a broad statement, a goal that describes a basic area of challenge in which the problem solvers efforts will be focused. It is important to keep this broad and to allow as many different alternatives to arise as possible. Brain storming and lateral

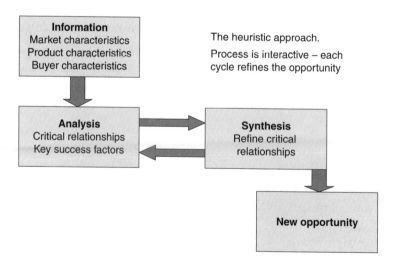

Figure 4.1   *Spotting opportunities*
Source: Wickham, *Strategic Entrepreneurship*, 4th edn (FT/Prentice Hall, 2006)

thinking are two tools that can be used in this process. Exploring the data involves generating the evidence to answer the question(s) set. In this case data may include hard measures drawn from reports but also qualitative and observational data. The purpose of this stage is to focus clearly on qualifying the opportunity.

Framing the problem involves seeking and specifying problem statements and making choices about the best options. This is a strategic decision-making process and one which is best undertaken as a team effort. A clear element of this approach is understanding the strengths and weaknesses, opportunities and threats.

The life cycle of opportunities

The degree of opportunity spotting that is available will tend to depend on product life-cycle. Arguably, the more mature an industry is, the less creative are the opportunities which are available. It could be said that the process of business enterprise is determined by which section of the life cycle the business is in (see Figure 4.2 below). There are usually four stages of the cycle. This means that introduction and growth are the most exciting stages for the entrepreneurial leaders of the social organization.

Enhancing business enterprise

Opportunity spotting must serve the purpose of moving an organiza-tion forward. It is suggested that business enterprise can be collated

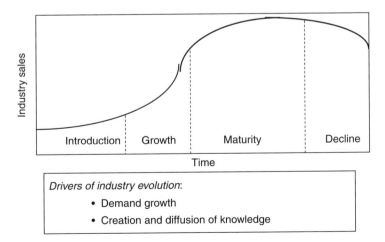

Figure 4.2   **The industry life cycle**

into sections in order to be successful. The stages outlined below provide a framework for opportunity spotting (Deakins and Freel, 1999).[17]

Knowledge base

In order to be enterprising, knowledge needs to be constantly improved and up to date. Information is power, and can be one of the critical success factors of an organization. Knowledge is one of the key components of the business operation. Scanning of the environment will enable the organization to adapt and to remain customer-focused. In the social economy this is particularly pertinent owing to the changes in legislation and the fact that they are reliant on government funding and public scrutiny.

Direction base

In order to use resources efficiently and effectively, it is useful to ensure a personal and business direction is established in a clear manner. This can be ensured through effective planning and by often (if necessary) creating a step-by-step approach, which can be set through out as per the following sequence.

1. Establish a business plan
2. List the activities which need to be done
3. Schedule a time to do them
4. As new ideas and strategies develop repeat the above
5. Amend the business plan to keep track of the activities needed to implement the ideas
6. Repeat the above.

As Dees (1998)[18] points out

where others see problems, social entrepreneurs see opportunity. They are not simply driven by the perception of a social need or by their compassion, rather they have a vision of how to achieve improvement and they are determined to make their vision work. They are persistent. The models they develop and the approaches they take can, and often do, change, as the entrepreneurs learn about what works and what does not work. The key element is persistence combined with a willingness to make adjustments as one goes.

Aside from the above, it is necessary to prioritize the opportunity ideas and the activities in terms of importance for the development of the enterprise and also to meet the needs of stakeholders (both internal and external). 'Often entrepreneurs see opportunities where others see problems. Whereas ordinary mortals dislike the uncertainty brought about by the change, entrepreneurs love it because they see opportunity and they do not mind the uncertainty' (Burns, 2007, p. 35).[19]

Creating an enterprising social organization requires continually scanning the business environment and continually being creative about new ideas and new ways to deliver services and raise revenue. Brown and Weiner (1988)[20] define environmental scanning as 'a kind of radar to scan the world systematically and signal the new, the unexpected, the major and the minor'. Environmental scanning (see Figure 4.3) is looking for and using information about events, trends, and relationships in external environment, the knowledge of which would assist management in planning the organization's future course of action (Choo et al., 1993).[21]

Scanning provides the insight into markets that is required to set out organizational strategies. The consequences of this activity include fostering an understanding of the effects of change on organizations, aiding in forecasting, and bringing expectations of change to bear on decision making (Morrison, 1992).[22]

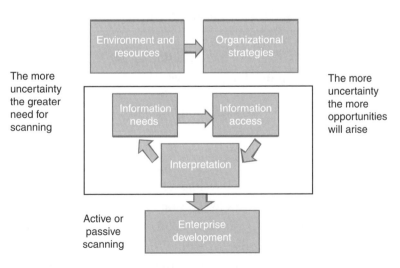

Figure 4.3   *Environmental scanning*
Source: Adapted from Choo et al. (1993)

This scanning (Aguilar, 1967)[23] can consist of intelligence gathering based on undirected viewing which includes reading a range of publications for no specific purpose other than to be kept informed of trends. Conditioned viewing is where there is a deliberate attempt to collate this information in terms of assessing its relevance to the organization. This is distinct from informal searching which consists of actively conducting research but doing it in an exploratory way to qualify a specific market opportunity. All of these searches are in contrast to formal searching, a proactive mode of scanning entailing formal methodologies for obtaining information for specific purposes. This is probably the least effective means of environment scanning since the data is time and context specific.

It has been argued that opportunity spotting is closely linked to enterprise development – the way in which individuals and their organization succeed through being creative and innovative. Opportunity spotting involves continually scanning the business environment to identify new opportunities that others might have missed. These opportunities provide a chance to add value and create a sustainable organization – one that is able to fulfil its vision for its stakeholders. Before finishing off this section on opportunity spotting, it is worth investigating 'where' opportunities arise from. Assuming that this is not a systematic search other methods may be employed.

Networks and external relationships

Social networking is a key interpersonal skill for the social leader. Social networking can be summed up as follows:

It not what you know, it is who you know that matters.

Building external relations is critical to establishing legitimacy with multiple stakeholders within a community. Social networks bind groups together and create a feeling of belonging. The interaction between the actors allows mistakes to be anticipated and commercial experience to be (partially) offset by good advice. The main part of a network for a social enterprise lies within the community. This is quite often reflected in the constitution of the Board of Directors. Apart from the beneficiaries of the enterprise, other client groups can include the funding agencies, the government and other social leaders. Networking with other groups within the locality as well as with similar organizations operating elsewhere is, arguably more crucial for social entrepreneur than for the small business.

Social networking is recognized as a key method for receiving relevant information, mutual learning, getting appropriate personnel, and for joining together for common causes. The close networks can provide the much needed emotional support for social entrepreneurial leaders in the face of tremendous pressure and adverse circumstances. As O'Donnell and Cummins[24] note, there is increasing recognition that traditional marketing theories are inappropriate for the smaller firm and that the quality rather than the quantity of a social network is critical to the success of a new venture. What matters about social networking is that knowing the right people will allow a growing social enterprise to compensate for a lack of commercial acumen within a management team. Ultimately, access to a social network is the defining characteristic that will allow an enterprise to spot new opportunities and leverage growth from them.

Example 4.1 provides a summary of key points of the chapter

| Examples | 4.1 Social entrepreneurs |

Example 4.1   Social entrepreneurs

Income generation and integration within a community are not complementary activities.
The success of a social firm may depend on its ability to balance these activities.
The aim of a social enterprise is to achieve economic success and the maximization of social benefits.
The pursuit of this is labelled as the pursuit of blended value. In doing do the social enterprise will find it difficult to raise funds through the normal channels of equity funding.
The search for opportunity is a key role of the social entrepreneur.
Opportunity spotting is closely linked to economic development
Environmental scanning and networking are crucial to opportunity spotting

Revision questions

1. Referring to an article in the *Guardian*[25] in which a charity body warns over transfer of services:

   'Charities should think twice before plunging into contracts to deliver public services, the umbrella body for the voluntary sector will caution tomorrow in a move to curb government expectations of large-scale transfers of services from state providers.'
      Your task is to present both sides of the argument on either:

   (i) opportunity spotting and delivery; that social organizations should 'chase' ever larger contracts in order to support their services and fulfil their mission or
   (ii) charities have a commitment to the groups that they serve and that they compromise service delivery through the taking on of a large government contract.

2. To what extent can you balance quality of service with the need to demonstrate economic viability?
3. Using the framework above, identify the opportunities for improvements in service delivery for a public sector organization you are familiar with, now and in the future. How can they be expected to respond to these opportunities? Justify your choices.
4. Please refer to the Centre for the Advancement of Social Entrepreneurship for examples of Teaching Case studies in the area of Social Enterprise and related materials. http://www.fuqua.duke.edu/centers/case/knowledge/casestudies/index.html. (See the case study on 'Futures for Kids' as an example of the problems of fund raising.)

References

1. Adapted from http://www.schwabfound.org/definition.htm, accessed June 2009.
2. J. Boschee, *Introduction to Social Entrepreneurship: Mapping the Social Purpose Business Sector* (2003), Institute for Social Entrepreneurs. http://www.socialent.org/intro.
3. J. Emerson, *The Nature of Returns: A Social Capital Markets Inquiry into Elements of Investment and the Blended Value Proposition*, Social Enterprise Series, no. 17 (Boston, MA: Harvard Business School, 2000).
4. A. Lingane and S. Olsen, 'Guidelines for Social Return on Investment', *Harvard Business Review*, vol. 46, no. 3 (2004), pp. 1–22.
5. J. A. Schumpeter, *The Theory of Economic Development*, 3rd printing, 1963 (New York: Oxford University Press, 1934).
6. P. Drucker, *Innovation and Entrepreneurship* (London: Heinemann, 1985).
7. J. A. Timmons, *New Venture Creation: Entrepreneurship for the 21st Century* (New York: Irwin McGraw-Hill, 1999).

8. J. Schumpeter, *Cycle of Creative Destruction* (Harvard University Press: Cambridge, MA, 1943).
9. D. Henton, J. Melville and K. Walesh, *Civic Revolutionaries: Igniting the Passion for Change in America's Communities* (Jossey-Bass Publishers, 2003).
10. J. G. Dees, *The Meaning of Social Entrepreneurship* (Durham, NC: Duke University, 1998). See www.fuqua.duke.edu/centers/case/documents/Dees_SEdef.pdf.
11. Schwab Foundation for Social Entrepreneurship, see http://www.schwabfound.org/whatis.htm, accessed December 2008.
12. H. Mintzberg, 'The Manager's Job: Folklore and Fact', *Harvard Business Review* (July 1975), pp. 49–61.
13. D. F. Muzyka, 'Spotting the Market Opportunity', in *Mastering Enterprise* (Essex: Pearson Education, 2000).
14. S. Bridge, K. O'Neill and S. Cromie, *Understanding Entrepreneurship and Small Business*, 2nd edn (Basingstoke: Palgrave Macmillan, 2003).
15. A. A. Gibb, 'Education for Enterprise: Training for Small Business Initiation – Some Contrasts', *Journal of Small Business and Entrepreneurship*, vol. 4 no. 3 (1987), pp. 42–7.
16. D. Carson, S. Cromie and P. McGowen Hill, *Marketing & Entrepreneurship: An Innovative Approach* (London: Prentice Hall, 1995), pp. 56–7.
17. D. Deakins and M. Freel, *Entrepreneurship and Small Firms* (Berkshire, UK: McGraw Hill 1999).
18. J. Dees, *The Meaning of Social Entrepreneurship*, (Kauffman Foundation 1998), available at www.fuqua.duke.edu/centers/case/documents/dees_sedef.pdf.
19. P. Burns, *Entrepreneurship and Small Business*, 2nd edn (Basingstoke: Palgrave Macmillan, 2007).
20. A. Brown and E. Weiner, *Supermanaging: How to Harness Change for Personal and Organisational Success* (New York: Mentor, 1988).
21. Choo, Chun Wei, and E. Auster, 'Environmental Scanning: Acquisition and Use of Information by Managers', in M. E. Williams (ed.), *Annual Review of Information Science and Technology* (Medford, NJ: Learned Information, Inc. for the American Society for Information Science, 1993).
22. J. L. Morrison, 'Environmental Scanning', in M. A. Whitely, J. D. Porter and R. H. Fenske (eds.), *A Primer for New Institutional Researchers* (Tallahassee, FL: The Association for Institutional Research, 1992), pp. 86–99.
23. F. J. Aguilar, *Scanning the Business Environment* (New York: McMillan, 1967), adapted.
24. A. O'Donnell and D. Cummins, 'The Use of Qualitative Methods to Research Networking in SMEs', *Qualitative Market Research: An International Journal*, vol. 2, no.2 (1999), pp. 82–91.
25. D. Brindle, 'Charity Body Warns over Transfer Services', *Guardian* 30 May 2005.

5 building an enterprise

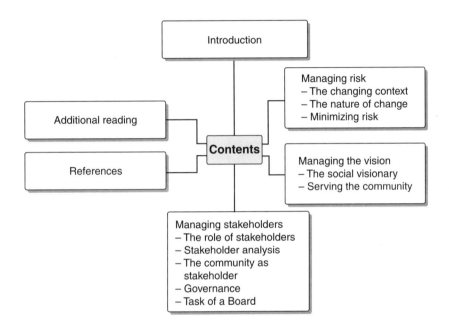

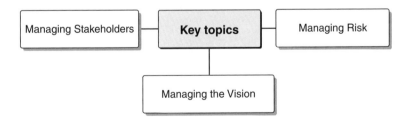

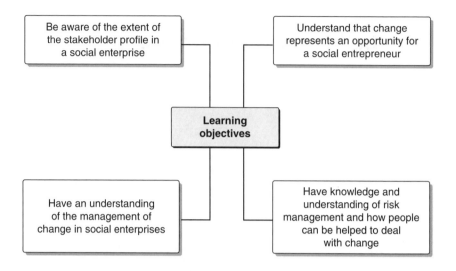

Introduction

It has already been argued (Chapter 3) that a social enterprise, like a conventional business, will go through stages as it grows. At each stage, the enterprise can be expected to change and the management will need to respond to events both inside and outside the firm. This process is part of the 'professionalism of management' as it moves from start-up into its second stage of development as an established business. The start-up stage, the earliest stage of business development, is replaced as trading activities take-off and the firm undergoes a transition. After this a firm may undergo further transitions before reaching the stage where the firm is managed at a divisional level.

As indicated, this chapter and this book concentrates on the second stage of growth – once a firm is established. It is this second stage of trying to develop and sustain the enterprise that offers the real challenge to those involved. The first part of this chapter looks at how an enterprise can accommodate risk and how change can be an advantage to an enterprise in terms of how it organizes itself. It draws upon the Varney report as an example of one of the drivers for change, and argues that 'punctuated change' is more difficult to manage than continuous change.

The second part of the chapter looks at stakeholders and the relationship between management and an efficient and well-governed enterprise. It is the vision that matches the external risks of the environment with a sense of purpose and direction. This direction then needs to be communicated to stakeholders. It is also the board of governors, not just the social entrepreneur, who are responsible for formulating strategy and managing resources.

Managing risk

The traditional tools of risk analysis are based on the ability to gather empirical information to allow the processing of uncertainty. Risk analysis is seen as a technical subject – one in which risks are framed and judged in terms of probabilities. Inherent in this approach is the idea that change is progressive and not disruptive.

> The traditional technical foundation of risk management is a risk analysis, a discipline whose strength consists in its machine-like

engineering quality. One standard conception of risk analysis focused on identifying, measuring and evaluating possible outcomes from both natural and technological hazards. The concern is to estimate the probability of the likely effects of specific events happening.

(Hutter and Power, 2005)[1]

This topic examines the impact that change and choice have upon social enterprises, especially in terms of their relationship with public sector enterprises. Previously, change might not have impacted seriously upon social enterprises – but that hardly seems to be the case anymore. This means that enterprises that were once risk averse are expected to innovate and embrace change. The risk profile of social enterprises is therefore changing.

The changing context

The environment within which social and public enterprises operate is changing. The Varney report (2006)[2] was commissioned by HM Treasury to advise the Chancellor on opportunities to transform service delivery within public sector enterprises.

> Much more innovation will be needed to meet the challenges of the fast-changing environment in which we live. The next ten years will bring considerable change within the UK in terms of demographics, socio-economics, customer requirements and expectations, as well as technological developments.
>
> For example:
>
> New technologies will continue to emerge, but the changes are difficult to predict.
>
> There will be an increasing need to show flexibility in adapting and responding to changes and opportunities as they arise. There is likely to be continuing adoption of new technologies such as advanced mobile devices, digital television and high speed Internet access. Customer preferences are changing as society becomes more prosperous and more diverse. At the same time the needs of lower income citizens must be met.

The Varney report, which looks for efficiency saving and a level of customer service that 'approximates' to the private sector, is already having an impact on NHS spending. The following are policy statements from the UK government outlining reforms within the health sector:

> NHS foundation trusts (often referred to as 'foundation hospitals') are at the cutting edge of the Government's commitment to the decentralisation of public services and the creation of a patient-led NHS. NHS foundation trusts are a new type of NHS trust in England that have been created to devolve decision-making from central government control to local enterprises and communities so they are more responsive to the needs and wishes of their local people. The introduction of NHS foundation trusts represents a profound change in the history of the NHS and the way in which hospital services are managed and provided.
>
> Department of Health[3]

Within the education sector, in schools, further and higher education, similar 'reforms' are taking place. Education and health are the two main areas of expenditure for the UK government. Given the pace and extent of the changes taking place, avoiding change and its passive management is not a viable strategy.

The argument here is that change of all types presents opportunities for social entrepreneurs and the social enterprises they represent.

The nature of change

Thompson and Martin (2005)[4] note, 'Effective organizations must be able to manage change. When strategies change they are often accompanied by change in structures and responsibilities and people are clearly affected'.

In theory, there are two types of change. Continuous change and punctuated change. Figure 5.1 provides an outline shape of each form of change.

Steady state and continuous change are comparatively easy to manage in the sense that the change is predicable and not disruptive. These situations are observed in mature industries and were, until recently, typical of the public sector. Continuous and predictable change has now become an exception rather than the rule, especially within the public sector. Most change is now punctuated: it happens as a series of disjointed but partially predictable policy changes.

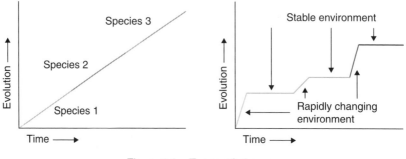

Figure 5.1 **Types of change**

Punctuated change is typical of the business environment of public sector and social enterprises. While this may be a relatively stable environment compared with commercial enterprises, it is still disruptive.

Whether change is continuous or punctuated, people resist change because it is seen as a threat to familiar patterns of behaviour as well as to status and financial rewards. Commitment to change is improved if those affected by it are allowed to contribute as much as possible to formulating and implementing the management of change. This strategy, of giving ownership directly, contradicts a top-down view that only top management are responsible for addressing change. This approach is closely related to Lewin's (1951)[5] Field Theory which stated that resistance to change can be overcome by the following approaches:

- Unfreezing – getting rid of existing practices and ideas that stand in the way of change.
- Changing – teaching employees to think and perform differently.
- Refreezing – establishing new norms and standard practices.

The aim is to encourage 'ownership' of the change as something that 'they' want and need. This commitment by involvement will only be successful if management is prepared to listen to staff and volunteers' views and suggestions, and to be willing to alter plans if the message is clear that something is unworkable or would benefit from alteration.

Ideally, the organization will seek to develop a culture where people do not feel threatened when they're constantly asked the question and challenged about existing behaviours and existing way of doing things, and change them a culture that sees innovation is changed as normal; a culture that is ideal for dealing with chaos; a culture where people do not automatically ask who is already doing this?

(Thompson and Martin, 2005)

Minimizing risk

It will often be the case that different subcultures and attitudes towards risk and risk management may exist within enterprises or within community groups. This is a conscious decision that managers take to encounter or to avoid risky situations. As Thompson and Martin (2005) point out,

the key elements in risk are potential upsides and downsides. The greater an enterprise's awareness, insight and understanding of emerging trends and opportunities the more informed they will be. Decisions and risks are linked irrevocably as the strategic decisions made by enterprises and managers reflect their management of the risk they face.

(Thompson and Martin, p. 766)

The fact remains that most enterprises are built to pursue strategies that deliberately seek to avoid, manage or minimize risk. Risk can be exhibited in four ways:

1. Personal risk.
2. Opportunity risk of not doing something.
3. Environmental risks associated with changing environments.
4. Resource-based risks involving the allocation of internal resources.

The characteristics of an enterprise (Clarke and Varma, 1999)[6] that avoids risk can be classified as:

- Centralized or co-operative decision-making structures without effective executive leadership.
- Adherence to formal planning systems, tight budget control and a reward-based system.
- Top down management by fear and intimidation, developing a culture of caution.

These are the characteristics of formal bureaucracies and they are the antithesis of the opportunity-seeking entrepreneurial enterprise. According to Carson et al. (1995),[7]

> entrepreneurship and marketing are focused on innovation and change. The really skilful entrepreneur sees things in a way no one else does. They perceive opportunities in the market place which perhaps are not yet fully formed but are currently no more than shapes and patterns arising from a new technology and fashion or trend, a possible cultural shift.

This would suggest that there are distinct differences between enterprises that avoid risk compared with those that embrace change. Thompson and Martin (2005)[8] argue that any enterprise must meet the needs of its stakeholders if it is to survive. This means being aware of change and having the vision to manage that change.

> The ability of the entrepreneur to break free from bureaucratic rigidities, fan the flames of innovation and create new situations has been the basis of the growth of many of today's great corporations. Ford, Durant, Kellogg, Krupp, Eastman, Siemens and Daussalt all built giant enterprises which are virtually synonymous with their industries.
>
> (Cannon, 1985)[9]

One of the ways in which a social entrepreneur can manage real change is through a vision. While the mission outlines the enterprise's purpose, the vision describes what the enterprise will look like in the future. The vision is the big picture and is generally promulgated by the founder. A vision statement (Figure 5.2) forms the internal framework for an enterprise's general philosophy, goals, strategies, ethical standards and performance criteria. Ideally, a vision statement improves the enterprise's effectiveness and productivity because it motivates and guides everyone involved to work towards a certain goal (Kirby, 2004).[10]

A vision statement should

1. be general in its sweep (which allows it to survive even in an unstable environment);
2. be short, precise and clear;

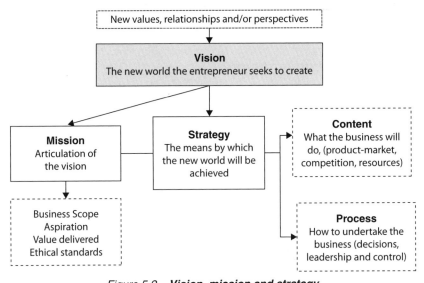

Figure 5.2   **Vision, mission and strategy**
Source: P. A. Wickham, *Strategic Entrepreneurship*, 3rd edn (FT/Prentice Hall, 1998), p. 133

3. include a promise that the enterprise will support its members' pursuit of the vision;
4. clarify the enterprise's direction and purpose;
5. focus on a better future;
6. reflect high ideals in challenging ambitions;
7. stress the enterprise's distinctive and unique components.

Once the vision is accomplished, an enterprise needs to re-evaluate itself as well as its environment, and decide whether to change the vision, mission, and programmes. An example of this is given as Minicase 5.1.

> I started blueEnergy because I wanted to build wind turbines and help people in the process. I eschewed corporate jobs, even ones in the renewable energy sector, because I didn't want to spend the next 10 years of my life behind a desk. How ironic then that I find myself behind a desk 16 hours a day.
>
> (Matthias Craig, co-founder of blueEnergy)

For background detail on the trials and tribulations of starting and developing blueEnergy, raising money, building an organization and the technical challenges involved, please see: http://www.socialedge. org/blogs/generating-blueenergy.

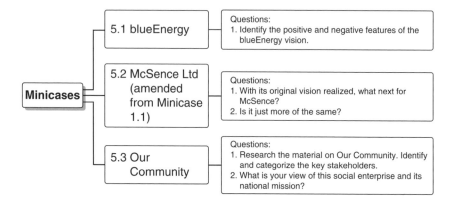

Minicase 5.1   blueEnergy

blueEnergy's mission is to provide *sustainable*, low-cost energy to communities in need.

blueEnergy is a nonprofit organization that provides a low-cost, sustainable solution to the energy needs of marginalized communities through the construction, installation, and maintenance of hybrid wind and solar electric systems. blueEnergy manufactures wind turbines that are specially designed for simple manufacturing, robustness and efficiency in low wind speeds. blueEnergy manufactures the systems locally, near their point of usage, to keep energy costs low, improve equipment serviceability, and create employment where it is desperately needed.

It is widely accepted that access to electricity is a necessary, although not sufficient, requirement for modern economic and social development. Electricity opens the door to a host of technologies that promote education, public health, and economic development, such as emissions-free light, refrigeration, and communication devices. Without electricity, communities are unable to participate in the benefits of modern advances and are left isolated and literally in the dark. In Nicaragua, blueEnergy's initial project country, half of the roughly 5 million inhabitants do not have access to electricity; the situation is particularly grim in the Caribbean Coast region of the country where nearly 80% of the inhabitants go without.

In part because of this, and in part the cause of this, the region is the poorest in Nicaragua, itself the second poorest country in the western hemisphere.

Several factors conspire to make the cost of grid extension, the most common method of extending energy services, prohibitive on the Caribbean Coast of Nicaragua: low population density, rugged terrain, and lack of general civil infrastructure. Diesel generators, the most common form of distributed generation globally, are cost prohibitive with fuel prices over $4 a gallon, and a logistical nightmare. Despite this, most development initiatives attempt to implement diesel mini-grids with predictably disastrous results. Other development initiatives rely on solar power only, which entails high costs and uncertain serviceability. Finally, some development projects use imported wind turbines, which tend to be very expensive and most often fail to meet production expectations or fail entirely due to the harsh environment and improper servicing. blueEnergy's approach to rural electrification focuses on manufacturing wind turbines on the Caribbean Coast, near the point of usage. This local, wind power centric focus keeps energy costs low, improves servicing feasibility, and provide jobs where they are desperately needed.

Source: http://www.blueenergygroup.org (accessed December 2008)

QUESTIONS

1. Identify the positive and negative features of the blueEnergy vision.

The social visionary

A social visionary will try to engender a heightened sense of accountability to the stakeholder constituencies served. This often involves 'selling a dream' – a vision of the future and the possibilities that new directions create for social enterprise.

> The entrepreneur's vision is a picture of the new **world** he or she wishes to create. The picture is a positive one. ... He or she is motivated to make their vision a reality.
>
> Wickham, (1998)[11]

The main features relating to the creation of such a vision are shown as Figure 5.3.

Vision must exist before strategy development and planning

• **The vision provides:**	• **The vision is constantly refocused:**
• Sense of direction. • Defines goals and objectives. • Provides focus when going gets tough. • Gives the venture a moral content and social priority. • It communicates and attracts venture support. • It forms the basis of the leadership strategy.	• What is source of value to be created? • Who will be involved? • Why will they want to be involved? • What rewards will they gain? • What new relations are needed? • What is the potential for self development?

*Figure 5.3   **Making the vision a reality***
Source: Adapted from P. A. Wickham (1998, p. 107)

The dream is encompassed by the vision and the mission statement for the enterprise. This places a responsibility on the enterprise to seek a sound understanding of the constituencies which they are serving. The vision of Brian Tannerhill led to the creation of McSence and this vision is outlined below and in Minicase 5.2.

> An entrepreneur sees and strives for the opportunity to make an idea a success. A social entrepreneur does exactly the same but allows the profit from this opportunity to be used for social good. I believe the mindset is the same. Business drives both the economy and all entrepreneurs to create wealth. It is how that wealth is distributed that changes an entrepreneur to a social entrepreneur. Our sector should exist to encourage, challenge and convert all entrepreneurs to become social entrepreneurs. This should include sharing good practice and ideas throughout the country and mentoring other entrepreneurs and business managers to produce the best profitable results to regenerate all our communities. I look forward to the day when we all accept profit as a social word.
>
> Tannerhill, Chief Executive, McSence Group,
> Senscot 26/6/2005 (http://www.mcsence.co.uk)

Visionaries make sure they have correctly assessed the needs and values of the people they intend to serve and the communities in which they operate. In some cases this requires close connections with those communities. They understand the expectations and values of their 'investors', including anyone who invests money, volunteers' time and/or expertise to help them. They seek to provide real social improvements to their beneficiaries and their communities, as well as attractive (social and/or financial) return to their investors. Creating a fit between investor values and community needs is an important part of the challenge. When feasible, social entrepreneurs create market-like feedback mechanisms to reinforce this accountability. They assess their progress in terms of social, financial, and managerial outcomes, not simply in terms of their size, outputs, or processes.

Minicase 5.2   McSence Ltd (amended from Minicase 1.1)

It was back in 1984 that Brian Tannerhill, a local resident in Mayfield, Midlothian, first initiated the idea of forming a Community Business that would provide employment and services to his local community. This business was to be called Mayfield Community Self Employed Natural Collective Exercise or, more simply, McSence.

Serving the community

The support of local businesses was crucial to the early development of McSence. At the outset, Brian Tannerhill persuaded local traders to commit £5 per week for the first year as a contribution to the start up costs of the community owned business on the condition that it did not compete with any of the contributors. This initiative raised £7500 and resulted in local business people being invited onto the Board to provide invaluable business experience.

Since those early days, McSence has grown into a group of companies that employ over 50 local people and generate an annual turnover of approximately £1.2 million. Profits generated by the companies are ploughed back into the local community with recent examples being the provision of a youth centre and sports equipment for local youngsters.

Source: http://www.mcsence.co.uk

QUESTIONS

1. With its original vision realized, what next for McSence?
2. Is it just more of the same?

Sykes (1999)[12] defines three key contributions to the growth of enterprises:

1. Envisioning a future state in an uncertain environment.
2. Enacting the vision by giving it direction and purpose and acquiring the necessary resources.
3. Enabling it to happen by harnessing the support of other key people.

In terms of traditional risk management the social vision can be more emotional than analytical. As Burns (2005)[13] points out, the vision is a key element of both entrepreneurship and leadership. It is a view of a 'new world and a shared world'. It is usually qualitative rather than quantitative and it should be inspiring and motivating, transcending logic and contractual relationships.

This chapter has looked at the management of change in social enterprises. A distinction has been drawn between enterprises that operate in a stable environment and those that operate in an environment where change is the norm. It is argued that in healthcare education and social policy, change is endemic. Most of this change may be punctuated but it is still important that an enterprise and the people who work in it understand and positively respond to change. While it may be true that enterprises in the public sector avoid risk, a social enterprise has the option of embracing change and being entrepreneurial and innovative. This will involve establishing a clear vision which provides a framework for the organization's philosophy, goals, strategies, ethical standards and performance criteria. The social visionary is the person in the enterprise responsible for selling the dream to stakeholders that the enterprise is opportunity-seeking rather than risk-avoiding.

It is the responsibility of the social visionary to ensure that everyone inside and outside the enterprise is not only familiar with but believes in the vision and that it becomes the guide for the enterprise's development.

Managing stakeholders

A stakeholder is anyone with a declared or conceivable interest in the activities of a social enterprise. An enterprise's position and its adoption of the vision can be determined through a stakeholder analysis. This includes both internal and external stakeholders and a consideration of the power influenced by different constituencies. Ultimately it is the board of governors' responsibility to reconcile any difference between the stakeholders' interpretation and the ethics and vision of an enterprise.

The role of stakeholders

The broadest way of defining social responsibility is to say that the continued existence of companies is based on an implied agreement between business and society. In effect, companies are licensed by society to provide goods and services which society needs. The freedom of operation of companies is therefore dependent on their delivering a balance of economic and social benefits which society currently expects of them. The problem for companies is that the balance of needs and benefits is continually changing.

(Cadbury, 2002)[14]

A stakeholder can be defined as:

> Those who depend on the enterprise for the realisation of some of their goals and in turn the enterprise depends on them for the full realisation of its goals.
>
> (Garavan, 1995)[15]

As indicated, a stakeholder is anyone with a declared or conceivable interest or stake in a community. Stakeholders can be individuals or enterprises within the public or private sector, and include customers, competitors, government, suppliers, the community, employees and lenders – it is a wide-ranging concept. The idea behind a stakeholder analysis is to identify the different expectations of the various stakeholders and to develop a map to manage these. It is based on the assumption that there are conflicts of expectation between the different groups and that there is an opportunity and a cost to keeping everyone happy.

Examples of 'conflicts of expectations' might include

- The need to concentrate on new trading activities to achieve short-term profitability as opposed to the more established and longer-term forms of additional funding. 'Short-termism' and a lack of strategic insight will preclude investment in long-term projects.
- The need to appoint external professional managers to manage growth versus the community's loss of control over day-to-day activities as the enterprise grows.
- Extending into markets outside the local areas which may generate revenue but which will require greater management input and may affect local service delivery.
- In public services, a common conflict is between mass provision and specialist services (e.g. preventive dentistry or heart transplants). In public services, savings in one area (e.g. disability allowances) may result in increases elsewhere (e.g. school meals, medical care).

Stakeholder analysis

A stakeholder analysis is the systematic identification of key stakeholders and the appraisal of their influence on strategy implementation. It may also involve creating a strategy to reshape the influence of

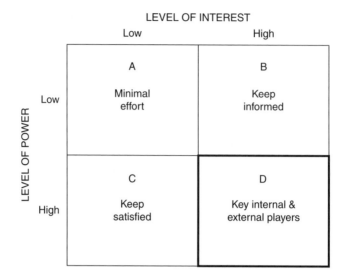

Figure 5.4   *Stakeholder interest*

existing or new stakeholders. Depending on their level of interest, and set against their level of power, each group of stakeholders can be expected to respond differently to conflicts. Shown as Figure 5.4.

The two key questions that need to be asked relate to power and interest.

1. Power
   'If I were to pursue this strategy with disregard to the views of this stakeholder, could they stop me?'
2. Interest
   'How high is this strategy in their priorities? Are they likely to actively support or oppose this strategy?'

Within the context of a social enterprise, external stakeholders might include

- The community and their representative bodies.
- Government agencies and funding bodies.
- Donors, private investors and sponsors.
- Governing bodies, unions, trade associations and other charitable enterprises.

An internal stakeholder might include

- Founding members, volunteers and staff. In the Health Service it can include patients, clinicians along with support staff and professional agencies directly involved in the delivery of services.
- Within an educational establishment it might include pupils, their parents, the Board, teachers and support staff.

The community as stakeholder

The most important members of the stakeholding constituency for social enterprises are those members of the community at whom the services of the social enterprise are directed. In an ideal world, in market-centred enterprises such as a hospitals or schools, it is patients and pupils that are the most important yet they often receive the least attention!

Internal and external stakeholders can be divided up into a table, and the relative importance of each stakeholder, in terms of their influence, can be assessed. This gives a set of primary and secondary stakeholders. A simple guideline to drawing up a stakeholder table consists of:

- Identifying and listing potential stakeholders.
- Assessing their interests in relation to the immediate issues, noting that stakeholders may have more than one immediate agenda.
- Assessing their likely impact on decision-making, especially their ability to block decisions.
- Measuring their relative importance in helping to implement decisions.

The main point of a stakeholder analysis is to identify and rate 'influencers' – those who directly and indirectly affect policy and influence delivery.

There are different ways of conducting a stakeholder analysis. The most direct way is to conduct a survey, asking the stakeholders about their needs and demands, how they evaluate the organization and its programmes (satisfactory or not, helpful or not, etc.), and what kind of additional projects they would suggest. Such surveys can also include an evaluation of the organization's impact on the stakeholders, for example by looking at how much money they had before as compared to after a project or how an employment strategy fits in with the demand for jobs or service delivery. Care is required when surveying certain groups, for example when interviewing vulnerable people, and external advice should be sought on ethical/appropriate ways of conducting these types of interviews.

Another approach is to use qualitative research i.e., going out and talking to the target audience about their demands, perceptions and suggestions. This approach requires more careful planning and execution. The results of the analysis will give the organization direction concerning its positive and negative aspects and the initial finding should certainly be circulated to stakeholders within the enterprise and presented during Board meetings. Assuming that conflicts are inevitable, and that they need to be managed, then a social enterprise can use two specific techniques to anticipate the impact of conflicts.

For an example of a stakeholder community at its widest sense please see Minicase 5.3.

Minicase 5.3   Our Community

Our Community is a world-leading social enterprise that provides advice and tools for Australia's 700,000 community groups and schools, and practical linkages between the community sector and the general public, business and government. The vision that has guided the development of Our Community is that every Australian should have easy and ready access to a community group that suits everyone from children, to adults, to grandparents. Our Community is a self-sustaining social enterprise and has been developed using investment provided by a forward-thinking group of social investors, led by Carol Schwartz. These are the first social investors in Australia to invest in the first major private company established solely to enhance the social good.

Social investment uses a new model of engagement with business and complements philanthropic foundations, which were established with profits made from business.

Source: http://www.ourcommunity.com.au (accessed December 2008)

QUESTIONS

1. Research the material on Our Community. Identify and categorize the key stakeholders.
2. What is your view of this social enterprise and its national mission?

Governance

In the social economy enterprises can grow too large for effective communication and control. There may be tensions between salaried staff and volunteers and this may be compounded by tension between head office and local community groups of stakeholders. The volunteers may have raised the bulk of the money for the social enterprise and are naturally keen to ensure that the money is spent in line with the vision they have for the enterprise. In a commercial environment an SME can be expected to be accountable to both those who provide the funding and to their customers. In not-for profit enterprises there are many more stakeholders to take into account when making decisions. As a result, accountability and the effective communication of management decisions become much more crucial.

Decision making within a social enterprise is influenced by the absence of an obvious owner. In many cases social enterprises are owned by local communities, and such local communities may have a range of different objectives. In this sense a social enterprise has guardians – people with a long-term commitment to the enterprise who bestow and sustain its basic principles and values. The founders and management of a social enterprise can therefore be considered as guardians, but guardians who are responsible for making decisions in the context of business strategies that are compiled by a Board.

Task of a Board (internal)

The task of a Board (which may also be referred to as the governing body, trustee or council) is to ensure that the enterprise remains true to the purpose stated in its constitution. Ideally, the role of the principal officers of the company, which includes the CEO and the senior management, should match exactly the aspirations of the community that they serve along with stakeholders, such as funding enterprises. However, as the enterprise grows, it is typical that conflict will develop between the principles, the community and the stakeholders.

The Board of a social enterprise has the same responsibilities as the Board of a commercial enterprise – to manage resources, to be accountable for the decisions and actions of the enterprise, and to formulate strategy. Compared with the Board of a commercial enterprise, a social enterprise has more constraints placed upon it because of its status. The most pressing of these are its objectives which are likely to encompass social as well as commercial goals. In many cases the social enterprise may be more involved in fund-raising and organizing volunteers to help it to fulfil its role within the community.

As Harris and Rochester (1996)[16] point out, the Boards of social enterprises often fail to perform from the perspective of the principles, the founders and the members of the community. Staff may feel marginalized in terms of decision making which is slow and often compromised by corporate social responsibility considerations. Some observers might argue that it is difficult to attract Board members who are able to work commercially and think socially. Their role is demanding and quite often there is no financial remuneration or thanks for making difficult decisions. Furthermore, successful managers drawn from the commercial sector are not automatically effective on the Board of a social enterprise. While this might be mitigated by training, the key issue is to ensure that Board members are aware of their, often changing, responsibilities and that there is a process for continually improving communications between the Board and staff. Ideally the Board of a not-for-profit (NFP) social enterprise should be a mix of the philanthropic and of skilled business people.

A weak Board means that managers and field workers have the scope to pursue their own agendas if the Board has no clear conception of the enterprise's objectives, or if the Board is unable or unwilling to exercise its role in monitoring and controlling the behaviour of staff and volunteers. Once the trust between managers, workers and the Board starts to disintegrate, direction becomes difficult to manage. However, different relationships exist between the guardians, Board, staff and beneficiaries (clients). In the traditional model, the guardians (who may themselves be Board members) empower the Board to reflect and represent their views. The Board employs the staff (either paid workers or volunteers) to deliver a service to the beneficiaries. There is therefore a clear chain of accountability and governance because of the likelihood of their sharing a commitment to the purpose of the enterprise.

For a summary of the main points covered in this chapter please see Example 5.1.

Examples —— 5.1 Building an enterprise

Example 5.1   Building an enterprise

Change represents opportunities for social entrepreneurs.

The Varney report is an example of the drivers for change.

Punctuated change is more difficult to manage.

Ownership of change is one of the keys to success.

Most large enterprises are built to pursue strategies that deliberately seek to avoid, manage or minimize risk.

Bureaucracies are the antithesis of the opportunity-seeking entrepreneurial social enterprise.

While a public sector enterprise might avoid risk, a social enterprise needs to embrace change by being entrepreneurial and innovative.

Vision is the distinguishing characteristic. Social visionaries envision, enact and enable.

As an enterprise, the Board, not the social entrepreneur, is responsible for managing resources, being accountable for the decisions and actions of the enterprise, and formulating strategy.

The appointment of Board members is critical to the success of the enterprise.

Revision questions

1. Identify a social enterprise that will allow you to draw up your own stakeholder table. How does it compare to what was described in this chapter?
2. By conducting your own research, identify the issues associated with how social enterprises mobilize volunteers. Consider the impact that this has on their enterprises and the potential impact on service delivery.
3. Seek out and interview a mix of Board members of at least two social enterprises.
   (a) What is the mix in the backgrounds of Board members?
   (b) How were they selected?

References

1. B. Hutter and M. Power (eds), *Enterpriseal Encounters with Risk* (Cambridge: Cambridge University Press, 2005).
2. D. Varney, *Service Transformation: A Better Service for Citizens and Businesses, a Better Deal for the Taxpayer* (2006). From www.hm-treasury. gov.uk/media/4/f/pbr06_varney_review.pdf.
3. Department of Health, 'Background to NHS Foundation Trusts', February 2009. Available at http://www.dh.gov.uk/publications, accessed November 2009.
4. J. Thompson and F. Martin, *Strategic Management: Awareness and Change*, 5th edn (London, UK: Thomson Learning, 2005), p. 801.

5. K. Lewin, 'Problems of Research in Social Psychology', in D. Cartwright (ed.), *Field Theory in Social Science: Selected Theoretical Papers by Kurt Lewin* (New York: Harper & Row, 1943–4/1951), pp. 155–69.
6. C. J. Clarke and S. Varma, *Strategic Risk Management, the New Competitive Edge, Long Range Planning*, 32 (4) (1999), pp. 414–24.
7. D. Carson, S. Cromie, J. McGowan Hill, *Marketing and Entrepreneurship in SME's, An Innovative Approach* (Hemel Hempstead: Prentice Hall, 1995), p. 155.
8. J. Thompson and F. Martin, *Strategic Management*.
9. T. Cannon, cited in P. Burns, *Entrepreneurship & Small Business* (Basingstoke: Palgrave Macmillan,1985), p. 304.
10. D. Kirby, 'Entrepreneurship Education: Can Business Schools Meet the Challenge?' *Education & Training*, vol. 46, no. 8/9 (2004), pp. 510–19.
11. J. W. Mullins and D. Forlani, 'Missing the Boat or Sinking the Boat: A Study of New Venture Decision Making', *Journal of Business Venturing*, 20, (2005), pp. 47–69.
12. P. A. Wickham, *Strategic Entrepreneurship* (London: Financial Times/ Prentice Hall, 1998), p. 133.
13. N. Sykes, 'Is the Enterprise Encoded with a 'DNA' which Determines its Development?' paper (unpublished) presented at The Visioneers, Conference, Putteridge, Bury Management Centre, April 1999.
14. P. Burns, *Entrepreneurship and Small Business*, pp. 223–6.
15. A. Cadbury, *Corporate Governance and Chairmanship* (Oxford University Press: Oxford, 2002).
16. T. N. Garavan, 'Stakeholders and Strategic Human Resource Development', *Journal of European Industrial Training*, vol. 19, issue 10 (1995), pp. 11–16.
17. M. Harris and C. Rochester, 'Working with Governing Bodies', in S. P. Osborne (ed.), *Managing in the Voluntary Sector* (London: International Thomson Publishing, 1996).

Additional reading

Davister, C., Defourney, J. and Regoire, O., *Integration of Social Enterprises in the European Union: An Overview of existing models in the European Union* (Toronto, Canada: International Society for Third Sector Research, 2004), April.

Prabhu, G. N., 'Social Entrepreneurial Leadership', *Career Development International*, vol. 4, issue 3 (1999), pp. 140–5.

Thompson. J. and Martin, F., *Strategic Management: Awareness and Change*, 5th edn, (Thomson Learning, 2005). (See chapter 17, 'Leading Change', pp. 795–839).

6 growing pains

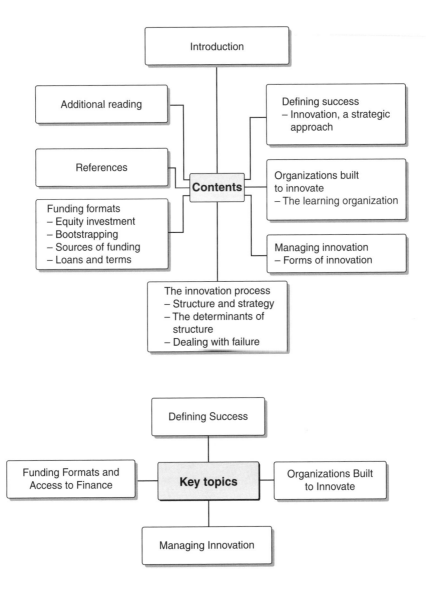

127

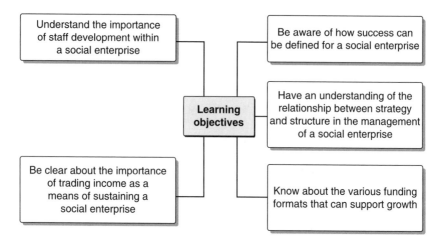

Introduction

This chapter examines the growth options and the dilemmas that face social enterprises as they grow. Two themes are addressed: the challenge of growing through innovation and the funding formats that might be available to support growth.

Covering the growth pains of a social enterprise means examining the role of innovation and how this influences the growth prospects of a social enterprise. The question of defining success is addressed and this is followed by a discussion about how flexible responses to opportunities affect organizational structure. The relationship between strategy and innovation is investigated along with the need to create an organizational format that encourages innovation. This is then matched into a discussion about funding formats and the impact that this has on business structures. It is argued that social enterprises have limited access to funding and that while there are loans and grants available, for an organization to grow it really needs trading income if it is to be sustainable.

Just because social enterprises have become a popular medium for policymakers to support and even when the public welcome them, this does not mean that social enterprises will automatically grow and succeed. Many within the sector would agree with the idea that both the management within, and boards of social firms, need access to better training to become more professional and commercial.

Defining success

The expectations for social enterprise are perhaps impossibly high.

> Because people are looking for something different to address challenges like climate change, there will be a trend towards social enterprises since they mix the economic, the social and the environmental. ... Social enterprise will transfer power to citizens over the things which affect their lives.
>
> (Smith Institute, 2007, p. 15)[1]

The definition of success for a social enterprise is difficult to untangle since it can be seen from a number of different perspectives. Some of these have been discussed in Chapter 3 where the argument centred on the role of the lead entrepreneur and what their vision was for the future. It has already been noted that not all social enterprises can be expected to become 'gazelles' and, if social enterprises reflect the successes and failures of the small business community, many will trundle along and many will fail. When discussing growth, we need to look at the larger picture of who the enterprise was set up to help. Therefore, it seems quite legitimate to leave behind the personal aspirations of the founding social entrepreneur. The questions are:

1. What are the characteristics of a social enterprise that grows beyond the vision of one person and becomes a viable business entity?
2. What distinguishes an organization with long-term growth potential from others?

Community-based social enterprises are not set up to achieve pure commercial success. They seek to provide *sustainable* economic activity in ways which ensure that the money and benefits from trading activities are redirected back into the local community. This is especially important when the social enterprise is based in a disadvantaged community or when it is dedicated to working with vulnerable groups. Even though a social enterprise is established to address a specific local or community need, this does not mean that it should not be ambitious to grow and extend its influence *beyond* the locality. A successful social enterprise may wish to replicate its business model by transferring its reach to other communities. For example it may wish to 'franchise' the business model and replicate it elsewhere. Alternatively it may wish to provide more services to an existing local market. In the case of Shetland Island-based Enviroglass it is growing its influence well outside its peripheral island locality to be a major UK-wide success story any business would be proud of. Innovation is a key aspect of the success of Enviroglass, as is ambition.

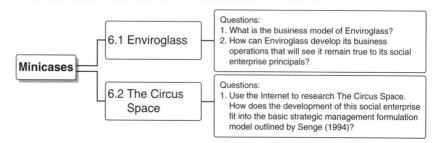

Minicases

6.1 Enviroglass

Questions:
1. What is the business model of Enviroglass?
2. How can Enviroglass develop its business operations that will see it remain true to its social enterprise principals?

6.2 The Circus Space

Questions:
1. Use the Internet to research The Circus Space. How does the development of this social enterprise fit into the basic strategic management formulation model outlined by Senge (1994)?

Minicase 6.1   Enviroglass

'Enviroglass, Shetland's award-winning social enterprise glass recycling company is set to export recycled glass paving slabs to a number of new project developments throughout England. It has emerged that two schools in Greater Manchester and a number of housing developments in Middlesex and London have all stipulated Enviroglass recycled glass pavers in their specification. It is expected significant orders will follow in the near future, making Enviroglass a major exporter from Shetland to the UK with regard to recycled glass products.'

Shetland has long been at the forefront of glass recycling throughout the UK with Enviroglass undertaking the first trials in the production of recycled glass pavers two years ago. This resulted in the launch of a wide range of recycled glass pavers throughout Shetland and the UK through their web site. The product has such a high environmental and sustainability rating that major developers and capital project providers are now seeking Enviroglass products to be included in their projects. With the onset of a large amount of recycled glass paving slabs to be manufactured, and with more and more architects showing an interest, Enviroglass are now looking at the possibility of expanding their operations to include a more mechanised method of production and of employing more staff to cope with the raised level of demand.

Mick Clifton, Project Officer with Shetland Amenity Trust, who oversees Enviroglass, commented 'this is really fantastic news and one which all staff at Enviroglass have been working very hard for. The prospect of exporting high quality recycled glass products to the rest of the UK is a huge success story. This is good for Shetland and good for the environment. We have developed a recycled product, which exceeds British Standards and which a large number of customers are fully embracing'.

Source: www.senscot.net/profiles (accessed December 2008)

QUESTIONS

1. What is the business model of Enviroglass?
2. How can Enviroglass develop its business operations that will see it remain true to its social enterprise principals?

What is clear is that a social enterprise, like any other small business, can be expected to go through a series of growth stages. In the earliest stage, that of business start-up, the social entrepreneur is involved in conceiving, planning, launching, implementing and assessing an idea. A great deal has been written about business start-up and this is not the central tenant of this book. It is what happens next that is important, since it is (comparatively) easy to start a social enterprise to meet an identifiable need, but much more difficult to fund and sustain it.

Innovation is central to this process. The Oxford English Dictionary defines innovation as '*making changes to something already established*'. Invention, by contrast, is the act of 'coming upon or finding: discovery'. Whereas inventors stumble across or make new things, '*innovators try to change the status quo*'. This partly explains why big corporations have a big problem with innovation. It is, however, accepted wisdom that smaller enterprises are more innovative and that it is this ability to be innovative that distinguishes them.

Early-stage innovations often remain local. Middle-stage is characterized by expansion, organizational development, and deeper institutionalization of a successful innovation, leading to the innovation being implemented on a broader scale, regionally or nationally. In late-stage social entrepreneurship, the innovation is widely accepted as a new pattern in society. Innovation in the provision of products and services, and the minimization of delay in turnaround from concept to market introduction, is a means by which an organization can create an advantage over competitors and maximize the efficiency of financial, personnel and material resources.

The innovative approach to growth can be characterized by both the life cycle and by stage models. These models are useful tools but they describe what is happening when an organization grows rather than why that organization is capable of growth. We need to see strategy as a way of thinking – an approach to decision making. This approach to decision-making depends on organization context and it has already been argued that social enterprises are a distinct form of business. Hence strategy in big companies is different from small companies. Public sector organizations also make different decisions than private sector organizations. By definition then, a social enterprise has elements of small business strategy and elements of not-for-profit (NFP) public sector strategy. Strategic thinking in social enterprise is therefore 'hybridised'. (Frumkin and Kim, 2000).[2]

Innovation, a strategic approach

Strategy is a management approach that has its roots in military thinking. Webster's New World Dictionary defines strategy as 'the science of planning and directing military operations'. Strategic manoeuvres use the principles of military strategy. Thus a business strategy is the set of policies used to anticipate and manage conflict and for securing of an advantage over the competition. It is however important to be careful with the military analogy. Modern warfare is based on the destruction of opposing forces and on the use of resources which are greater than that of the enemy so as to give an overwhelming advantage, presenting the victor with the opportunity to destroy the enemy.

> Success in business is usually about adding value of your own, not diminishing that of your competitors, and is based on distinctive capability, not destructive capacity. ... The second area in which the military analogy misleads is in inviting excessive emphasis on leadership, vision, and determination.... Fighting against overwhelming odds may sometimes be a necessary military strategy. It is almost always not a sensible business strategy.
>
> (Kay, 1993)[3]

Social enterprises thrive because they do not take their purpose from traditional measures of commercial success, whether these are performance targets, job creation measures or profitability. Social enterprises are guided, usually informally, by a 'scorecard' in which financial performance has to be blended alongside their role in boosting human and social capital.

The idea here is that social enterprises can be fast-growing and highly competitive, market-led businesses – if they choose to be. For an example of this see Minicase 6.2 The Circus Space. From the web site it would not be easy to identify that this was indeed a social enterprise.

Minicase 6.2   The Circus Space

The Circus Space is one of the top 3 circus schools in Europe. The founders of the Circus Space have customized a huge derelict power station in Hackney. From this facility the organisation runs degree courses as well as private training and ensures all its operations are commercially viable. The Circus Space has been an active contributor to the creative buzz that now dominates this part of East London. It is also an important anchor of the local social community having recently initiated an extensive programme for local young people. The group's turnover growth of 380% in the last 5 years is further evidence of its Europe leading performance.

Source: www.thecircusspace.co.uk

QUESTION

1. Use the Internet to research The Circus Space.
   How does the development of this social enterprise fit into the basic strategic management formulation model outlined by Senge (1994)?

Organizations built to innovate

If strategy is one part of the formula for success, developing an organization that is capable of being innovative is the second part. (Please refer to Chapter 9 for more discussion on strategy.)

It is argued that 'successful organisations develop a culture of change that just keeps moving' (Kanter, 1999).[4] It can also be argued that when change occurs in the business environment, at either the societal or industry level, it is the ability of an organization to manage the process at a human or micro-level that determines its ultimate success.

According to the Senge (1994),[5] 'Learning Organizations' include:

- A learning approach to strategy formulation, implementation, evaluation and improvement must be structured as learning experiences with continuous improvement in the light of experience.
- Participative policymaking shared with all stakeholders. The aim of the policy is to satisfy customers and the differences of opinion and values that are revealed in the participative process are seen as productive tensions.
- Learning climate: that encourages experimentation and learning from experience. This may require a change in culture to one that encourages information sharing and shared learning.

The defining characteristic of the learning organization is the link between individual performance and organizational performance. According to Mason (2008),[6] there are seven steps to achieving a Learning Organization:

1. Communication system to facilitate the exchange of information
2. Commit to developing and facilitating an atmosphere for learning
3. Create a vision for the organization
4. Through training and awareness expand stakeholder's behaviour
5. Communicate a change in the company's culture
6. Allow staff and stakeholders to question key business practices and assumption
7. Develop workable alternatives for future actions and expect small setbacks!

The Learning Organization, in its attitude towards failure, engagement and vision, shares many of the characteristics of the social enterprise. Please see Figure 6.1 for the outline of an entrepreneurial organization.

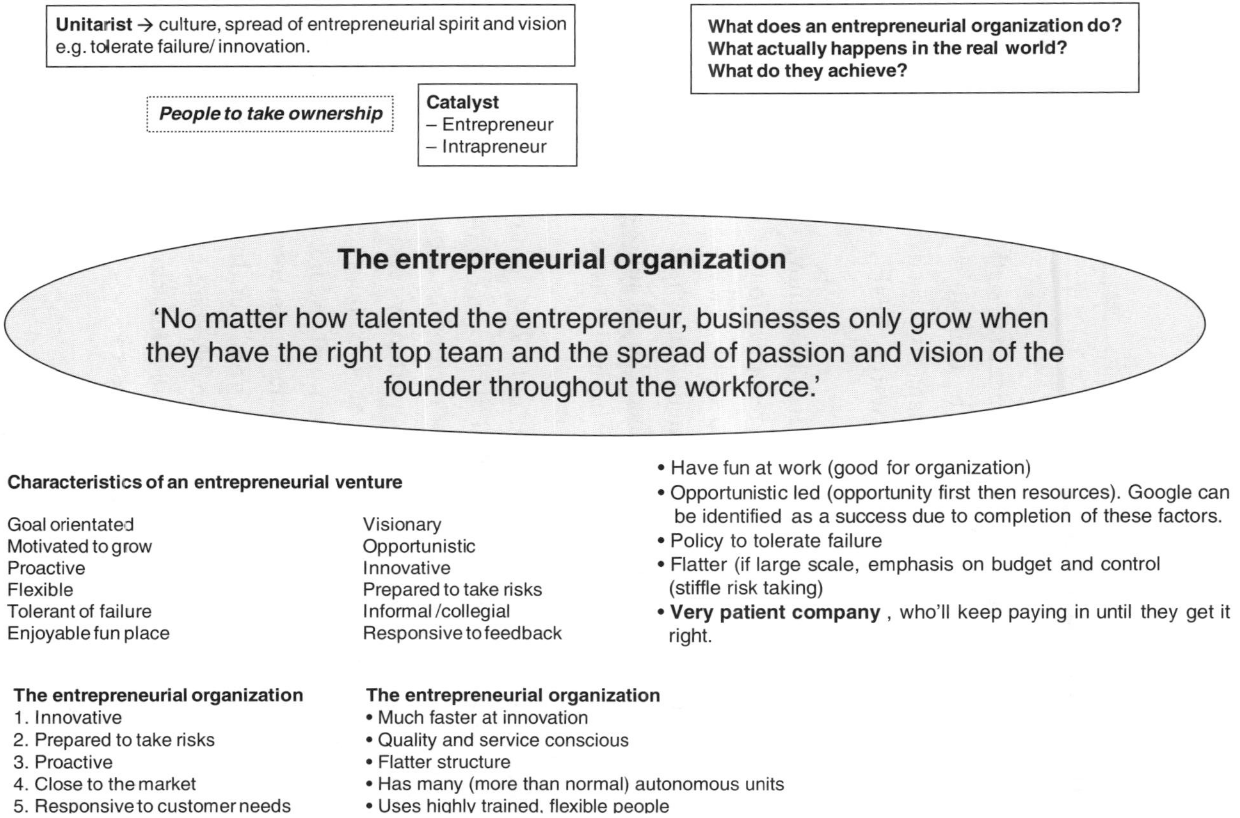

Unitarist → culture, spread of entrepreneurial spirit and vision
e.g. tolerate failure/ innovation.

What does an entrepreneurial organization do?
What actually happens in the real world?
What do they achieve?

People to take ownership

Catalyst
– Entrepreneur
– Intrapreneur

The entrepreneurial organization

'No matter how talented the entrepreneur, businesses only grow when they have the right top team and the spread of passion and vision of the founder throughout the workforce.'

- Have fun at work (good for organization)
- Opportunistic (opportunity first then resources). Google can be identified as a success due to completion of these factors.
- Policy to tolerate failure
- Flatter (if large scale, emphasis on budget and control (stiffle risk taking)
- **Very patient company**, who'll keep paying in until they get it right.

Characteristics of an entrepreneurial venture

Goal orientated
Motivated to grow
Proactive
Flexible
Tolerant of failure
Enjoyable fun place

Visionary
Opportunistic
Innovative
Prepared to take risks
Informal/collegial
Responsive to feedback

The entrepreneurial organization
- Much faster at innovation
- Quality and service conscious
- Flatter structure
- Has many (more than normal) autonomous units
- Uses highly trained, flexible people

The entrepreneurial organization
1. Innovative
2. Prepared to take risks
3. Proactive
4. Close to the market
5. Responsive to customer needs

Figure 6.1   The entrepreneurial organization

It is about creating, through sharing knowledge and ideas, actions which will contribute to the interests of the whole rather than the individual or the department (Thompson and Martin, 2005).[7] This approach is entirely consistent with a social enterprise's blended values, combining economic success with social benefits (see Chapter 4).

Managing innovation

As well as creating the right environment for staff and stakeholders, a successful social organization should be built to respond to change by being innovative in the way that it manages its activities. Social organizations are as capable of being innovative in this sense as any other enterprise format.

Leadbeater (2007)[8] argues that 'all innovation involves the application of new ideas – or the reapplication of old ideas in new ways – to devise better solutions to needs. Like learning, innovation is a cumulative, collaborative activity in which ideas are shared, tested, refined, developed and applied. Social innovation applies this thinking to social issues: education and health, issues of inequality and inclusion'.

According to Thompson and Martin (2005), 'innovation takes place when an organisation makes a technical change, e.g. produces a product or service that is new to it, or uses a method or input that is new and original'. Thus innovation implies opportunity-seeking and responding to change through the introduction of something new. While innovation is usually associated with new or novel technology, it may also be related to service processes, approaches to marketing a product or service, or the way in which jobs are carried out. In other words, innovation relates to the creation of sustainable long-term advantage. Like becoming a Learning Organization, being innovative is an approach to enterprise, rather than a management process.

There are four forms of innovation:

1. New products or services, which are either radically new or which extend the product lifecycle.
2. Process innovation leading to reduced operating costs, and affected partially by the learning and experience effect.

3. Marketing innovations, which rely on finding new groups of customers or sponsors or new channels through which a service can be delivered.
4. Organizational changes, which reduce costs or improve the quality or consistency of delivery.

One of the issues that becomes clear when developing an action-centred approach to innovation is that it cannot be prescribed. An innovative organization can be expected to adopt the Learning Organization concept because of the increasing pressure to change with developments in globalization, changes in customer expectations, different competitive landscapes and technology. An organization needs to continuously develop to maintain competitive advantage and learning is the only way of obtaining and maintaining a competitive edge, during periods of upheaval.

Goffin (2005, p. 8)[9] describes innovation as the creation of something 'new' that creates and adds value for customers and clients. Something 'new' does not indefinitely mean something revolutionary; it can mean updating an existing product or service and taking advantage of changes in demand within a market segment. These innovations are what Christensen (2004, p. xv–xx)[10] identifies as disruptive or sustaining innovations. The disruptive innovation introduces a new value proposition: it can create new markets or reshape existing markets. Sustaining innovations are improvements to existing products, processes or markets, and will typically maintain the status quo within a given market. What this means is that innovation can be either radical or incremental. Innovation in the modern organization is multi-dimensional and should be thought of as an on-going process rather than a management activity. Creating an organization built to innovate requires an understanding of how innovation is to be achieved.

For an organization to become innovative it must allow original thinking and creativity to flourish. As Trott (2005, p. 11)[11] points out, this is 'invariably a team game'. Being able to innovate means appointing the right people and giving them the opportunity to perform creatively – to find new solutions to doing things differently. When organizations foster the right conditions then innovative behaviour will flourish.

Innovation strategy should be set out in the 'vision' statement, together with a set of objectives that seek to implement this new approach. Innovative organizations require a set of core competencies and capacities which enable them to embrace innovation. These competencies are usually located within the organization as resources, or they can be accessed externally as part of technical collaboration or knowledge-sharing initiatives. The values which encourage an innovation culture need to be embedded within the organization and throughout its stakeholders. When building an innovative organization its management is a complex and detailed process. As Louis Pasteur observed 'chance favours the prepared mind'. In other words, if organizations develop their understanding of the creative process they can help set up the conditions within which 'serendipity' can take place and be capitalized on.

For the social enterprise, it is important to note that learning, knowledge and innovation need not rely entirely upon the ability of staff or volunteers to be creative. Social innovators can tap into external networks – knowledge-based relationships that are funded on collaboration and the exchange of mutual ideas. This exchange takes place between all the different levels of stakeholders – direct and in direct. This mutual exchange of ideas should, in theory, be easier within the third sector than within commercial organizations. There is less commercial sensitivity and a great incentive to respond to social welfare and public choice by sharing ideas, by sharing information and by jointly developing new forms of services. When discussing innovation it is important to distinguish between ideas, inventions and innovations. Ideas are relatively easy to come by; inventions are more difficult.

The innovation process

There are three players in the innovation process: inventors, lead entrepreneurs and business managers. Each must possess a very different set of skills that at times conflict. Social enterprises will fail if they are unable to build value propositions with their customers and stakeholders. According to Piercy (2005, p. 9):[12]

> Frederick Webster suggests that we should think about how we design and bring together all the business processes that: define customer value (e.g. market research, analysis of our core competencies, economic analysis of customer use systems): develop customer value (e.g. new product development, design of distribution channel, selection of partners, develop price mid-value positioning), and deliver customer value (e.g. logistics, sales, transaction processing, after-sales service, applications engineering and customer training).

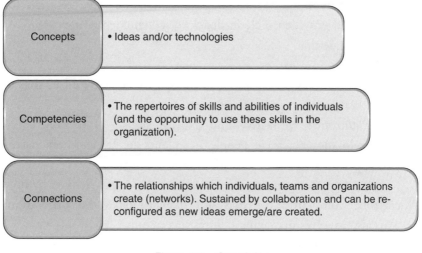

Figure 6.2 **Creativity**
Source: Based on Kanter, *When Giants Learn to Dance* (New York, Simon & Schuster, 1989)

However, the processes also have a behavioural dimension (e.g. interpretation and understanding in value definition, motivation and commitment in value development, and attitudes and behaviour in value delivery). The challenge is not just to manage techniques but also people.

Piercy is presenting a scenario in which innovation is not just about new technologies or processes, but is about creativity and how people and their organizations manage innovation, and how these processes add value to service delivery. It is argued that a creative organization (Figure 6.2) is better positioned to be innovative and to be creative in achieving this process of adding value. What this suggests is that innovation is not accidental and it has to be part of a business culture that focuses on opportunity-seeking and opportunity-spotting.

Dealing with failure

Assuming that an organization is subject to external change, the best test of innovation is to deal with failure. Extensive bureaucracy demotivates staff and volunteers and reduces personal power. In an entrepreneurial organization, (Figure 6.1) new ideas would be supported and failure would be the subject of review and learning, not recrimination. This ability to accommodate and learn from failure is implicit within the 'Learning Organization'. These organizations have clearly stated visions and values, they (re)align goals and make them relevant for their staff, and provide timely feedback to stakeholders. Birley (1997)[13] goes on to argue that

> [l]eaders of successful customer transformations have told us that to make them work, organizations must:
>
> Develop new, proactive and process skills – this may entail pulling in more creative people from outside. It definitely means letting people go with their instincts and feeling.
>
> Encourage experimentation and reward success as defined by how customer competitive it makes (or is likely to make) the corporation. This also involves managing failures successfully.
>
> Learn how to work on twin tracks – do what needs doing better now and, simultaneously, new things that may take longer.
>
> Unlock the enterprise within, defining risk differently and having 'venturesome' people make key resource decisions.
>
> Develop new leadership skills with a new set of language and tools to reflect not the entrepreneurial or management world of yesterday, but what is needed today and in the future.
>
> The corporation's responsibility is to support and reward this in new and innovative ways.

It is important to note that the discussion in this chapter is about the relationship between innovation and strategy, between innovation and organization and ultimately the relationship between strategy and structure. This section has outlined the principles and readers are encouraged to develop their own understanding about innovation and their own understanding about strategy. The important thing to realize in this discussion is that strategy, entrepreneurship and innovation are linked. Both are an attitude and an approach to growing a successful social enterprise.

They are the antithesis of a process of formally planned business growth. In terms of developing this attitude, there is no indication that the entrepreneur and the social entrepreneur need to think differently. To succeed, to create a sustainable business, both need to be 'disruptive' in their thinking. Both need to be creative. Entrepreneurs think in non-conventional ways, to challenge existing assumptions and to be flexible and adaptable in solving problems. They see opportunities and make them happen. Entrepreneurs are intuitive rather than rational thinkers.

> Instead of adopting a structured, analytical approach to problem solving, which requires attention to detail, adherence to rules and systematic investigation, it is believed that they prefer a more intuitive approach that requires more holism and synthesis, lateral rather than sequential reasoning and random methods of exploration.
>
> (Kirby, 2004)[14]

Funding formats

Creating a learning-style organization and one that is built for innovation and creativity takes resources to put a vision into place. One critical resource for growing a social enterprise is access to finance and sources of funding. Compared with SMEs, social enterprises are more limited in their choices. This means that access to alternative sources of funding to supplement donations, sponsorship and grants is critical to sustaining a social enterprise. Unless a non-profit organization is generating earned revenue from its activities, it is not acting in an entrepreneurial manner. It may be doing social good, creating new and vibrant programs, but it is innovative, not entrepreneurial (Boschee, 2003).[15] This distinction is important because a social organization needs to be sustainable – it has to generate trading income – not just donations or sponsorship. In certain circumstances there is a conflict with the need to generate funding and income from commercial enterprise while at the same time serving the needs of a community. This inherent conflict means that social firms can exist at different growth stages, in terms of their ability to match income with social integration. It is the ability to manage this conflict between integration and income that is one of the main factors that determine the success of a social venture.

This implies that the social capital element of a social enterprise has an impact on financial performance. Social capital refers to the intangible social networks and shared values that are often associated with the third sector. The concept has been widely applied by the World Bank (1999)[16] which sees it as a means of creating social cohesion. One component of social capital that is particular to the third sector are the volunteers who contribute human capital to offset costs and

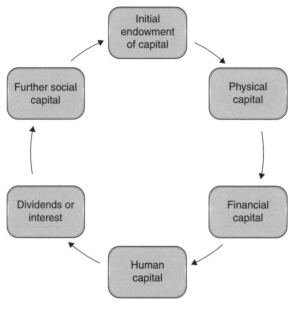

Figure 6.3 ***Social capital***
Source: Based on Leadbeater (2007)

improve service delivery. The connections between the different elements of social capital are shown as Figure 6.3.

Equity investment

The Venture Financing Chain is the ability of a business to access outside sources of assistance to fund growth (Lingane et al., 2004).[17] There are a range of sources available for profit-driven SMEs, but these are constructed to provide investors with a return on their capital. The most fundamental form of external investment is known as bootstrapping often in the form of 'family and friends' who invest in a new business. Leaving this aside, the more sophisticated from of equity investments are through business angels and then venture capital firms or even an Initial Public Offering (IPO). As one moves through the different options the potential sums to be raised increase. In other words equity investment is the capital source that allows accelerated growth.

Business angels, and possibly venture capitalists, are equity investors and they are often used by fast growth commercial business to fund the 'second stage of development', that is the period two or three years after the business was set up. However, due to the concept of 'blended values', equity-based investments are not a funding source that is readily available to a social organizations. Within the US, venture philanthropy exists, whereby individuals of high net worth deliberately invest in social enterprises. In Europe this phenomena is mainly evident in investors who specialize in supporting green technologies. It however remains the case that most social enterprises are still excluded from equity investments because of the nature of the ownership of their social enterprise.

This is because an investor cannot usually expect a return on investment through a dividend or sale. Furthermore, all forms of equity investment require the current owners to give up part of the ownership, and when control of the firm is invested in a community rather than a group of individuals the opportunity for dispersal of shareholder value to outside investors is limited. One possibility to deal with this is to obtain the agreement of the community to sell the venture so as to secure funds to invest in other activities that are of a greater priority to the community.

Bootstrapping

This problem with the equity investment route means that 'bootstrapping' is a financial reality for starting-up most social enterprises. The term is an allusion to the expression '*pulling oneself up by one's bootstraps*'. Bootstrapping can be described as a creative means of financing a venture through the leverage of resources without the need to raise equity from traditional sources or borrowing extensively from a bank. It is characterized by a reliance on internally generated retained earnings and customer advances.

One of the most common financial disciplines employed in bootstrapping is the positive cash flow – which means slowing down payments to suppliers and speeding up the collection of payments from customers. Apart from any ethical consideration that a social organization might face in delaying payments, bootstrapping requires sophisticated management of the supply chain and it will ultimately generate negative cash-flow as outgoings exceed income streams. The point to realize is that social enterprises may have more limited sources of funding available and are more likely to rely on internally generated funds for a longer period of time than an SME. As a growth strategy bootstrapping and the use of internally generated funds has its limitations. It may be appropriate as a short-term source of funding, but it is unlikely to create a sustainable venture.

The alternative to bootstrapping is to seek debt finance. This includes bank debt such as overdrafts, short and long-term loans, asset based finance and trade credit. In this sense social enterprises are like the majority of small firms – they rely on short-term finance to maintain their business. Unlike small firms, though, they do not have the choice of accessing longer term venture finance that can support longer-term growth. Compared with small technology-based businesses, for example, the collateral available to grow a social enterprise model looks to be compromised. An over reliance on bootstrapping and grant funding will inevitably limit the growth potential. This is why income streams from commercial activity such as bank finance or support from private individuals or private companies is so important to creating a sustainable business.

Sources of funding

Access to finance is one of the most important issues facing social enterprises of all shapes and sizes. This section provides generic background information on this topic and it is important to note that funding sources will vary locally, regionally and nationally.

The following is a summary of the recommendations that were reported in the DTI[18] Finance for Social Enterprise Seminar, July 2004.

- A greater use of risk sharing mechanisms.
- Financial education for social enterprises so start-ups and developing social enterprises are better able to prepare business plans and management accountants are more investment ready.
- Improved delivery of dedicated technical assistance and business support. This needs a specialist support for social enterprises rather than generic.
- Better links between business support provision and access to finance through CDFI's and other financial institutions and local authorities.
- Education and training.
- All front-line bank staff, networks and support organizations in social enterprising to use visits to social enterprises to understand their needs for finance.
- For credit risk departments in banks to understand the potential of the social enterprise sector. Demonstrate to banks that risk/return ratio levels are within excepted norms and social enterprises are not that different from any other SME in terms of repayment.

- Persuade bankers to use a cash flow lending techniques.
- To have movement of staff between banks and CDFIs to get practical hands-on experience and understanding of lending to the social enterprises.
- More innovation and financial packages.

The tone of the DTI recommendations indicates that it is not just access to finance but it is the financial sectors understanding of social enterprise that limits their ability to raise long-term funding and especially equity-based funding. The very real challenges of accessing funding are likely to be further exacerbated in the present economic climate.

Loans and terms

Most commercial loans to social enterprises involve terms and security similar to those made to mainstream businesses. However, many social enterprises have little in the way of physical security, but often have a dependable turnover or other cash flow. This implies that there is a need for more lenders to offer unsecured overdraft lines, although again, is this likely to happen in the present economic climate? The relative lack of cash flow lending to social enterprises (most of which are quite small) is comparable to the lending position to standard small and medium size enterprises. At least the impression is that of a difficulty of raising bank finance.

In the past the banks have tended to focus their lending on the larger enterprises. Within the social economy, the larger social enterprises and voluntary organizations look likely to attract a proportionately greater amount of funding to the detriment of the newer, smaller social enterprises.

A study published as part of the 2006 UK survey of SME finances contained a social enterprise booster survey (Fraser, 2007).[19] Overall the sample consisted of 2455 UK based businesses with fewer than 250 employees and 1002 UK based social enterprises. In terms of bank funding when comparing SMEs and social enterprises, no significant difference was found with respect to

- Amount received relative to amount sought
- Rejection rates between SMEs and social enterprises
- Loan terms

It was however the case that social enterprises made significant use of grant financing: 71.7 per cent of social enterprises surveyed made use of grant financing as opposed to 6.3 per cent of mainstream SME businesses that did not. The study suggested that this was in part due to the preference of social enterprise managers to avoid debt finance. It may also be the case that social enterprises, in searching for funding, are much more geared to seeking out the grants that are available to them. It is also possible that the general problems perceived by SMEs in trying to obtain bank financing have caused social enterprises to doubt their ability to obtain bank funding whereas the study indicates that social enterprises can access bank lending quite successfully. The report also observes that there is a marked perception among smaller social enterprises that they will be rejected by mainstream finance providers. It is suggested this pessimism – as well as a lack of good financial advice, and their tendency to be located in deprived areas – may contribute to the greater reliance of social enterprises on grant finance.

The report recommends that better communication between social enterprises and finance providers must be fostered to counter the unwarranted perception that banks are unwilling to lend to the sector.

Even taking into account limited access and the pessimism discovered by Fraser (2007), many social enterprises fail to search out the best terms. This suggests that many social enterprises do not have a good understanding of commercial bank funding and that knowledge of the financial systems will continue to be a barrier to future growth and success. For example the trustees of social enterprises may be reluctant to take on asset debt finance. This allows the finance available to businesses to grow in line with sales. Factoring and Invoice Discounting services primarily provide these facilities. It is also possible to extend the finance available to include Asset Based Lending – facilities secured against stock, plant, machinery and property.

Furthermore many social enterprises do not distinguish between grants and contracts for services on their financial statements. Being able to analyse these sources of income separately is key to assessing the stability and self-sufficiency of the organization. The strength of management and of relationships with other funders (primarily government agencies) will tend to influence the banks' decision to lend. For this reason social enterprises need to network with potential funders including the banks. The most entrepreneurial social firms seek to influence public, corporate, media, academic and other thought leaders around the world. In the case of for-profit social entrepreneurs, their focus is clearly on social value creation with part of their profits being re-invested in scaling up their social return on investment.

The argument presented in this section is that social enterprises have many of the characteristics of small businesses. They may have limited access to funding and may often have a poor understanding of sources of finance. Generally, they are dependent upon bootstrapping with some limited use of debt financing preferring instead to try and access grant funding. They are, however, generally unlike small businesses who in some cases have the option of equity financing. This difficulty is compounded by the fact that many social entrepreneurs have, as indicated, limited knowledge of how to access bank financing.

All of these challenges are compounded when there are problems in the external environment. For this reason the generation of revenue from external trading activities will become all the more important for social enterprises. It will change the blended values.

Example 6.1 provides a summary of the main points in this chapter.

| Examples | — | 6.1 Growing Pains |

Example 6.1   Growing Pains

The support of politicians and policymakers does not guarantee success.
Social enterprise has elements of small business strategy and elements of not-for-profit public sector strategy.
The defining characteristic of the Learning Organization is the link between individual performance and organizational performance to provide continuous learning opportunities.
Extensive bureaucracy de-motivates the workforce and reduces personal power.
Innovation, creativity and enterprise are key cultural values of a sustainable social enterprise.
Learning and innovation are closely linked.
Innovation cannot be prescribed. It is an approach not a process.
Like SMEs, social enterprises have limited access to funding. Compared with SMEs social enterprises are more likely to use grant funding than debt funding limiting their choice of finance and funding.
At different stages of growth social enterprise require different funding formats and access to different sources of finance.
They are unlikely to have access to equity funding.
Bootstrapping may be used during start-up but alternative forms are required to grow a business.

Revision questions

1. We have indicated that there are seven steps to achieving a 'Learning Organization'. Select a social enterprise you are familiar with. Conduct research into what these steps are and apply these principles to this social enterprise.
2. From the four forms of innovation identified in this chapter characterize 'innovations' from an organization that you are familiar and assess the impact that these innovations might have in terms of adding value to a social enterprise.
3. Select a local charity or voluntary organization and conduct a social audit of their capability. It is important that you speak to the person in charge – either the chief executive or a main board member. It is also important that if you are working in a tutorial group that you co-ordinate your approach to conducting interviews, the questions that are asked and the weighting that is put onto the responses.

   You may wish to build your questions around the following themes:

   (a) What are the key areas of support that would assist your organization in becoming fully able to sustain itself over the medium to long term? Can you give examples of good practice?
   (b) What areas of support would your organization require to be able to function more effectively and deliver a better service? Can you give examples of good practice?
   (c) In what ways would your organization wish to engage with policy-makers and other key stakeholders? Can you give examples of good practice?
   (d) What are the continuing barriers to equality/social justice/community development as identified by the communities your organization supports and represents? Can you give examples of good practice in removing such barriers?

Compare and contrast the responses with others and develop recommendations to remove barriers and promote social entrepreneurship by citing examples of best practice within the sector.

References

1. A. Westall and D. Chalkley, *Social Enterprise Futures* (Smith Institute: London, 2007), p. 16.
2. P. Frumkin and M. T. Kim, 'Strategic Positioning and the Financing of Nonprofit Organizations', Hauser Center for Nonprofit Organisations, Working paper No. 2, October, Harvard University, 2000).
3. J. Kay, *Foundations of Corporate Success* (Oxford University Press: Oxford, 1993).

4. R. M. Kanter, 'Change in Everyone's Job: Managing the Extended Enterprise in a Globally Extended World', *Organisational Dynamics*, 28, 1 (1999), pp. 7–23.
5. P. Senge, *The Fifth Discipline: The Art and Practice of the Learning Organisation* (New York: Doubleday, 1994).
6. M. Mason, *New Directions: The Learning Organisation.* Available at http://www.moyak.com/researcher/resume/papers/var21mkm.html, accessed April 2008.
7. J. Thompson and F. Martin, *Strategic Management: Awareness and Change*, 5th edn (Thomson Learning, 2005), p. 232.
8. C. Leadbeater, *Social Enterprise and Social Innovation: Strategies for the Next Ten Years*, Cabinet Office, Office for the Third Sector, November 2007.
9. K. Goffin and R. Martin, *Innovation Management: Strategy and Implementation Using the Pentathlon Framework* (Basingstoke: Palgrave Macmillan, 2005).
10. C. M. Christensen, S. D. Anthony and E. A. Roth, *Seeing What's Next: Using Theories of Innovation to Predict Industry Change.* (USA: Harvard Business Review, Cambridge, MA, 2004).
11. P. Trott, *Innovation Management and New Product Development*, 2nd edn (London: Prentice Hall, 2002), Chapter 1.
12. N. Piercy, *Market-Led Strategic Change*, (Reed, Elsevier NV, 2005), p. 9.
13. S. Birley, 'The Corporate Entrepreneur: Leading Organisational Transformation', *Long Range Planning Journal*, June 1997, vol. 30, issue 3 (1997), pp. 345–52.
14. D. Kirby, 'Entrepreneurship Education: Can Business Schools Meet the Challenge?' *Education and Training*, vol. 46, no. 8–9 (2004), pp. 510–19.
15. J. Boschee, *Introduction to Social Entrepreneurship, Mapping the Social Purpose Business Sector* (Institute for Social Entrepreneurs, 2003). See http://www.socialent.org/intro_to_se.htm - mapping.
16. The World Bank, 'What is Social Capital?' *PovertyNet* (1999). See http://www.worldbank.org/poverty/scapital/whatsc.htm.
17. A. Lingane and S. Olsen, 'Guidelines for Social Return on Investment', Harvard Business Review, vol. 46, no. 3 (2004), pp. 1–22.
18. Access to Finance for Social Enterprises is available at the following URL, http://www.cabinetoffice.gov.uk/third_sector/research and statistics/social_enteprise_research.aspx.
19. S. Fraser, *Finance for Small and Medium Sized Enterprises: Comparisons of Social Enterprises and Mainstream Business* (University of Warwick, Centre for Small and Medium Sized Enterprises, 2007).

Additional reading

Dees, J., Emerson, J. and Economy, P., *Strategic Tools for Social Entrepreneurs* (New York: Wiley, 2002), Chapter 10: 'The Question of Scale: Finding An Appropriate Strategy For Building On Your Success'. Textbook site is www.enterprisingnonprofits.org.

7 marketing for social enterprises

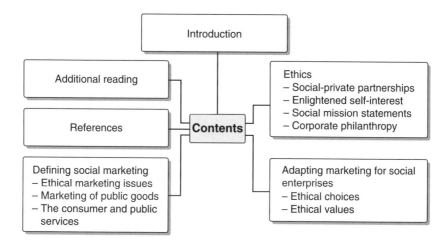

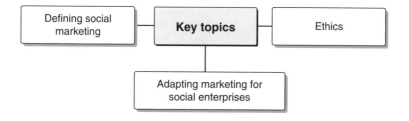

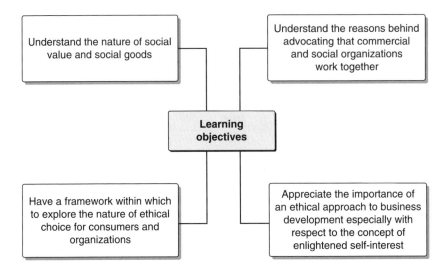

Introduction

Social enterprises, unlike charitable organizations or the public sector, operate fully or partially within the market economy. Like many 'third sector' organizations, they are obliged to show a return on their efforts and they are obliged to compete for funds, sponsorship and support resources. This means that they exhibit many of the organizational characteristics of for-profit organizations.

Any business, whether it is profit-making or non-profit-making, has responsibilities. While making a profit (or surplus) is one of the first priorities, it can be argued that businesses are not purely profit-seeking – some at least see themselves as having social responsibilities not just to their customers but also to their employees, their suppliers, the community, society in general and the environment. This is important to the social economy since a relationship with the private sector may mean that a private business is willing to work alongside social organizations to supports their activities within the community.

Finally, this chapter examines the means by which social firms provide social value to their customer groups and the service delivery and support infrastructures that they draw upon.

Ethics

The first topic begins with a discussion about why commercial organizations should be willing to support and work alongside social organizations. The issue of neo-liberalism is discussed, along with the social responsibility of the wider business community. The next topic examines how corporate firms manage themselves in terms of business ethics. The question of social and private partnerships is examined along with the idea of enlightened self-interest. This looks at the conflict between profit and social responsibility and contrasts private and public sector principles. Social mission statements are examined as a way of managing a Corporate Social Responsibility (CSR) strategy and examples are given of firms' own social missions. Codes of practice as well as ethical strategic frameworks are also examined.

In the 'sustainable market' topic, the discussion moves onto the different ethical choices that companies and individuals make and the trade-offs that are involved. The argument is that ethical standards are a management responsibility and that social marketing is a tool that is used to communicate these standards. In the final topic, the role of stakeholders is examined. A stakeholder is anyone with a declared or conceivable interest in a social organization. The issue of conflicts is addressed along with ways of assessing the power and the interest of direct and indirect stakeholders. The management of stakeholders through governors is then examined.

> If you think in a deeper way that you are going to be selfish, then be wisely selfish, not narrow-mindedly selfish.
>
> Dalai Lama of Tibet (1997)[1]

Social-private partnerships

There is an acceptance at a governmental level in many countries, including the UK, that public sector and voluntary organizations should seek to behave in a more business-like manner (i.e. more like the private sector). The argument is that the efficiency of service provision is enhanced where a public or voluntary agency conducts its affairs in accordance with business principles. This includes a move towards rewarding enterprise as well as adopting flexible working practices.

The acceptance of the enterprise economy suggests that private firms perform better because of market mechanisms. However, one area where concern has arisen is the unfettered transference of the profit motive from private to social organizations. The question remains whether private sector work and profit motives really are relevant to social organizations, and ultimately it comes down to an argument about free-market or interventionism. With hindsight we can argue that social organizations may need to be closely regulated by their boards to ensure that the community does gain.

Hartigan and Martin (2004)[2] summarize the argument into two perspectives:

The only 'social responsibility of business' is to increase profits. The corporation is an instrument of the stockholders who own it. If the corporation makes a contribution, it prevents the individual stockholder from himself deciding how he should dispose of his funds. – Friedman (1962)	Economic performance is the first responsibility of a business. [...] But economic performance is not the only responsibility of a business. – Drucker (1975)

Enlightened self-interest

The concept of 'enlightened self-interest' is a philosophy in ethics which states that persons or corporations who act to further the interests of others (or the interests of the group or groups to which they belong), ultimately serve their own self-interest. Yet in terms of the present banking crisis it would appear that greed triumphed over self-interest in that the activities of many of the senior people within banks brought about the collapse of the bank they worked for. In this case it is easy to say that there should always be a trade-off between business profit objectives and the ethical orientation of an organization. Ethical orientations can include employment rights, environmental performance and equal opportunities and is sometimes classified as enlightened self-interest.

As indicated above, the banks have demonstrated the wrong kind of self-interest by seemingly ignoring the impact of their selfishness on the rest of society. Many third sector organizations, including social enterprises, have been accused of using public funds to insulate them from market forces. This is the very thing the banks have so clearly taken advantage of, especially in the UK.

Doing good for others in one's own interest could be described as enlightened self-interest; it makes individuals feel better about themselves (see Minicase 3.4 on OneWorld Health). The social entrepreneur operates in the area of enlightened self-interest in that being successful leads to the feel-good factor of doing something meaningful for others. The social enterprise needs to make use of individual philanthropists if and where it can.

However, we advocate that a sustainable social enterprise is created when it takes advantage of market forces to create profits, and through this puts resources back into the community it serves rather than relying directly on philanthropy for funding.

Within the UK public sector, the Nolan Committee (May 1995), suggested a number of important principles that the public sector should follow:

- Selflessness – holders of public office should take decisions solely in terms of public interest, without any concern for personal financial gain.
- Integrity – holders of public office should not place themselves under any financial or other obligation to outside individuals or

organizations that might influence them in the performance of their official duties.

- Objectivity – in carrying out public business, including making public appointments, awarding contracts or recommending individuals for rewards and benefits, holders of public office should make choices on merit.
- Accountability – holders of public office are accountable for their decisions and actions to the public and must submit themselves to whatever scrutiny is appropriate to their office.
- Openness – holders of public office have a duty to declare any private interests relating to their public duties and to take steps to resolve any conflicts arising in a way that protects the public interest.
- Leadership – holders of public office should promote and support these principles by leadership and example.

The implication of the Nolan Committee is that public bodies should be expected to behave in an ethical manner. The question then remains as to what the motivation for private firms to operate selflessly is, and, through enlightened self interest, to work alongside social organizations.

Social mission statements

Werther and Chandler (2005, p. 44) argue that for companies in the business sector, Corporate Social Responsibility (CSR) needs to be linked into the vision that the organization is seeking to achieve. In turn this links into the mission statement in terms of what the organization is going to do to achieve its mission. Both CSR and strategy are concerned with a firm's relationship to the environment and this means that it must be linked into internal operational capability in terms of finance and marketing operations. Once the external and internal have been matched, the firm can come up with CSR imperatives in the form of objectives. These in turn can be converted into community-based action plans.

Figure 7.1 provides an overview of the process.

Many multinational enterprises employ social mission statements. Ben & Jerry's operate three statements: one for product, one economic and one social. Their social mission is expressed in their value statement:

We have a progressive, nonpartisan social mission that seeks to meet human needs and eliminate injustices in our local, national and

Figure 7.1 **Corporate social responsibility**
Source: Werther, W. B. and Chandler, D., *Strategic Corporate Social Responsibility: Stakeholders in a Global Environment* (London: Sage, 2005)

international communities by integrating these concerns into our day-to-day business activities. Our focus is on children and families, the environment and sustainable agriculture on family farms.[3]

What is interesting is that Ben & Jerry's is owned by Uniliver but, arguably, it still appears to retain its original founding values. The same argument might apply to other absorbed business such as the Body Shop which is owned by L'Oreal, and Green and Blacks which is now owned by Cadbury-Schweppes. To examine the social mission concept further we have picked Starbucks as an example of a multinational enterprise, and we have provided a question box at the end of this chapter on Starbucks.

This discussion would seem to indicate that the third sector does not occupy the high ground on ethics exclusively. In fact both small businesses and corporations can create a valuable social partnership, one which is of mutual benefit.

Corporate philanthropy

In terms of a business approach to ethics, company donations and behaving responsibly can be seen to improve financial results. It is a marketing tool. Another perspective is that a company can build relationships with social organizations and with local communities to maintain its influence at local or national levels.

This form of altruism is one stage on from 'enlightened self-interest'. In taking an altruistic perspective a company that generates profit can present itself as being responsible for benefiting the wider society – not just its own customers. Altruism implies that a firm works with and donates to local causes that are not directly associated with its core business.

This altruism is translated into sponsorship, donations and joint working agreements. The Clinton Foundation recently joined with the Microsoft Foundation to support 'a business-oriented approach to the problem of climate change' (Microsoft, 2008).[4]

In the UK, the Hunter Foundation[5] has set itself the objective of 'effecting positive, long-term cultural change to deliver a "can do" attitude', initially in Scotland, via major investment in, largely, educational programmes. The Foundation has committed £35 million and this, it is claimed, has leveraged an additional public and private sector investment of £175 million.

> A recent study by Indiana University on Philanthropy reported that across the nation with household income above $200,000 or a net worth of at least $1 million, found that entrepreneurs donated an average of $232,206 per year'. 'Rather than seeking tax shelters, more than 86 percent of respondents said they were motivated to give by the opportunity of 'meeting critical needs' in society, while 82.6 percent said they were moved by a 'feeling that those who have more should give to those with less'.[6]

The schemes outlined are examples that grab the headlines. What this translates into are two types of funds that are available to social organizations (Pepin 2005).[7]

1. Corporate strategic giving. Funding and resources seen as an investment to achieve corporate business aims (cause-related marketing, co-branding and sponsorship).
2. Venture philanthropy. Human resources and funding invested in a social organization or charity by entrepreneurs, venture capitalists and corporations in search of a social return on their investment.

At the local level this provides the opportunity for social organizations to work with local private companies and leverage funding, sponsorship and resources for good causes. The Big Give is an example of organized giving that matches private donations with charities internationally. It is a free-to-use website that helps donors quickly and discreetly find charity projects in their field of interest. An example of a UK project listed under the Big Give scheme is Minicase 7.1.

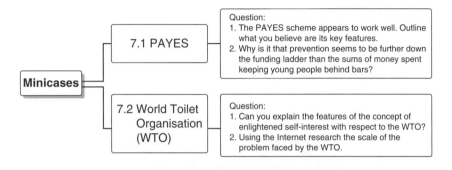

Minicase 7.1   PAYES

PAYES is a youth and community initiative aimed at young people from the Sefton area of Merseyside who are at risk of becoming involved in criminal activity.

PAYES targets young people aged 12 or 13 who have not come to the attention of the Police themselves, but are considered to be at risk of doing so. Risk factors include the presence of young offenders amongst their peers, regular truanting from school, and/or sharing a home with a known offender. Young people can be referred to the Scheme by a number of agencies. Once their eligibility has been confirmed, they are interviewed at home and invited to sign a contract committing them to good conduct, a proviso of remaining involved in the Scheme.

PAYES was launched by volunteers from Merseyside Police in 1993, prompted by the tragic murder of two-year-old James Bulger. PAYES takes the form of a three-year personal development programme. Police volunteers organise a variety of educational and leisure activities in Sefton, and if participants demonstrate good behaviour and do not become involved in criminal activity, they will be invited to attend a Level 1 residential programme provided by Brathay Hall Trust (Brathay). This pattern continues throughout the three years, with attendance on the Level 2 and Level 3 courses also being contingent on the young people's good conduct. The three Levels follow a curriculum development model and are designed to offer increasing levels of challenge and responsibility within a supportive environment.

The outcomes of PAYES can be described under three headings, the first of which is crime diversion. The Scheme encourages young people to stay out of trouble in spite of their 'at risk' status. They are offered an incentive to behave well during their adolescence, when statistically they are most likely to begin experimenting with crime. PAYES spans these vulnerable years, providing long-term support rather than a 'quick fix'. Since the Scheme was founded, Sefton has benefited from a steady decrease in the levels of street crime and anti-social behaviour involving young people.

The second broad outcome is personal development. Past PAYES participants have reported improvements in confidence and self-esteem, social and team skills, self-awareness and relationship to others, and broadening personal aspirations.

The third outcome is community cohesion. Through the Scheme, the young people have frequent contact with the Police volunteers, giving the young people the chance to see the 'human side' of Police work. The Police volunteers also learn to relate better to young people's experiences. The mutual trust which develops has a significant impact on their perceptions of one another within the community, and also has a positive influence on the peer groups of those involved.

108 young people took part in the 2008 Scheme. In 2009 we would like to work with a similar number of young people, but this is entirely dependent upon funding. The non-profit cost of 7 Brathay courses (2 at Level 1, 3 at Level 2, and 2 at Level 3) is £54,910.

PAYES is a registered charity and the Police volunteers carry out local fundraising, but given the demands of their full-time policing responsibilities Brathay has undertaken to assist them by seeking funding for this highly beneficial programme. As such all funds received by Brathay for this programme are held by Brathay in a restricted fund in the name of PAYES, for expenditure only on the various PAYES courses.

Source: www.thebiggive.org.uk

QUESTIONS

1. The PAYES scheme appears to work well. Outline what you believe are its key features.
2. Why is it that prevention seems to be further down the funding ladder than the sums of money spent keeping young people behind bars?

Adapting marketing for social enterprises

In the same way that it is often assumed that all businesses are motivated by profit so it is also assumed that all consumers are motivated by cheap prices. If this was the case then the decision to install energy efficient heating in a home would rely entirely on cost benefit analysis and alternative forms of energy would not be considered. The same concept would apply to organic food which is more expensive to purchase than intensively farmed food. This suggests that both companies and consumers make ethical choices. By understanding how companies and individuals make ethical choices, social organizations can tap into the goodwill generated and how public goods can be marketed.

Ethical choices

In 1962 Friedman noted that 'there is only one social responsibility of business – to use its resources and engage in activities designed to increase its profit so long as it … engages in open and free competition without deception and fraud' (Friedman, 1962, p. 69).[8] Friedman went on to assert that *'the social responsibility of business to only increase profits is no longer sufficient'*.

Corporate greed, post Enron, is frowned upon by the public. The free-market viewpoint of profit at any cost is now considered out-moded by society, governments and trade bodies. Yet this did not stop the banking crisis of 2008 happening where the banking and invest-ment sectors' greed for profit and individual bonuses brought down some of the major investment and mortgage banks in the US, UK and to a lesser extent in Europe. This has caused panic on a large scale for investors and for governments, and was not enlightened self-interest.

But smaller and larger organizations operate differently in terms of their ethical choices. In the small-firm sector, decision-making control remains in the hands of the business owners, enabling them to make personal choices about the allocation of resources. In addition, the ten-dency for small firms to be dominated by personal relationships and the preferred absence of bureaucratic controls may enhance relation-ships of trust and openness in business relationships (Spence et al., 2001).[9] This implies that smaller organizations have the ability to make ethical choices because they retain individual control over their decision-making processes. This is highlighted in Figure 7.2

Broadening this concept of individual choice and ethics in the small firm, the term Corporate Social Responsibility defines the relationship between an organization and the societies with which it interacts.

Figure 7.2   ***The ethic-profit trade-off***
Source: Goldsmith, W. and Clutterbuck, D., *The Winning Streak* (London: Weindenfield and Nicolson, 1984)

It implies an ethical consideration of attitudes towards the environment and a willingness for the firm to be seen as 'doing its bit' to help the environment and the community.

The factors that go to make up the broad spectrum of ethical determinants and pressures are as follows: What is legal or not legal? What can business do to operate ethically? What should individuals do to act ethically?

In many cases, especially when a major industrial incident occurs and lives are lost, we ask ourselves two questions. Was it legal? How can they get away with it? The UK government was forced to introduce the Corporate Manslaughter and Corporate Homicide Act of 2007 because of gross failures in health and safety by prominent big businesses.

In terms of business operations the growth of Fairtrade products in the supermarkets has been brought about firstly because of media and public pressure and secondly because their customers want and expect to be able to buy them. The UK supermarket chain Waitrose has recently come under pressure from members of the public to not stock products grown by Israeli settlers who it is argued are operating in land confiscated from Palestinian farmers.

As individuals we have a range of ethical behaviour pressures acting upon us, including family and peer pressures and our own experiences and values built up over time, allied to the powerful force of public opinion. From this the pressure grows on government and business to protect the environment for others.

Ethical values

So far this discussion has concentrated on business ethics. The Theory of Reasoned Action (Ajzen et al., 1980)[10] is one theory that links attitudes and behaviour of consumers. Individual purchasing behaviour is seen as a function of intention and a purchasing decision is a function of attitude and subjective norm. Attitude towards performing the behaviour is further deemed to be a summed product of the individuals' beliefs and their evaluation of those beliefs. Bluntly speaking, consumers and businesses do not respond rationally by seeking the lowest price but instead seek products that are statements based on lifestyle and values.

This heat pump and boreholes cost GBP 17,544 minus a GBP 4000 government grant, and the solar panel system was GBP 6500 minus a GBP 2500 grant,' he says. 'Yes, the economic payback is marginal, and a lot of cynics ask what is its worth and why are we doing it. I say well, it is a way forward and you can either sit on the fence and do nothing, or you can say, let's contribute. If you do good, you feel good. And the house will still have a smaller carbon footprint.

(The Scotsman Newspaper, 26 January 2008)

Ethical values are the embodiment of what an organization or individual stands for. For example, it should not be difficult for organizations and individuals to support the aims and objectives of the World Toilet Organization (WTO) (Minicase 7.2). They should set the standards by which its individual members, including staff, management and suppliers, operate to. If individual members' values disconnect with the organization's corporate values, that organization will be dysfunctional. It will say one thing and do another. Potentially worse, an organization may publish an ethical code which presents itself in a positive image while unethical values and the pursuit of profit guide organizational behaviour in a different way. A disconnect between individual members and corporate ethical values can be seen as a management failure rather than an attempt to be deliberately misleading.

As Schubert (1979)[11] points out,

management has to do more than establish codes of conduct. We have the primary responsibility to motivate and inspire employees to conduct themselves honestly and fairly. Starting at the top, we have to set the example for others to follow by acting in a morally proper way. We have to practice what we preach.

This discussion on ethics has centred on the idea that both businesses and individuals are capable of making ethical choices. It refutes the idea of free market economics and suggests that social enterprises can market themselves to take advantage of enlightened self-interest and altruism.

Defining social marketing

Kotler et al. state that 'marketing is more than an isolated business function – it is a philosophy that guides the entire organisation'. The authors go on to state that 'Marketing, more than any other function, deals with customers. Creating customer value and satisfaction are at the heart of modern marketing thinking and practice'. It tends to divide into three parts:

> Marketing strategy which defines who you want to sell to and what they want to buy from you while recognizing the ability to offer products or services, profitably.
>
> Marketing management which means managing the five 'Ps' [product, price, promotion, place and people]
>
> Market communications which means making customers aware of what you have to offer and how easy it is for them to buy from you.

The central core of marketing is customers. There is a basic distinction between an organization that is market-led rather than product (or service) driven. The distinction is recognized in entrepreneurial research, which separates the entrepreneur from the craftsman, the opportunistic professional from the professional manager.

According to Drucker,(1975)[12]

> Marketing is so basic a function that it cannot be considered a separate function within the business, on a par with others such as manufacturing or personnel. Marketing requires separate work and a distinct group of activities. But it is first, a central dimension of the entire business. It is the whole business seen from the view of its final results, that is from a customer's point of view. Concern and responsibility (for Marketing) must therefore permeate all areas of the enterprise.[13]

The key questions to be addressed are:

> Compared with others, how good are you at delivering value added to your customers?
>
> What segment of the market are you part of?
>
> How powerful or attractive is that segment in terms of its growth and sustainability?
>
> How powerful are you within this segment or niche?

It is important to understand the need to deliver value to the customer. An organization that does so can usually be credited with having a core competence that is – what the enterprise is inherently capable of, and is good at doing. The fact is, a social enterprise may be good at many things, but unless those competencies can directly be leveraged to create stakeholder value, they do not necessarily offer the best balance of social mission and commercial viability.

For a social enterprise to grow, it requires a vision. Somehow this must translate into *entrepreneurial marketing*, a distinctive approach to management. Without this the enterprise will remain ineffective.

> The skill is to be able to reconcile the vision with actual possibilities, by articulating that vision so it may be communicated to others by defining the actions that are necessary to progress the venture.
>
> Wickham, 1988).[14]

> The vision is a defining characteristic of entrepreneurial management. The entrepreneur's vision is a picture of the New World he or she wishes to create.[15]

This enterprising style is exhibited by an intuitive and opportunistic approach to strategy formulation and market management. Carson[16] describes this process as 'adaptive marketing'. This is the process whereby 'formal marketing' of the sort in most textbooks is adapted to suit the characteristics of the entrepreneur. Carson maintains that

> 'a normative model of market planning is inherently informal, follows sequential and structured steps and requires discipline' and that this is 'inherently unsuited to entrepreneurial decision-making'. 'Thus, what needs to be done is to match (this) technique to suit the characteristics and capability of the entrepreneur'.

Dees (1998)[17] notes that

> markets do not work as well for social entrepreneurs. In particular, markets do not do a good job of valuing social improvements, public goods and harms, and benefits for people who cannot afford to pay. As a result, it is much harder to determine whether a social entrepreneur is creating sufficient social value to justify the resources used in creating that value. The survival or growth of a social enterprise is not

proof of its efficiency or effectiveness in improving social conditions. It is only a weak indicator, at best.

The following section is extracted from *A Synopsis of Social Marketing* by Lynn MacFadyen, Martine Stead and Gerard Hastings (1999) from the Institute of Social Marketing, University of Stirling. A full copy of the paper is provided from the library of the University of Stirling.

The term social marketing was first coined by Kotler and Zaltman in 1971 to refer to the application of marketing to the solution of social and health problems.

According to McFayden et al. (1999),[18]

Social marketing, like generic marketing, is not a theory in itself. Rather, it is a framework or structure that draws from many other bodies of knowledge such as psychology, sociology, anthropology and communications theory to understand how to influence people's behaviour (Kotler and Zaltman, 1971). Like generic marketing, social marketing offers a logical planning process involving consumer oriented research, marketing analysis, market segmentation, objective setting and the identification of strategies and tactics. It is based on the voluntary exchange of costs and benefits between two or more parties (Kotler and Zaltman, 1971). However, social marketing is more difficult than generic marketing. It involves changing intractable behaviours, in complex economic, social and political climates with often very limited resources (Lefebvre and Flora, 1988). Furthermore, while, for generic marketing the ultimate goal is to meet shareholder objectives, for the social marketer the bottom line is to meet society's desire to improve its citizens' quality of life. This is a much more ambitious – and more blurred – bottom line.

Figure 7.3 provides an outline of the features of social responsibility in the context of marketing.

Ethical marketing issues

Ethical marketing is now receiving much more attention, especially in the popular press. A few of the ethical marketing issues that businesses and social organizations face in presenting their credentials to the public

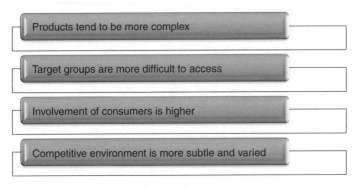

Figure 7.3 **Social responsibility in marketing**
Source: From MacFadyen et al. (1999)

are: carbon emissions and climate change; ecological sustainability and biodiversity; renewable resources and energy; sound sourcing and fair trade; recycling, waste minimization and waste disposal; employee rights and welfare; animal welfare; social issues such as health, obesity and diversity; and supply-chain integrity, whereby independent suppliers are asked to match their corporate customers' ethical criteria.[19] And, in presenting themselves, businesses and social organizations face two choices: to be explicitly linked to specific issues or else to play down the public presentation and concentrate on stakeholder values.

For example, in 2007 Marks & Spencer[20] announced the introduction of Plan A – a £200 m, 100-point, five-year eco plan. The plan is to be rolled out internationally and across all stores and it has measurable targets set within a specific timeframe. Will the credit crisis on the UK high street derail this eco-plan on the basis that Marks and Spencer, in common with most retailers, is suffering reduced sales? Or will the 'ethical bargain' that Marks and Spencer have struck with the public carry the day?

MacFadyen et al. go on to argue that 'existing models of consumer decision-making are only partly satisfactory, since they tend to emphasis hedonic, self-interested outcomes, in contrast to the more societal-centred viewpoint of ethical consumers'. The term 'green consumer' first appeared in the early 1990s. Since then research studies have moved the debate towards wider environmental concerns by noting that ethical consumers were concerned about areas including animal issues, irresponsible selling, armaments and oppressive regimes. This shift in consumer behaviour partly explains the moves towards corporate social responsibility. It also encourages volunteers and facilitates social marketing.

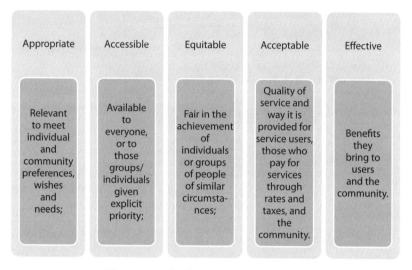

Appropriate	Accessible	Equitable	Acceptable	Effective
Relevant to meet individual and community preferences, wishes and needs;	Available to everyone, or to those groups/ individuals given explicit priority;	Fair in the achievement of individuals or groups of people of similar circumstances;	Quality of service and way it is provided for service users, those who pay for services through rates and taxes, and the community.	Benefits they bring to users and the community.

Figure 7.4 **Social and ethical delivery**
Source: R. J. Marshall and L. Letrone, 'Positioning Social Marketing', *Social Marketing Quarterly*, Vol. 10, Issue 3 & 4 (2004), pp. 17–22

The principle behind ethical marketing detailed in Figure 7.4, is that being a good company would attract consumers to that company and make a profit, while unethical behaviour would result in customers avoiding that product or organization. Some would argue (Beardshaw 1991)[21] that marketing is 'an ethically neutral system serving in an unequivocal market'. However, according to Sheth (1988)[22] it is only recently that marketers have become interested in the idea of social responsibility. This may be in response to the aggressive marketing tactics adopted by pressure groups such as Greenpeace and Friends of the Earth. It may also be in response to the use of the Internet to organize opinion as exampled by blog websites which encourage the boycotting of Nike and McDonald's.

Social responsibility in marketing encompasses areas such as how consumers behave, the role of regulations along with environmental and sustainable marketing. The Bodyshop and the Co-operative Bank ought to be businesses that have a high recognition amongst the public for ethical behaviour. But, social and ethical marketing is much more than having a brand that consumers recognize.

An example of a key area of concern on a global scale that requires action by both the public and by major corporations is to be found in Minicase 7.2 The World Toilet Organisation. Over 2.6 billion people worldwide including 980 million children do not have access to basic sanitation.

Minicase 7.2   World Toilet Organisation (WTO)

World Toilet Organisation (WTO) is a global non-profit organisation committed to improving toilet and sanitation conditions worldwide. WTO is also one of the few organisations to focus on toilets instead of water, which receives more attention and resources under the common subject of sanitation. Founded in 2001 in Singapore by Jack Sim, with 15 members, it now has 190 member organisations in 56 countries working towards eliminating the toilet taboo and delivering sustainable sanitation. WTO was created as a global network and service platform wherein all toilet and sanitation organisations can learn from one another and leverage on media and global support that in turn can influence governments to promote sound sanitation and public health policies. WTO is the organizer of the very successful series of World Toilet Summits and World Toilet Expo and Forum. To-date, 8 World Toilet Summits and 2 World Toilet Expo & Forum have been hosted in 10 different cities around the world. Each summit addresses the critical issues of toilet and sanitation from technologies, development, funding, to design, maintenance, social entrepreneurship, capacity building, research and various other related topics, creating massive media coverage and momentum.

In 2006, the Schwab Foundation, a family of the World Economic Forum, awarded the Outstanding Social Entrepreneur of the Year to WTO and made its founder, Jack Sim, a Schwab Foundation permanent fellow. In 2007, WTO was honored as an Ashoka Global Fellow for its excellence in social entrepreneurship. In addition to advocacy, capacity building and sanitation projects, WTO is now driving a market-based strategy to address the dysfunctional sanitation market for the poor, by installing efficient market infrastructure.

Sanitation brings benefits of health and dignity to humanity especially to the slums, and rural areas. Promotion of ecological sanitation through recycling of excreta helps prevent environmental pollution into water ways.

Source: www.worldtoilet.org

QUESTIONS

1. Can you explain the features of the concept of enlightened self-interest with respect to the WTO?
2. Using the Internet research the scale of the problem faced by the WTO.

Social goods, social values

As marketing is based on the concept of exchange relationships, it can be argued that as a society becomes more concerned about social and environmental issues the social marketing opportunities will increase.

An ethical checklist for Social Ethical Marketing (Donovan and Henley, 2004)[23]	Code of Ethics (Rothchild, 2001)[24]
1. Ensure that the intervention will not cause physical or psychological harm.	1. Do more good than harm.
	2. Favour free choice.
2. Does the intervention give assistance where it is needed?	3. Evaluate marketing within a broad context of behaviour management (giving consideration to alternatives of education and law).
3. Does the intervention give those who need help the freedom to exercise their entitlements?	
4. Are all parties treated equally and fairly?	4. Select tactics that are effective and efficient.
5. Will the choices made produce the greatest good for the greatest number of people?	5. Select marketing tactics that fit marketing philosophy (that is meeting the needs of consumers rather than the self-interest of the organization).
6. Is the autonomy of the target audience recognized?	6. Evaluate the ethicality of a policy before agreeing to develop a strategy.

Of course consumers always have a choice in the private marketplace at least, of buying or not buying a product or service, and where competitive markets exist they can choose according to their own preferences. They carry weight, therefore, only as the sum of their individual choices. In the social economy this same level of choice may not apply since goods are not traded at full economic cost to the consumer – they are subsidized and non-competitively provided.

> To shift the balance of power in favour of consumers, those representing their interests have isolated the five key principles, which provide a structure defining consumerism. These are the principles of access, choice, information, redress and representation. People or potential consumers first of all have to have access to the benefits offered by a product or service.
>
> (Potter, 1988)[25]

When choice exists in a 'free' market, individuals can influence the profits and the behaviour of producers to select goods and services with the right mix of price and quality. The existence of competition tends to work in favour of consumers by operating to keep prices down while delivering high quality. In the social economy, market distortions can occur.

The consumer and public services

Most public and social services are provided because they are in the public interest and contribute towards the public good. There are two forms of public service:

1. those designed to give people access to services they would not otherwise be able to enjoy;
2. those concerned with some form of social distribution of resources.

At the same time, resources within the public and voluntary sector are limited and depend upon political patronage or corporate support for distribution. The consumer principles of choice do not apply. The interest of individual consumers must be balanced against the interests of the community as a whole, and of other stakeholders.

The dilemma of service delivery in social marketing centres around five principles (Potter 1988):

1. Access
   Those who pay for public services and those who benefit from them are not necessarily the same people, the main consumer principle of access cannot be classed a consumer right.
2. Choice
   Consumer choice exists within the social economy but usually involves redistributing costs and benefits within society, meaning individual consumer choice cannot be the sole driving force that dictates who benefits and who pays. Indeed, it is plainly not relevant to some services at all.

   This means that consumers cannot express their preferences directly through exercising their choices.

   Where there is competition, individuals have the power to choose and services can become sensitive to their real needs and preferences. But because of the re-distributive nature of the public sector, consumer choice cannot be the sole mechanism for reconciling competing claims on the public purse. Where individuals are not able to make choices directly, other mechanisms must be developed to ensure that their interests are taken into account.
3. Information
   Information takes on an even greater importance in the public sector because the services at stake are likely to be crucial to

consumers' welfare, and because the imbalance in the amount of information processed by providers and consumers is often so wide.

They need information about goals and objectives; about the standards of service authorities aim to provide, and the standard achieve; about their rights to a service, and their responsibilities in using them; about the way authorities or structured and the decision-making process; about why decisions are taken and about what those decisions actually are. Information of this kind can confer real power, if by power one means the ability to influence change.

4. Redress

Individuals have an obvious need for mechanisms to settle their grievances quickly, simply and fairly. But the existence of redress mechanisms can bring wider benefits, by acting as checks on the actions of social providers, and by constituting a form of quality control that allows services to identify and put right any underlying problems in their management systems, policies and practices.

5. Representation

Taken literally, it means simply that the views of consumers should be adequately represented to decision-makers at all points in the system where decisions are taken concerning their interests. The traditional consumer response has been to argue that while members are elected to take decisions on behalf of individuals and the community, they cannot possibly hope to know everything about consumers' preferences. These need to be identified and represented to them, so that they can base their political decisions on facts rather than untested assumptions. The current crop of opinion surveys carried out among local government residence and service users, and patients in the health service, can be seen as a form of representation by research.

The debate about choice is evident within health service reforms. 'Choice and consumer power as the route to social justice not social division' is a central theme that now appears as the government seeks to allocate scarce health care resources.

Social care is an area where 'choice' has been a major policy aim for over a decade, for politicians of all parties. So it may be helpful to see if this experience casts any light on choice in health services.

A 'Positive Choice', as the Wagner committee on residential care reported in 1988, would provide people with the necessary information and support to make decisions about one of the most important moves in later life: the giving up of one's own home and much independence. Has this happened? Over the past decade people have been able to choose between residential homes, but their quality is highly variable and there are great differences in availability at local level. The extent of their choice may be limited and, since most care is publicly funded, strict limits exist on the funding to pay for these services. Small-sized homes are closing or being taken over by large corporations. A market in social care has undoubtedly led to more flexible services that can provide help with problems related to illness and disability. More people are able to stay at home, particularly if they have a high level of disability. But in reality there is often little choice – and many people find their circumstances are not 'bad enough' for care of any type. Development of direct payments may produce wider choices for disabled people and carers, and here social care will have much to show health services. But the lessons may be about the limits of choice, as well as its benefits.

(Healthmatters.com 2003)[26]

Example 7.1 provides a summary of the issues covered in this chapter.

| Examples |————| 7.1 Marketing for social enterprises |

Example 7.1   Marketing for social enterprises

Social enterprises, unlike charitable organizations or the public sector, operate fully or partially within the market economy.

Private firms are seen as performing better because of the market mechanism.

There is always a trade-off between business profit objectives and the ethical orientation of an organization.

Public and social services are provided because they are in the public interest and contribute towards the public good.

But resources are limited and interest of individual consumers must be balanced against the interest of the community.

Consumer and businesses do not respond rationally by seeking the lowest price but instead seek products that are statements based on lifestyle and values.

> The basic principle behind ethical marketing is that being a good company would attract consumers to a company and make a profit whilst unethical behaviour would result in customers avoiding that product or organization.
>
> As marketing is based on the concept of exchange relationships, it can be argued that as a society becomes more concerned about social and environmental issues, the marketing of goods will respond accordingly.

Revision questions

1. Starbucks[27] have an environmental mission statement as well as a social mission statement which states that 'corporate social responsibility runs deeply throughout our company'.

   They go on to say that 'contributing in a positive way to the communities we operate in is one of our guiding principles – and this means local communities, as well as those in coffee growing countries'.

   Conduct research to identify the extent of Starbucks' contribution to local communities in your country or region.
2. Using the database, pick a Sector, Location and Beneficiaries and search through The Big Give[28] projects and choose one or more projects. Investigate, by following the links, the extent of giving and the range of sponsors.

References

1. Dalai Lama, quoted in Matthew Bunson ed., *The Wisdom Teachings of the Dalai Lama* (London: Penguin Books, 1997).
2. P. Hartigan and R. Martin, *Social Entrepreneurship: Understanding the New Strategic Space for Social Value Creation*, Session 10: CISCO – Corporate Philanthropy and Corporate Social Responsibility, HEC Geneva, 2004.
3. See http://www.benjerrys.com/our_company/our_mission/index.cfm.
4. Microsoft, 'Clinton Foundation, Microsoft to Develop Online Tools Enabling the World's Largest 40 Cities to Monitor Carbon Emissions', 2007, see http://www.microsoft.com/presspass/press/2007/may07/05-17Clinton FoundationPR.mspx.
5. Hunter Foundation at http://www.thehunterfoundation.co.uk/news.
6. A. Loten, 'Entrepreneurs are Twice as Charitable as Heirs', 2008, reported in Inc.com http://www.inc.com/news/articles/200611/charity.html.
7. J. Pepin, 'Venture Capitalists and Entrepreneurs become Venture Philanthropists', *International Journal of Nonprofit and Voluntary Sector Marketing*, vol. 10, issue 3 (2005), pp. 165–73.
8. M. Friedman, *Capitalism and Freedom* (Chicago: Chicago University Press, 1962).

9. L. J. Spence and R. Rutherford, 'Social Responsibility, Profit Maximization and the Small Firm Owner Manager', *Journal of Small Business and Enterprise Development*, vol. 8, no. 2 (2001), pp. 126–39.

10. I. Ajzen and M. Fishbein, *Understanding Attitudes and Predicting Social Behavior* (Englewood Cliffs, NJ: Prentice-Hall, 1980).

11. Schubery (1979) cited in Chonko, L., *Ethical Decision Making in Marketing* (London: Sage, 1995), p. 129.

12. P. Drucker, *Management: Tasks, Responsibilities and Practices* (Woburn, MA: Heinemann, 1995), p. 65.

13. Drucker, *Management*.

14. P. A. Wickham, *Strategic Entrepreneurship* (London: Pitman, 1988), p. 131. For a discussion on the relationship between the Vision, the Mission and Strategy, see chs 9, 10 and 11.

15. Wickham, *Strategic Entrepreneurship*, p. 107.

16. Carson et al., *Marketing and Entrepreneurship* (Harlow, England: Prentice Hall, 1995), pp. 174–96.

17. J. G. Dees, The Meaning of Social Entrepreneurship, Stanford GBS News and Information. www.gsb.stanford.edu/services/news/DeesSocentrePaper.html, accessed December 2009.

18. L. McFadyen, M. Stead and G. Hastings, *A Synopsis of Social Marketing* (University of Stirling; Institute of Social Marketing, 1999), see www.ism.stir.ac.uk/pdf_docs/social_marketing.pdf.

19. H. Edwards, *Ethical Marketing* (London: Brand Republic, 2007).

20. 'Marks & Spencer launches a £200 m Eco Plan – Plan A'. See http://www.marksandspencer.com/gp/node/n/51361031?ie=UTF8&mnSBrand=core, accessed April 2008.

21. J. Beardshaw, *The Organisation in its Environment* (London: Pitman, 1991).

22. J. N. Sheth, D. M. Gardner, and D. E. Garrett, *Marketing Theory: Evolution and Evaluation* (West Sussex, England: Wiley, 1988).

23. R. Donovan and N. Henley, 'Social Marketing: Principles and Practice', *Social Marketing Quarterly*, Vol. 10, Issue 1 (2004), pp. 31 4.

24. M. L. Rothschild, 'Review of "Building Strong Brands" by D. Aaker', *Social Marketing Quarterly*, Vol. 7, Issue 2 (2001), pp. 36–40.

25. Potter, 'Consumerism in the Public Sector', *Public Administration* 66 (2) (1988), pp. 149–64.

26. 'How will Consumer Choice Impact on the NHS?' Health Matters (2003), available at http://www.healthmatters.org.uk/issue54/consumerchoice.

27. See http://starbucks.co.uk/en-GB/Social+Responsibility/.

28. The Big Give, see http://www.thebiggive.org.uk.

Additional reading

Werther, W. B. and Chandler, D., *Strategic Corporate Social Responsibility: Stakeholders in a Global Environment* (London: Sage Publications, 2005).

8 the changing roles of social enterprises

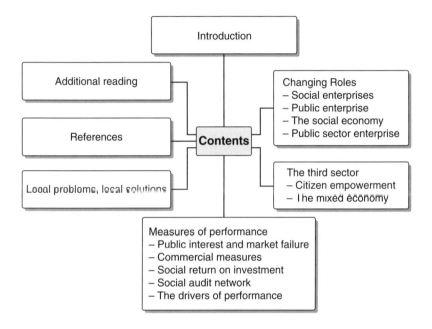

Introduction

Additional reading

References

Local problems, local solutions

Contents

Changing Roles
– Social enterprises
– Public enterprise
– The social economy
– Public sector enterprise

The third sector
– Citizen empowerment
– The mixed economy

Measures of performance
– Public interest and market failure
– Commercial measures
– Social return on investment
– Social audit network
– The drivers of performance

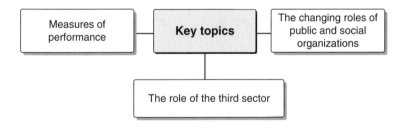

Measures of performance

Key topics

The changing roles of public and social organizations

The role of the third sector

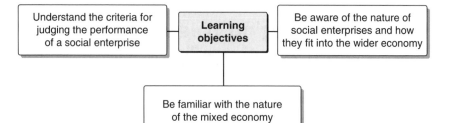

Introduction

A great deal has been written about globalization and the changing role of multinational corporations. Prior to the 1980s and into the 1990s, little was written about entrepreneurial ventures and their role in creating wealth. It is also only recently that interest has focused on not-for-profit organizations, their role in society and how they can balance the need for a commercial operation while still serving the community. In the current economic climate this is driven by a crisis of confidence in the 'real economy' where the private sector has struggled to generate and distribute equitably, the wealth sought by its main stakeholders.

The literature on multinational corporations and international business is not particularly helpful in providing an insight into the management of a social enterprise. This is already apparent in the definitions discussed in Chapter 1. This is because the business environment and the resources available to a multinational corporation are different from those available to a social enterprise. The starting point for this chapter is to look at how the literature on management and enterprise can help us understand social enterprises and how models and ideas in the mainstream can be used to create sustainable businesses.

The first topic of the chapter looks at the way in which the management and policy expectations of not-for-profit organizations are changing. It looks at traditional views of the firm as profit maximizers and contrasts this with the commercial aspirations of social organizations and public enterprises. The terms 'social enterprise' and 'public enterprise' are seen as part of the social economy, and this helps to provide definitions of this part of the 'third sector' economy and the business formats that are now evolving. It also looks at ways in which government policy encourages enterprise within the third sector and the dilemmas that social enterprises face in responding to this challenge.

The 'Third Way' looks at social enterprises and the influence of policy and government initiatives on providing, or constraining, choice within the social economy. It considers the conflicts that are created when public sector 'actors' seek to maximize their own interests and considers the view that all social entities are fundamentally sets of individual actors. One of the most influential of these actors, consumer and citizen empowerment, is introduced as a major driver of change.

The final topic looks at economic, financial and commercial measures of performance and how these might apply within a social enterprise. It is argued that there is no immediately accessible measure of performance for a social organization, so it can be difficult to judge whether it is operating efficiently in terms of meeting needs within the community. Despite this, social enterprises find themselves subject to considerable external scrutiny from funders, clients, sponsors, and the media.

Changing roles

Social enterprises can be expected to make different types of decisions than for-profit organizations. They are not in the business of making profit at any expense and have an obligation to try and create a surplus, but to do so responsibly.

> Business must fight as if it were a war. And, like any good war, it should be fought gallantly, daringly, and above all, not morally.
> (Levitt, 1958, p. 43)[1]

Traditional views of the firm as a profit maximizer are becoming outdated and the social enterprise is seen as a new business format that is evolving in response to changes in the relationship between the government, the business community and the publics that they serve. The argument that is used throughout the book is that social enterprise is a hybrid business format that has developed because of changing business and societal expectations. A social enterprise is one of a number of not-for-profit formats that include voluntary, co-operative and publicly owned enterprises. Because these formats overlap, the term social organization is now used to embrace these third sector organizations. So while all share the first two elements of a 'triple bottom line' of social aims and social ownership, it is the enterprise element that distinguishes the social enterprise format (Social Enterprise London).[2]

Public sector and not-for-profit organizations are expected to behave like and work alongside private sector organizations to deliver services. This means that they perform in a 'market economy' and that they share some but not all of the characteristics of profit making organizations.

Understanding the social market and enterprise economy and how it changes is critical to understanding the role of social enterprises and how they are expected to perform.

Social enterprises

As we have already indicated, the term 'social enterprise' refers to any organization that trades with a social purpose, using business principles and management approaches to achieve socially explicit goals. This goal is usually to create a financially self-sustaining organization – one that reduces its dependency on public funding and one that chooses to operate with minimum interference from government and agencies in providing a service. As discussed in Chapter 4 and like any 'entrepreneurial' organization, it will seek to be independent and follow its own vision.

The term 'public enterprise' is linked to and shares many of the characteristics of a social enterprise. It refers to a public owned organization that may be formally constituted and which provides a chargeable public service, but not for profit.

Public enterprise can be broadly defined as including any undertaking which:

1. has its own accounts; and
2. has income related to services provided (unlike defence, tax collection, social security); and
3. is owned wholly or partly by central, regional or local government (unlike private enterprise).

A range of legal definitions from the EU, UN, OECD can be found in a report carried out for the European Parliament in 1996.[3]

The BBC is an example of an incorporated public enterprise. It has public service broadcasting obligations but its governors are expected to fulfil these without becoming extensions of the established state bureaucracy [sic]. The same approach is now being applied to the health and education sectors.

So an administrative core remains responsible for the management and delivery of services which are not marketed or traded freely. But, other parts are public enterprises that receive revenue from the sale of its service. Examples include parking, passports, and TV licences. Public enterprises may receive support from the government in the interests of wider social objectives, and services may be offered at low or below-market prices to certain classes of consumers.

The term 'social organization' can be used to encompass *both* social and public enterprises. It encompasses 'social enterprise' which has a separate legal constitution and 'public enterprise' in which public authorities exercise indirect control over income generation, dispersal and managerial decisions.

Both social and public enterprises are part of the 'social economy'. European governments have an interest in fostering this 'social economy' that delivers services that cannot, for economic reasons, be delivered by either private sector or by public sector organizations.

> There has been a subtle shift in emphasis between the public and private sector and this has resulted in the emergence of social organisations, that provide public and voluntary services but which operate as commercial 'enterprises'. The emergence of social organisations has moved aspects of public sector management from an administrative role to a more performance orientated one which is becoming more 'business like'. This has been the case in health, education, general welfare provision, the criminal justice system, local government and the civil service.
>
> (Carr, 2000)[4]

This process can be seen as the introduction of private sector 'enterprise' management into the public and not-for-profit sector. There is an assumption (again) that public sector organizations will work better if commercial practices are adopted.

> There have been significant improvements to public service delivery over recent years. The Government's programme of investment and reform has delivered real improvements in the way that services are delivered, many of which are highlighted in this report. However, social, demographic and technological changes continue apace and there are increasing challenges to keep up with the best in the private sector. Differences between the public and private sector are likely to grow over the next decade unless public sector service delivery is further transformed. Over the next ten years, there is an opportunity to provide better public services for citizens and businesses and to do so at a lower cost to the taxpayer.
>
> (Varney, 2006, p. 8)

The OECD (1997)[5] endorses the UK Government's perspective on the relationship that exists between the third sector, the public sector and the private sector. According to the UK's Department of Health (2009),[6] many parts of the public sector are actively looking to form delivery partnerships with a third sector organization where the public sector is unable to take on the full costs of service delivery. It notes:

> Social enterprise can offer health and social care organisations the opportunity to deliver high quality services in ways that are flexible, non-bureaucratic and have the potential to deliver good value for money.

An extension of this model is where individual consumers and the agencies working on their behalf are prepared to make some payment towards healthcare but this payment is insufficient to be attractive to the private sector as the payment does not cover full costs and generate profits. Here social organizations draw down grants, raise funding or seek sponsorship to pay for additional and marginal services. This support can come from public or private sector organizations as well as donations from the public. This 'self-sufficiency' funding model runs alongside a partial, non cost-covering charge on customers. A key element of this emerging 'social economy' is the capacity to deliver effectively, and to sustain services through a range of volunteers and donors, rather than relying on public sector support.

The social economy can be cast in a wider role by focusing on the 'economic' dimension of voluntary organizations. Organizations making one or more of the following contributions would fall within the social economy.

- Creating paid employment or educational opportunities for disadvantaged groups.
- Raising employability and healthcare delivery.
- Impacting on the social well-being of beneficiaries by facilitating access to services or support.
- Contributing to sustainable development through recycling, energy efficiency, or other means.
- Supporting community learning and development, active citizenship and volunteering.
- Preventing subsequent economic exclusion especially working with disaffected young people.

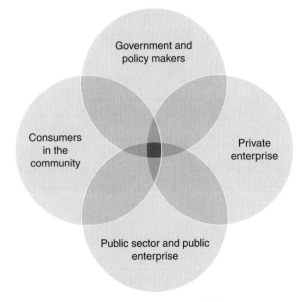

Figure 8.1   ***Social economy influencers***

This broader specification of the social economy would include organizations providing a wide range of services to a diverse set of groups of the population – and this would go back to the notion of the social enterprise and the voluntary sector occupying the ground that sits between the private and the public sectors. Figure 8.1 shows the diverse range of influencers within the social economy.

It is important to note that the UK government attitude and policy towards social enterprise is influenced by the European Union. The European Union sees the social economy as an essential part of the European economic model and important in promoting social cohesion and democracy. The European Commission uses the Co-operatives, Mutuals, Associations and Foundations (CMAF)[7] definition based on the registration of the company to define the social economy. It has established the presence of a Social Economy Unit in the Directorate General for Industry to provide a stronger focus on social enterprise.

What is entirely consistent with both public and social enterprise is that service provision in education, healthcare and social work will increasingly be challenged by the creation of social organizations to deliver services and goods for communities. This can range from a school being expected to raise funds to extend its sports activity, a hospital raising funds for specialist equipment to rural communities raising funds for a new hall. Some projects are for large capital items and some projects are small revenue items – the fact is that these projects may well be fulfilled through some form of social organization, part-way between the public and private sector.

Public sector enterprise

The discussion above has suggested that there exists a relationship between the public sector, whose role it is to allocate resources, and a social enterprise nominated to undertake delivery. That interface can be described as public enterprise.

> The decentralisation of control in public services has begun to take shape, through greater independence for public services with a stronger emphasis on community representation (for example through foundation hospitals). This process offers a new vision of public ownership   and one that is very different to the highly centralised 'nationalised industry' model that has characterised the NHS to date.
>
> (Lewis, 2006)[8]

Within this new vision, it becomes increasingly difficult to distinguish a social organization, even one within the public sector, from a private sector business.

In the UK, the government still operates public corporations, an example of which is the Post Office. Typically, when public corporations are established an independent body is set up to protect the consumer's interests. In theory the managers have control over the day-to-day running of the business while the government maintains control over long-term strategic investment. In this form of organization, the government is a stakeholder rather than the principal owner. Borrowing on this experience, there has been a move away from full government control being exerted over all administrative functions towards a performance-based system designed to create greater public choice. This has been the case in health, education, welfare provision, the justices system, local government and the civil service (Carr, 2000).

The main criteria driving the public enterprise agenda is that management in the public sector should seek, as far as possible, to behave more like the private sector. The concept is that a public service provision is enhanced where a public sector agency conducts its affairs in accordance with business principles. Therefore, public service agencies should adopt reward structures for their employees, much like those in the private sector, encompassing such mechanisms as performance-related pay and more flexible working practices. The 'shift' from public administration to public 'enterprise' management means that the boundaries between the public sector become less distinctive from the private sector. It also means that the discretionary power (particularly over staff, contracts and money) enjoyed by public sector managers is increased, as the rules and policies emanating from central government are relaxed. In an ideal world, this 'shift' consists of:

- Reworking budgets to be transparent in accounting terms, with costs attributed to outputs not inputs, and outputs measured by quantitative performance indicators.
- Viewing organizations as a chain of low-trust principal/agent relationships (rather than fiduciary or trustee-beneficiary ones), with a network of contracts linking incentives to performance.
- Disaggregating separable functions into quasi-contractual or quasi-market forms, particularly by introducing purchaser/provider distinctions.
- Opening up provider roles to competition between agencies or between public agencies, firms and not-for-profit bodies.
- De-concentrating provider roles to the minimum-feasible sized agency, allowing users more scope for 'exit' from one provider to another, rather than relying on 'voice' options to influence how public service provision affects them (Dunleavy and Hood, 1994, p. 9).[9]

New Public Reform Management (NPRM) refers to this move away from 'traditional' forms of public administration using government departments to deliver public services. This move was evident in a set of OECD countries, including the UK, during the 1990s. A key description of the process of NPRM reform is:

> NPRM reform involves radical change to these 'traditional' structures. First, splitting up departments into corporate units with distinctive tasks and resources. The units are free from many central government-wide rules and day to day interference by ministers and operate with generic, rather than specifically central government,

management styles. Second, changing accountability and control systems. Instead of primarily controlling detailed inputs including budget topics or staffing, the systems use contractual frameworks specifying an overall budget level and a set of desired outputs against which the performance of the unit is monitored. Third, more use of competitive and market-like structures for provision of goods and services. These structures include competition with private firms, splitting purchasers of services from providers and charging users individually for the goods and services they receive rather than funding from general taxation. Fourth, reducing the reliance on a distinct group of civil service employees to deliver services by opening competition for appointments to candidates from other parts of government and the private sector.

(James, 2003)[10]

The changes that are taking place between the public sector and the private sector represent a new paradigm. This is 'a new world' where publicly and socially owned organizations are expected to play a role in the delivery of the service and to be rated in a free market economy on this performance. This is not a question about the legitimacy or the effectiveness of these social organizations as a delivery mechanism – but it is realistic to judge that policies now being introduced throughout Europe will encourage, rather than discourage, the formation of many more social organizations.

The third sector

Social enterprises can be seen as organizations that are subject neither to the commands of the government nor to the commands of the market economy; they exist in no man's land. They trade in selected social markets, selling their services and products, but they do so out of a sense of social purpose. Social enterprises start from the insight that much of what provides quality of life – health, a clean environment, opportunities to learn, take leisure and enjoy culture – depends on shared civic spaces and public goods. Social enterprise can therefore be seen as an innovative format (or social experiment) in the delivery of public goods and services. This sector is often referred to as the Third Sector.

The UK National Audit Office[11] has published a definition of the Third Sector:

> The Third Sector describes the range of institutions which occupy the space between the State and the private sector. These include small local community and voluntary groups, registered charities both large and small, foundations, trusts and the growing number of social enterprises and co-operatives. Third Sector organisations share common characteristics in the social, environmental or cultural objectives they pursue; their independence from government; and in the reinvestment of surpluses for those same objectives.

According to Pharoah and Scott (2002)[12]

> Contemporary policy initiatives appear to have adopted the terms 'social enterprise' and 'social economy', and asserted their significance as mechanisms for a variety of forms of regeneration, i.e. in relation to local neighbourhood urban regeneration, and different categories of low-income group. Specifically in relation to voluntary and community organisations, a move towards greater entrepreneurialism and a sustainable income base is increasingly perceived as a way of meeting funding gaps and continuing dependence on grant funding.
>
> This suggests that social enterprise is being offered as a policy response to an almost serendipitous mix of social policy goals – to use the existing voluntary and community infrastructure to provide goods and services, to create employment, to build individual and social capacity, and to generate an income base.

Discussion on the Third Sector relates to the relationship between government, service provision and the extent of public to private enterprise formats. However, a fourth party exists within this relationship namely that of the consumer and the choices that they exercise.

Social enterprises do add a dimension to service delivery and they are distinct from private firms. Figure 8.2 illustrates the difference in the formats.

Citizen empowerment

Citizen empowerment means that members of the public provide their politicians or the state with resources and power for which they expect

Figure 8.2 ***Growth versus vision***
Source: Adapted from Timmons (2002) and Kirby (2003)

goods and services in return, as well as laws regulating society that match what they are giving up.

> The power of government can never substitute for the power of people. The days of Whitehall ever thinking it knows better are over.[13]

This gives local people and local community groups opportunities not only as potential employees but also as consumers, encouraging participation in the development of the local economy. They can contribute to the distribution of better facilities and so improve the economic and social infrastructure of their area. The concept of empowerment is embedded in the NHS Health Plan[14] which talks about expert patients and patient empowerment.

> The plan is to move from a service that does things to and for its patients to one that is patient-led, to deliver a service that works with patients to support them with their health needs.

Many people believe that private and commercial organizations are capable of providing services that are regarded as 'public goods', such as healthcare and education. Others would argue that this would lead to a multi-tiered system and a restriction of access to high-quality services for a significant portion of the community. They further argue that the indirect benefits of a healthy and well-educated population are shared by all and as such that the costs should also be shared. Additionally, those who oppose the idea of a market economy argue that the conditions necessary for perfect competition rarely, if ever, exist. It is also suggested that competition in the provision of many public services, such as healthcare, is morally unacceptable and practically unworkable.

For the present, the social economy would seem to be gaining-ground. Within the Health Service, from April 2007, the Department of Health[15]

> is holding a Social Enterprise Investment Fund (SEIF) of £100 million over a four year period (£63 million capital and £27 million revenue from 2008/09 to 2010/11). In 2007/08, £1.7 million revenue and £8.9 million capital money was available to new and existing social enterprises, delivering health and social care services, who applied successfully for this funding.

The mixed economy

However, in many circumstances the market is a sound and appropriate mechanism for the allocation of scarce resources. Therefore the market place, via the price system, allocates goods and services to individuals and organizations. It is increasingly being recognized, especially since the collapse of communism in Eastern Europe, that the market is the most efficient system of allocation of many, but not all, goods and services. Although the market economy is far from faultless, and this has been illustrated by recent failures in the banking system where major private institutions, namely the banks, have been taken, at least in part, into public ownership. However, public ownership is no longer seen as necessarily guaranteed to be more efficient or effective in servicing the needs of society or individuals. It can be argued that public ownership is essentially a means of protecting the public from the results of failures in the market economy where the effects of failure cannot be tolerated by a just society.

In the current political climate, public–private partnerships are again part of the political agenda. The BBC describes public–private partnerships as 'any collaboration between public bodies, such as local authorities or central government, and private companies tends to be referred to as a public-private partnership'.[16]

Public–private partnerships provide the state with a form of funding capital projects that some sectors of society may see as controversial. Looking behind the execution of the policy, the principle being exposed is a relatively simple one. Housing Associations are one example and another is the Social Enterprise Investment Fund (SEIF) which has two aims:

1. To encourage the development of a vibrant social enterprise sector in the delivery of health and social care services.
2. To provide start-up funding and longer term investment to emerging and existing social enterprises* in the health and social care sector with a view to their sustainability.

An essential element to this argument is that local people and local communities can take control of their own destinies by creating third sector organizations that operate within a mixed economy to deliver local services for local people. However, as the saying goes, the road to hell is paved with good intentions and littered with sloppy analysis.

Measures of performance

Social organizations operate in a challenging business environment in which they are expected to behave commercially but may not have the resources or freedom to make the choices necessary to fulfil such expectations. This topic looks at traditional measures of control and performance within for-profit organizations and compares them with the responsibilities within social organizations to deliver for the communities they serve.

Public interest and market failure

In the 'public interest' means that governments take control of private enterprises as per the control being presently exerted, tentatively, over the banking system. Traditionally it is argued that enterprises were to be taken into public ownership to correct the inefficiencies that would otherwise arise. It was argued that sources of possible market failure included:

- The negative exploitation of a natural monopoly.
- The inability of markets to spread risks as efficiently as the state (thus rationalizing public ownership of high-technology – and high-risk – firms).

- The failure of normal commercial enterprises to consider external effects and the wider social consequences of their decisions.
- Stakeholders not acting rationally in the overall interests of the organization.

A public enterprise, it was argued, would be able to take account of all social costs and benefits in its decision making.

To cope with market failure, economists developed a set of rules for the conduct of public enterprise which it was thought would produce a better allocation of resources. This process, has until recently been sacrosanct. However, recently 'public interest' and 'market failure' have been linked in the thinking of governments world wide. Another widely held belief is the fundamental concept that publicly owned firms will operate more efficiently when subject to market competition, a fact which was implicit in the 1990s privatization programmes. Yet the 2008 credit crunch is based initially on the lending-based profiteering of the banks leading to huge losses and where, as a result, governments believe they cannot afford the consequences of allowing market forces (failed banks) to operate unchecked. Poor performance can now mean public ownership under certain conditions. Again, it is the concept of the public interest at work. In essence, capitalism is being bailed out by socialism – again. Essentially success means rewards; failure leads to compensation.

Accepting that social enterprises are hybrid organizations, the challenge is to come up with ways that measure performance in a social enterprise. Expecting a social organization to maximize social welfare creates challenges in terms of the public interest. There are general commercial economic and financial target measures that can be applied to judge social maximization – but neither of these is exclusive. Economic performance may be judged by a number of criteria:

1. The *technical* efficiency of operations (achieving the greatest output from given inputs in a engineering sense).
2. The overall *productive* efficiency of operations (achieving the lowest cost for a given output at the prevailing factor prices).
3. The *allocative* efficiency of the enterprise (ensuring that the price to consumers reflects the social costs of production and that enterprise output and quality maximize net social benefits.

Financial targets can be supported on a number of grounds including:

- They offer clear and easily measurable criterion of performance.
- It improves management morale by clarifying objectives, and avoids the psychological disadvantages which are associated with managing loss-making concerns.
- It provides a crude ex-post check that, in total, consumer benefits are as great as the costs of production.

Both economic and financial targeting need to be combined with other measures of monitoring performance in social organizations and theses can be borrowed from the commercial world.

> We need to make sure that the highest level of public spending in Scotland's history delivers the changes needed to close the gap between our poorest communities and the rest of the country. The time for talking is over. Nearly a third of Scotland's children still live in poverty. There are still too many neighbourhoods where crime and the fear of crime are commonplace and too many streets scarred by litter and graffiti. There are still too many Scots who feel excluded from the economic prosperity and social and cultural benefits the rest of the country enjoys at the start of the 21st century. ... To deliver this we will carry out more work to improve how we measure the effect of community learning and development services in building social capital and improving core service outcomes.
>
> (Scottish Executive, 2002)

Table 8.1 provides an outline of how a set of commercial performance measures could be determined. While these may be prescriptive they are part of the discipline required to measure performance.

A performance measure is a means of objectively assessing programmes, products, activities or services it needs to relate to mission and goals and it should be objectively measurable. As part of their overall management strategy, social and public managers can use performance measures to evaluate, control, budget, motivate, promote, celebrate, learn, and improve performance of an organization (Behn, 2003).[17]

Table 8.1   **Commercial performance measures**

Evaluate	Outcomes, combined with inputs and with the effects of exogenous factors
Control	Inputs that can be regulated
Budget	Efficiency measures (specifically outcomes or outputs divided by inputs)
Motivate	Almost-real-time outputs compared with production targets
Promote	Easily understood aspects of performance about which citizens really care.
Celebrate	Periodic and significant performance targets that, when achieved, provide people with a real sense of personal and collective accomplishment
Learn	Disaggregated data that can reveal deviancies from the expected
Improve	Inside-the-black-box relationships that connect changes in operations to changes in outputs and outcomes

Source: Behn, 'Why Measure Performance? Different Purposes Require Different Measures', *Public Administration Review*, 63, (5) (2003), pp. 586–606

Thompson and Martin (2005) identify three strategic measures of performance.

1. *Economy* refers to doing things cost effectively to manage the resources at the lowest possible cost consistent with achieving quality and quality targets.
2. *Efficiency* implies doing things right and means resources should be deployed and used to get the best return.
3. *Effectiveness* is also known as doing the right thing. This implies allocating the scarce resources to those activities which best satisfy the needs and expectations of the stakeholders.

It is important to note that economic and efficiency measures tend to be quantitative and objective measures of performance. Effectiveness on the other hand relates to outcomes and the satisfaction of needs.

Commercial measures

Within the private sector, profits, share price and dividends are visible, if partial, commercial measures of performance of corporate and private sector firms to those outside the business. In the City of London the most used measure of performance, among the deal-makers, is a multiple of earnings before interest, tax, depreciation and amortization (ebitda). Poor performance and the threat of takeover serve to concentrate management attention on shareholders' interests sometimes. If the business continues to under-perform it will ultimately go bust. In a social enterprise it can be argued that such external market disciplines are absent. It may see a reduction in its funding but the market will not impose any immediate sanctions. This may encourage a culture of inefficiency.

There is no immediately accessible commercial measure of performance[18] that can be applied to a social organization, so it is difficult to judge whether an organization is operating efficiently in terms of meeting service needs within the community or the intended purpose.

> Measuring outcomes pre-supposes that charities drive for quantifiable results or products, yet in this sector there is a recognition that a mere attempt to act is a positive outcome, even though an attempt is not measurable. Within the sector there has been some discussion of how to measure the impact of charities and not-for profit organisations outside of the usual financial and economic parameters, focusing upon other purposes such as advocacy and social capital.
>
> (Dunn et al., 2004)[19]

Despite these points, social organizations find themselves subject to considerable external scrutiny from funders, clients, sponsors, and the media.

Social return on investment

One of the key measures of performance of a social enterprise is in the use of Social Return on Investment (SROI). It is a process and a method for understanding, measuring and reporting on the value created by an organization. It examines the social, economic and environmental benefits of the organization's work, and estimates a value for its social and environmental impacts. SROI analysis assigns a monetary value to the social and environmental benefit that has been created by an organization by identifying the indicators of value which can be 'financialized'. Such a study was conducted on the activities of a social firm within the overall operations of The Forth Sector (see Minicase 4.1). This was a study of the operation of Six Mary's Place Guest House outlined below as Minicase 8.1.

Social audit network

It is possible to use the principles developed by the Social Audit Network (SAN) to assist a social enterprise to account fully for its

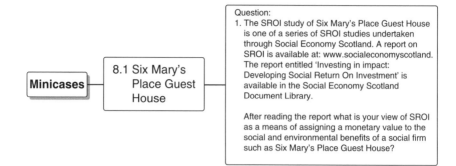

Question:
1. The SROI study of Six Mary's Place Guest House is one of a series of SROI studies undertaken through Social Economy Scotland. A report on SROI is available at: www.socialeconomyscotland. The report entitled 'Investing in impact: Developing Social Return On Investment' is available in the Social Economy Scotland Document Library.

After reading the report what is your view of SROI as a means of assigning a monetary value to the social and environmental benefits of a social firm such as Six Mary's Place Guest House?

Minicase 8.1   Six Mary's Place Guest House

The guest house is based in a Georgian townhouse located in the Stockbridge area of Edinburgh. It offers accommodation in 9 en-suite rooms, and can host up to 17 guests. The guest house is not marketed as a social firm and guests are not told of the mental health and employment aims of the business unless they enquire. However, the success of the guest house is such that many customers actively use it because of social aims and word of mouth is now the main marketing method. Within the guest house up to 20 training places are offered to individuals with mental health issues on a part-time basis covering either the breakfast shift or the housekeeping shift. The key aims of Six Mary's Place are:

- To improve the mental health of the trainees.
- To move individuals into the local labour market.
- To provide a supportive working environment.
- To manage Six Mary's Place as a sustainable business.

To achieve this objective, the guest house employs four full-time supervisory staff, two of whom have direct living experience of health issues. The supervisors work shifts and sleep over on a rota basis, with the manager responsible for the business functions supported by the social enterprise hub that is Forth Sector.

Source: www.forthsector.org.uk

The context
People with mental health issues are among the most disadvantaged groups in the UK labour market and now constitute the largest single group of claimants on incapacity benefit and as such a major cost to government. In turn people with mental health problems face real problems within society based on stigma and discrimination.

The SROI findings
The SROI report on Six Mary's Place is one of a series of SROI reports undertaken by Social Economy Scotland supported financially by the European Union. The analysis within the report indicates savings to mental

health and support services in Edinburgh of £420,000 per annum, and savings on welfare benefits and gains in employment income and tax income of almost £50,000 per annum. Social added value per participant is almost £25,000 per annum for and investment of £3500. For the period under study, for every £1 invested in Six Mary's Place almost £6 is returned in social value added.

For an online copy of this SROI report please visit: www.socialfirms. org.uk/resources/quality&impact

QUESTION

1. The SROI study of Six Mary's Place Guest House is one of a series of SROI studies undertaken through Social Economy Scotland. A report on SROI is available at: www.socialeconomyscotland.info. The report entitled 'Investing in impact: Developing Social Return On Investment' is available in the Social Economy Scotland Document Library.

   After reading the report what is your view of SROI as a means of assigning a monetary value to the social and environmental benefits of a social firm such as Six Mary's Place Guest House?

social, environmental and economic impact and to report and review its performance and to provide the information essential for planning future action and improving performance. In carrying out a Social Audit one of the aims is to be able to build in accountability by engaging with the enterprises's key stakeholders.

The SAN social accounting and Audit process consists of three steps, preceded by a 'getting ready' stage. This is shown as Figure 8.3. SAN conducts social accounting audits of social enterprises for a fee. Examples of enterprises who have had a social audit conducted are provided on the website (www.socialauditnetwork.org.uk).

In the UK, charities are monitored by the Charity Commission. Their boards are legally accountable for the solvency and continuing effectiveness of the charity and the preservation of its endowments. An annual report and accounts are demanded in the interests of informing the general public. The Charities Commission is empowered to intervene whenever the board is considered to lack management skills or financial ability to revive an ailing charity. Board members can be suspended and assets taken into possession of the Official Custodian.

Bowen (1994)[20] concludes that: 'Overall, it is fair to say that non-profits as a group are less closely monitored externally than the profit focused organisation'. As a result, there is a more pressing role for the

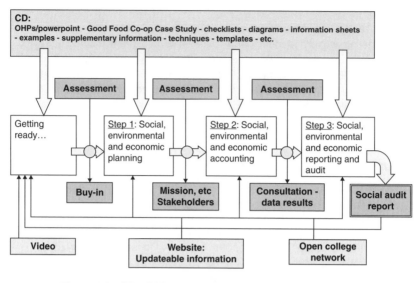

Figure 8.3   *The SAN social accounting and audit process*
Source: www.socialauditnetwork.org.uk

board to ensure good governance in the social economy than in the corporate sector. This position is generally accepted and the Charity Commission is undertaken a major review into the issue.[21]

While governance is not an area that is addressed in depth in this chapter or this book, the argument being presented is that good governance is the key to setting viable performance standards.

The drivers of performance

Rather than delve into economics and statistics, it is better to examine the 'drivers' – the economic, social and political factors that are encouraging the emergence of performance-related social organizations within the third sector of the economy. An understanding of these drivers will provide an understanding of what type of support new and existing social enterprises require and from whom. Understand the drivers and you will understand how you can access the formal, and possibly informal, support network.

Traditionally, there have been three different sectors within the economy; the public sector (government and its various agencies), the private sector (for-profit companies of all sizes) and the non-profit sector. The non-profit sector can be variously defined as the voluntary sector, charities and not-for-profit enterprises and the public as the consumer of services. The interests of all three sectors overlap.

The Institute for Social Entrepreneurs (2002)[22] argues that the

boundaries are beginning to merge: Nonprofits are adopting entrepreneurial strategies and starting businesses; for-profits are invading territory previously occupied only by nonprofits and government; and public sector agencies are forming partnerships with the other sectors and developing entrepreneurial strategies of their own.

They state:

Social enterprises are hybrids mixing social values and goals with commercial practices, operating in the market. They are constitutionally uncomfortable; there is always a tension between their social goals and their commitment to commercial operation. For precisely that reason, they have to question how they operate, and that is what makes them innovative. Social enterprises are driven by social goals – to provide education, childcare, family support – but they often deliver most of that through the market by selling services and products.

The argument presented is that performance measures need to be localized to the individual enterprise and the community that it serves.

Local problems, local solutions

The early Victorian philosophies were based on the idea that the solution to a community's problems is in the community's own hands – in their own localities. This concept is central in public choice that the consumer is given control over, and the option to buy-in to, whichever services it uses. This value is reflected in the 'localization' of community decisions through social enterprises that are created to be owned by, and have a local impact on, a specified part of a community. This is the antithesis of a public sector administration and governmental department that delivers social policy centrally through its civil servants.

From a policy perspective, social enterprises can therefore be seen as an ideal state for politicians; locally grown and locally controlled businesses with local stakeholders – the ultimate in community self-help that requires the minimum of interference from the public sector. This does tend to accord with some of the thinking on entrepreneurship. De Vries (1977)[23] views the entrepreneur as a social deviant 'a non-conformist poorly organized and not a stranger to self destructive behaviour'. This sociological perspective is consistent with the need to create a not-for-profit organization that directly addresses a social problem that is not currently being addressed by public sector organizations. So, while the public sector may embrace the social entrepreneur as a hero, the social entrepreneur is often at odds with the public sector – and is capable, sometimes, of biting the hand that feeds it.

The philosophical association between today's social organizations and the early co-operative movement partly explains their present role as agents for change when it comes to regenerating urban economies. The agent for change is expressed in an emphasis in social investment such as jobs, training with and re-investment with social-economic output.

Where the social enterprise can be seen to be different from the voluntary sector generally is on their level of dependency. Boschee (2006)[24] argues that 'the traditional business model for non-profits, depends solely or almost entirely on charitable contributions and public sector subsidies, with earned income either non-existent or minimal'. He goes on to state that the social enterprise is 'any organization, in any sector, that uses earned income strategies to pursue a double or triple bottom line, either alone (as a social sector business) or as part of a mixed revenue stream that includes charitable contributions and public sector subsidies'.

This concept of a 'triple bottom line' through mixed revenue sources creates a dilemma in terms of the support structure needed to nurture social enterprises. One side of the argument says that support should be directed within the existing (for-profit) support network since social enterprise compete and trade within laissez faire marketplaces. There is an equally compelling argument that support should be provided by specialist organizations which are dedicated to responding to the special needs of social organizations that generate revenue from trading and fundraising activities.

Regardless of whether the support delivery comes from an existing or a new dedicated support network, there are two issues that need to be addressed in terms of any support infrastructure. The first of these is sustainability, which refers to the ability of the business to identify long-term and growing areas of revenue generation that do not conflict with the organization's ethical values in terms of the delivery of services and deployment of resources. The second area is that of capacity building, which refers to the ability of staff within a social enterprise to marry commercial and social objectives to create an organization which generates and distributes a surplus.

As McPhee[25] points out,

> capacity building is a popular term these days – too popular and expansive a term, in fact, to mean much to individuals making specific decisions about programs and grant strategies. As a result, everyone – from practitioners to foundation CEOs – is calling for increased attention to the capacity-building needs of non-profit organizations. So far, however, the rhetoric is ahead of the work.

For a summary of the points of this chapter, please refer to Example 8.1.

Examples —— 8.1 The changing roles of social enterprises

Example 8.1   The changing roles of social enterprises

The term social and public enterprises are linked together as part of the 'social economy'.

The term 'social enterprise' refers to any organization that trades with a social purpose, using business principles and management approaches to achieve socially explicit goals.

Public Organizations in health and education are responsible for the delivery of services which are not marketed or traded freely.

The third sector occupies the ground that sits between the private and the public sectors.

Social organizations exist in no man's land between government and the private sector.

The market economy means that public services are being run through public-private partnerships.

Social enterprises are part of this third sector partnership.

The Board of a social enterprise is responsible for the performance of their social enterprise and are the key to setting viable performance standards.

'Local solutions to local problems' infers that general performance measures are often inappropriate measures of performance.

The challenge is to come up with ways to measure performance in a social enterprise.

Revision questions

1. Referring to the Varney Report, discuss the challenges of transformation associated with making the public sector 'business focused' and the impact that this can be expected to have on services. 'There have been significant improvements to public service delivery over recent years. The Government's programme of investment and reform has delivered real improvements in the way that services are delivered, many of which are highlighted in this report' Varney (2006, p. 8). Can you find an example of such an improvement?

2. For an introduction towards policy, refer to The Office of the Third Sector, The Cabinet Office, Social Enterprise, available online.[26] Pay particular attention to the Action Plan. What is your judgement of this plan?

3. 'The shift in power from public sector bodies towards social enterprise is to be welcomed.' Discuss this statement based around the principles of the public's access to services, choice, information, redress and representation.

4. Using economic, financial and commercial measures, assess their effectiveness (not efficiency) in measuring g the performance of a social enterprise.

    (Read Thompson, J. and Martin, F., Strategic Management: Awareness and Change, 5th edn, Cengage (2005), Chapter 7, pp. 315–33 for an insight into the strategic role of measuring performance.)

References

1. T. Levitt, 'The Dangers of Social Responsibility', *Harvard Business Review*, Sep–Oct (1958), pp. 41–50.
2. Social Enterprise London, available at http://www.sel.org.uk/knowledge.html, accessed June 2009.
3. 'Public Undertakings and Public Service Activities in the European Union', European Parliament, Directorate-General for Research, Economic Affairs series W-21 (May 1996).
4. P. Carr, 'Understanding Enterprise Culture: The Fashioning of Enterprise Activity within Small Business', *Journal of Strategic Change*, 9 (7) (2000), pp. 405–14.
5. OECD, *In Search of Results: Performance Management Practices* (Paris: OECD, 1997).
6. Department of Health, 'Transforming Health and Social Care – the Social Enterprise Investment Fund' (June 2009), www.dh.gov.uk/en/publication andstatistics, accessed December 2009.
7. European Commission, Enterprise and Industry, available at http://ec.europa.eu/enterprise/entrepreneurship/coop/ccmaf/pec-cmaf.htm, accessed June 2009.
8. R. Lewis, *Social Enterprise and Community-Based Care* (London: King's Fund, 2006).

9. A. Dunleavy and C. Hood, 'Old Public Administration to New Public Management', *Public Money and Management*, July–September (1994), pp. 9–16.
10. O. James, *The Executive Agency Revolution in Whitehall Public Interest Versus Bureau-Shaping Perspectives* (Basingstoke: Palgrave Macmillan, 2004).
11. Available at National Audit Office, http://www.nao.org.uk/our_work_by_ sector/third_sector.aspx, accessed June 2009.
12. C. Pharoah and D. Scott, 'Social Enterprise in the Voluntary and Community Sectors. Changes for Policy and Practice', International Third Sector Research Conference, Capetown, South Africa, 2002.
13. G. Brown, 'Choice & Empowerment', *Guardian*, 27 June 2007.
14. NHS Health Plan (2000) available at http://www.dh.gov.uk/en/ Publicationsandstatistics/Publications/AnnualReports/Browsable/DH_5277 178, accessed June 2009.
15. Department of Health, Social Enterprise, available at http://www.dh.gov. uk/en/Managingyourorganisation/Commissioning/Socialenterprise/DH_073 426.
16. BBC, 'What are Public Private Partnerships?' BBC News, 12 February 2003, http://www.news.bbc.co.uk/hi/uk/1518523.stm.
17. R. Behn, 'Why Measure Performance? Different Purposes Require Different Measures', *Public Administration Review* 60 (5) (2003), pp. 586 606.
18. S. Wainwright, *Measuring Impact: A Guide to Resources* (London: NCVO, 2002).
19. A. Dunn and C. A. Riley, 'Supporting the Not-for-Profit Sector: The Government's Review of Charitable and Social Enterprise', *The Modern Law Review*, 67 (4) (2004), pp. 632–57.
20. W. Bowen, *The Charitable Nonprofits: An Analysis of Institutional Dynamics and Characteristics* (San Francisco: Jossey Bass, 1994).
21. Charity Commission, 'The Code of Governance for the Voluntary and Community Sector' (London: 2005), www.charitycommission.gov.uk/ enhancingcharitiesgovernancecode.asp. Consultation Review, November 2009, accessed December 2009. For an insight into emergency issues refer to http://www.volresource.org.uk/briefing/govern.htm, accessed November 2009.
22. Institute for Social Entrepreneurs, see http://www.socialent.org/definitions. htm.
23. M. Kets de Vries, 'The Entrepreneurial Personality: A Person at the Crossroads', *Journal of Management Studies*, vol. 14 (1977), pp. 35–57.
24. J. Boschee, *Migrating from Innovation to Entrepreneurship: How Nonprofits are moving toward Sustainability and Self-Sufficiency*, 2006, see www.socialent.org.
25. P. McPhee, *Building Capacity in Non-profit Organisations* edited by C. De Vita and C. Fleming (The Urban Institute: Washington, DC, 2001), p. 6. www.urban.org/Uploaded PDF/building_capacity.pdf.
26. Social Enterprise Unit, Office of the Third Sector, Cabinet Office, 'Social Enterprice Action Plan 2006' (London, 2006) from www.cabinetoffice. gov.uk/third_sector/social_enterprise/action_plan.aspx, accessed December 2009.

Additional reading

Needle, D., *Business in Context*, 4th edn (London: Thomson Learning, 2004).

Thompson, J., Martin, F., *Strategic Management: Awareness and Change*, 5th edn (London: Cengage, 2005), Chapters 4, 5, and 7.

Varney, D., 'Service Transformation: A Better Service for Citizens and Businesses, A Better Deal for the Taxpayer' (2006). Available at www.hm-treasury.gov.uk/media/4/F/pbr06_varney_review.pdf.

9 enterprising social organizations

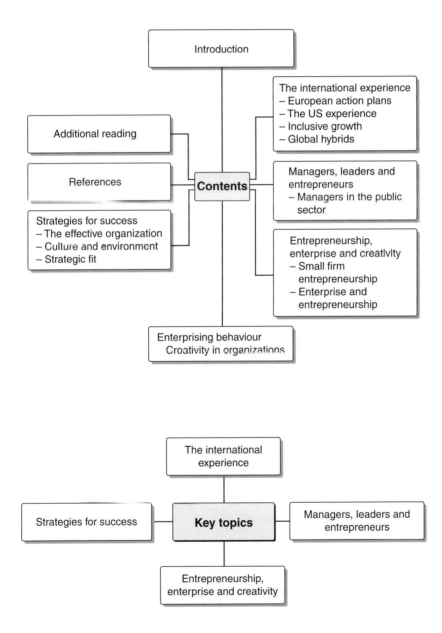

Introduction

The international experience
– European action plans
– The US experience
– Inclusive growth
– Global hybrids

Additional reading

References

Contents

Managers, leaders and entrepreneurs
– Managers in the public sector

Strategies for success
– The effective organization
– Culture and environment
– Strategic fit

Entrepreneurship, enterprise and creativity
– Small firm entrepreneurship
– Enterprise and entrepreneurship

Enterprising behaviour
Creativity in organizations

The international experience

Strategies for success

Key topics

Managers, leaders and entrepreneurs

Entrepreneurship, enterprise and creativity

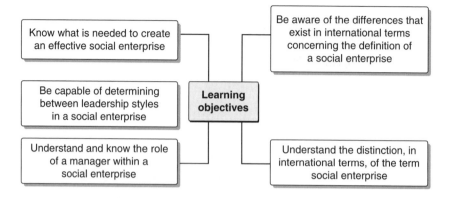

Introduction

This chapter starts by looking at international approaches to supporting European, US and global forms of social enterprise. It is argued that social enterprises are hybrid organizations that do not lend themselves to national definitions. Europe, through the policies of the European Union, places an emphasis on the social in comparison to the US emphasis on the enterprise element, and both can learn from each other's approach.

Assuming that geography or nationality is not the distinguishing factor for social enterprise, the management perspective is taken. This chapter goes on to examine the different roles of 'manager' and 'entrepreneur', and it is also looks at what it takes to create an 'enterprising' social organization. The argument is that leadership is more important than good management in times of change and growth. However, social organizations are different from private sector firms in terms of the leadership that they require. In terms of sustainability, creating an enterprising organization is seen as being more important than having an entrepreneurial leader.

The international experience

Each member state within the European Union has a different regulatory framework and this means that the social economy within Europe is developing at different speeds.

The Europa site states:

> Social enterprises are part of the social economy sector. They constitute a collection of organisations that exist between the traditional private and public sectors. Although there is no universally accepted definition of a social enterprise, its key distinguishing characteristics are social and societal purpose combined with an entrepreneurial spirit of the private sector.
>
> http://europa.en.int/comm/enterprise/entrepreneurship

So while the notion of 'social enterprise' has become widely used throughout the 27 member states in the last decade, it refers to different national contexts. In the US, for example, the social entrepreneur is closely associated with an individual developing an initiative with social aims. But in Europe, 'social enterprise' is applied to businesses engaged in social and occupational integration activities. This is referred to as 'WISE' — Work Integration Social Enterprise. These are autonomous firms engaged in work integration. Davister et al. (2004)[1] refers to 39 different types of WISE and notes that many of these are variants of national models. In Italy, for example, there are 2000 social co-operatives/firms, employing nearly 16,000 disabled people (1998). Germany also has a strong social firm sector with 248 social firms employing 3100 people with disabilities, delivering benefits for their members and to the local community.

The European Research Network (EMES) has a working definition of what form of activity constitutes a social enterprise for its member states. Their definition distinguishes between criteria that are more economic and those that are predominantly social. Four factors have been applied to corroborate the economic and entrepreneurial nature of the planned initiatives.

(a)   A continuous activity producing goods and/or selling services

Social enterprises, unlike the traditional non-profit organizations, are not normally engaged in advisory activities as a major goal, or in the redistribution of financial flows (as, for example, grant-giving foundations). Instead they are directly involved in the production of goods and the provision of services to people on a continuous basis. The provision of services represents, therefore, the reason, or one of the main reasons, for the existence of social enterprises.

(b)   A high degree of autonomy

Social enterprises are voluntarily created by a group of people and are governed by them in the framework of an autonomous project. Although they may depend on public subsidies for revenue it is the case that public authorities or other organizations (federations, private firms, etc.) do not manage them directly or indirectly. They also have the right of participation and to terminate the project.

(c)   A significant level of economic risk

Those who establish a social enterprise assume totally or partly the risk of the initiative. Unlike most public institutions, their financial viability depends on the efforts of their members and workers to secure adequate resources.

(d) A minimum amount of paid work

As in the case of most traditional non-profit associations, social enterprises may also combine monetary and non-monetary resources, voluntary and paid workers. However, the activity carried out in social enterprises requires a minimum level of paid workers.

To encapsulate the social dimensions of the initiative, four indicators are used:

(1) An initiative launched by a group of citizens.

Social enterprises are the result of collective dynamics involving people belonging to a community or to a group that shares a certain need or aim. They must maintain this dimension in one form or another.

(2) A decision-making power not based on capital ownership.

This generally means the principle of 'one member, one vote' or at least a voting power not distributed according to capital shares on the governing body which has the ultimate decision-making rights. The owners of the capital are obviously important, but the decision-making rights are shared with the other stakeholders.

(3) A participatory nature, which involves the persons affected by the activity.

Representation and participation of customers, stakeholder orientation and a democratic management style are important characteristics of social enterprises. In many cases, one of the aims of social enterprises is to further democracy at local level through economic activity.

(4) Limited profit distribution

Social enterprises not only include organizations that are characterized by a total non-distribution constraint, but also organizations like co-operatives in some countries, which may distribute profits only to a limited extent, thus avoiding a profit-maximizing behaviour.

European action plans

Europe has an action plan for social enterprise. The European Agenda for Entrepreneurship introduced the commission's action on promoting entrepreneurship in social sectors. It notes that the policy should take account of the differing needs of entrepreneurs, who run businesses ranging from university spin-outs to family-owned SMEs and social enterprises. Social economy enterprises already provide examples of delivering services in sectors alternative to, or complementing, the public sector. In the Communication on the promotion of co-operative societies in Europe (COM (2004), 18 final, 23.02.2004) the European Commission emphasizes the role of social co-operative enterprises. The effectiveness of co-operative forms in integrating social objectives has led certain member states to adopt specific legal forms to facilitate such activities. These have experienced considerable success and generated interest in other member states.

In order to promote social enterprises across Europe, the commission created, in 2004, a project promoting social entrepreneurship in Europe and launched a study on national policies and good practices concerning social enterprises in Europe in 2005. The European Parliament officially supports the need for community actions to take full account of the social economy's potential for economic growth, employment and citizen participation.

The commission's communication on promoting the role of voluntary organizations and foundations in Europe is aimed at illustrating the growing importance of voluntary organizations and foundations within the European Union and to show what problems and challenges these organizations are facing. A series of national conferences and experts' meetings have taken place, each of which addressed one of the communication's themes.

Examples include the:

- setting aside of 1 per cent of the European Social Fund for a Local Social Capital Fund open exclusively to non-profit organizations;
- stronger emphasis on the role of social economy organizations in the Structural Funds and in Community Initiatives;
- proposals for a European Volunteer Service programme similar to the US Peace Corp;

- third system and employment budget line;
- Liaison Committee of Development NGO's.

(http://www.oneworld.net/)

At present the European experience of social enterprise is fragmented and despite the commission's best intention to co-ordinate it, activity and policy is still derived at a national level in member states. While this may provide an opportunity to develop country specific models of social enterprises, this fragmentation is in distinct contrast to the US.

The US experience

According to Harvard Business School's Social Enterprise Initiative,[2]

> the nonprofit sector comprises 7 percent of US gross domestic product – a number that grows even larger when health care and public education are included. There are more than a million non-profit organizations in the US and their inception rate exceeds that of private businesses. They employ approximately 8.6 million people and mobilize another 7.2 million unpaid volunteers, which together constitute 14 percent of the labor force.

Many of the strongest US organizations – some with turnovers of up to $50 m a year were started in the early 1960s to address the causes of inner city riots, cutbacks in public services or the long-term decline of traditional industries. The regulatory environment is different from that of Europe. Some organizations offering training to disadvantaged groups are exempt from the US equivalent of National Insurance payments. In addition, under the Jarvits-Wagner-O'Day Act, passed by the 92nd United States Congress in 1971, US government departments are required to procure goods and services from organizations employing blind people or people with severe disabilities, providing they are able to compete on price and quality with other suppliers. The Community Reinvestment Act of 1977 also required the US banking sector to invest in poor communities.

Another significant difference between the US and Europe is the amount of direct benefits US organizations receive from the 'mainstream' business community. Charitable giving by individuals, foundations, and corporations was over $240 billion in the US in 2003.[3] The philanthropic capital markets are also significant. Over the next fifty years there will be an estimated six trillion dollars of intergenerational wealth transfer that will be flowing into this sector. Additionally, most corporations are involved with social sector issues and non-profit organizations. They do not see themselves as functioning in isolation from the society around them especially with respect to a segment of the US economy contributing 10 per cent of all jobs and 7 per cent of GNP.

The US environment for social enterprise has a number of advantages over Europe. In the US, the term is 'commonly understood to mean the use of non-governmental, market-based approaches to achieve social ends. Complicating matters further, definitions of social enterprise often vary within the US and Europe respectively. In the US, business schools favour a broad definition of social enterprise while espoused practitioners of social enterprise understand it simply as non-profit earned income activities' (Kerlin, 2006).[4]

The comparison is that the US emphasize the 'enterprise' element whereas in the EU it is the 'social' element that is promoted through policy. In the US, it can be argued that social enterprises have become more integrated with the business framework and have a higher level of commercial acceptance than in Europe. Europe, by emphasizing the social component of this form of business organization, is especially strong in the multi-stakeholders community-based initiatives. Both approaches have their advantages and their disadvantages and create a diverse range of variations.

Inclusive growth

Throughout the developing world one of the main issues for governments is the desire to try and balance globalization with what can be termed 'inclusive growth'. The definition of inclusive growth is growth that is fairly shared and corresponds to equality and equity. In essence, it is the attempt to spread economic growth more equitably across society – not just wealth, but also infrastructure and educational opportunity. In the third world, opportunities exist for the creation of social enterprises based for example around agriculture where the income generated through product sales will be retained within the community to try and create the wealth needed for inclusive growth to take place. In the case of Rwandan coffee growers, philanthropic funding from the Clinton Hunter Development Initiative (CHDI) is being used to fund start-up capital and provide, among other things, marketing expertise to allow Rwandan coffee growers' products to reach British supermarkets. The nature and structure of a social enterprise offers one vehicle to address the issue of inclusive growth on an international basis. In the UK, the Department for International Development (DFID) is supporting projects in countries such as Nepal and Afghanistan to help local farm producers create the basis for improving living standards through wealth creation and income retention (www.dfid.gov.uk).

A discussion on inclusive growth at the national level in India is available at www.weforum.org/summitreports/india2007.

Global hybrids

As discussed above, the functioning of social enterprises is closely linked to the concept of social responsibility and social equity. In fact, the social economy reflects what many are now referring to as the ethical economy, corporate citizenship and activities that promote economic and social wellbeing, inclusion, and justice, and in doing so might just provide a measure of inclusive growth.

Emerson (2005)[5] argues that markets and business, capital and commerce can be harnessed not simply for the creation of individual wealth, but rather the creation of value in its fullest. He notes that social entrepreneurs have created a diversity of approaches and strategies, all of which are coming together within a unified, global parade. This shown as Figure 9.1.

On the right-hand side of the spectrum are for-profit entities that create social value but whose main motives are profit-making and distribution of profit to shareholders. On the left-hand side of the spectrum are non-profits with commercial activities that generate economic value to fund social programmes but whose main motive is mission accomplishment as dictated by stakeholder mandate. You should be able to identify some of these organizations in your own local community. Emerson's typology indicates that social enterprises are hybrid organizations that do not lend themselves to national definitions. Europe may well place the emphasis on the social compared with the US emphasis on the enterprise element. Both parties can learn from each other's approach.

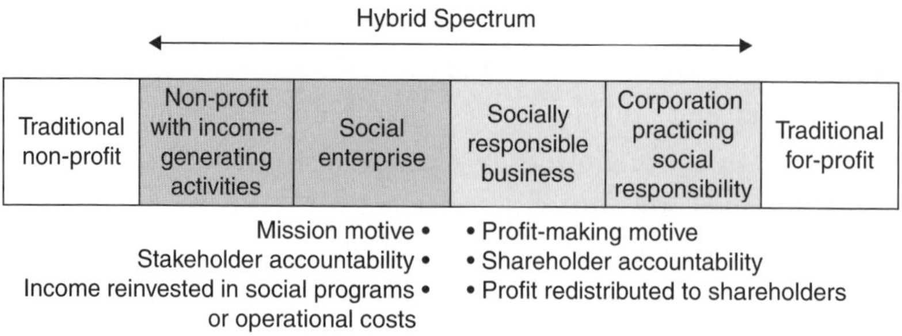

Hybrid Spectrum

Traditional non-profit	Non-profit with income-generating activities	Social enterprise	Socially responsible business	Corporation practicing social responsibility	Traditional for-profit

Mission motive •   • Profit-making motive
Stakeholder accountability •   • Shareholder accountability
Income reinvested in social programs •   • Profit redistributed to shareholders
or operational costs

*Figure 9.1   **Hybrid spectrum***
Source: Alter, S., Dawans, V., Morgan, W. and Miller, L., Virtue Ventures LLC (2007)

An examination of European, US and global hybrids presents a problem for developing a typology of the international experience. There are apparent differences between the North American experience and that of Europe. It is unclear whether there is a convergence or divergence of the model. Europe's predilection for 'social' and the US liking of 'enterprise' does, in global terms, indicate a diversity of different business models. The fact remains, however, that most social enterprises are community-based and, despite Europe's efforts at integration and member cooperation, the main influences will continue to come from the local community.

In this sense international comparisons may or may not be fruitful yet they do offer rich insights into how things actually work. To do so please compare and contrast the Minicases listed in this text starting with Chapter 1.

Managers, leaders and entrepreneurs

Regardless of cultural geography, there are differences between being a manager (somebody who is responsible for executing company policy) and a social entrepreneur (someone who initiates and innovates).

According to Hill and Jones (2004):[6]

Our understanding of modern management is enhanced if we remember the fundamental managing process: 'managers' perform basic 'managing functions' (of planning, organising, staffing, influence and controlling), which are facilitated by the fundamental 'linking processes' of decision making and communicating, to achieve the basic managerial purpose of organisational effectiveness.

Mintzberg (1975)[7] sees a manager as the person in charge of an organization or of one of its component parts. He or she is given formal authority over that unit and holds responsibility for its efficient production of goods or services and for the controlled adaptation to changes in its environment. The manager is also concerned with issues of effectiveness and of meeting goals and objectives.

Mintzberg's approach highlights the changing, uncertain environment in which the modern manager operates. Many things occur which cannot be predicted or controlled on a day-to-day basis. The modern manager has little time to reflect on strategy and must cope with numerous challenges each day. This means that professional managers are task-orientated.

Management in the public sector

Within the public sector there is a belief that managers should operate business tasks efficiently, borrowing on the means of private sector organizations. The fundamental nature of the shift from public administration to new public management is illustrated by Dunleavy and Hood (1994)[8]. They suggest that the 'shift' from public administration to 'social management' redefines the role of the manger within public sector organizations. On the one hand, social organizations that are part public sector and part social enterprise becomes less distinctive from the private sector, while on the other hand, the degree of discretionary power (particularly over staff, contracts and money) enjoyed by public managers is increased, as the rules and control coming from the centre are relaxed.

The public sector has long assumed distinctive goals from those of most private firms, such as the pursuit of equity, justice, fairness and accountability, and the enhancement of citizenship (Isaac-Henry et al., 1997).[9] It can, and often is, argued that the fundamental values of public administrators and organizational objectives differ from those of the private sector. Differences in values encourage a divergence in managerial behaviour such that the private sector model of management fails to 'fit' many public organizations. McKevitt and Lawton (1994)[10] have identified roles for private and public sector models. These roles are abbreviated and simplified below in Table 9.1.

From Table 9.1 it can be argued that private sector models are useful but not sufficient for social enterprises. The distinctive conditions

Table 9.1 **Private versus public sector**

Private sector model	Public sector model
Individual choice	Collective choice
Demand and price	Need for resources
Market need	Awkwardness (public domain)
Search for market satisfaction	Search for justice
Competition	Collective action

Source: McKevitt, D. and Lawton, A., *Public Sector Management: Theory, Critique and Practice* (London: Sage, 1994)

within the social enterprise economy, such as the greater role of collective choice, citizenship and engagement along with social justice, are not evident in the private sector. In Table 9.2 Hood (1996)[11] summarizes the changing role of the manager in social organizations.

Throughout this discussion it is important to note that managers are task-driven and that managers are essentially responsible for the control and efficient management of a business. This means that they report to someone who is responsible for their leadership. Creating a sustainable organization is about having good managers. More importantly, it is about the sort of entrepreneurial leader discussed in Chapter 3.

The problem with any discussion of public and private sector management is that it tends to concentrate on traditional, larger organizations or traditional public sector bodies. But social organizations are expected to innovate. Neither of the traditional formats embraces the concept of 'enterprise'.

Entrepreneurship, enterprise and creativity

There is a common agreement on the importance of entrepreneurship to the socio-economic and political stability of a nation (Westhead and Matlay, 2004).[12] One topical subset includes discussion about the challenge of teaching entrepreneurship (Kirby, 2004)[13]. Figure 9.2 provides an overview of the role of the entrepreneur (Thompson).[14] The entrepreneur spots an opportunity, and from this organizes the land, labour and capital to take advantage of the opportunity.

Enterprise and entrepreneurship

Gibb (1996)[15] was one of the first to make a distinction between small-firm entrepreneurship and enterprise. As he notes, 'not all

Table 9.2   **Management role change**

Doctrine	Meaning	Justification
Hands-on professional management of public organization.	Visible managers at the top of the organization, free to manage by use of discretionary power.	Accountability requires clear assignment of responsibility, not diffusion of power.
Explicit standards and measures of performance.	Goals and targets defined and measurable as indicators of success.	Accountability means clearly stated aims; efficiency requires a 'hard look' at objectives.
Greater emphasis on output controls.	Resource allocation and rewards are linked to performance.	Need to stress results rather than procedures.
Shift to disaggregation of units in the public sector.	Disaggregate public sector into corporatized units of activity, organized by products, with devolved budgets. Units dealing at arm's length witheach other.	Make units manageable; split provision and production, use contracts or franchises inside as well as outside the public sector.
Shift to greater competition in the public sector.	Move to term contracts and public tendering procedures; introduction of market disciplines in public sector.	Rivalry via competition as the key to lower costs and better standards.
Stress on private-sector styles of management practice.	Move away from traditional public service ethic to more flexible pay, hiring, rules, etc.	Need to apply 'proven' private sector management tools in the public sector.
Stress on greater discipline and economy in public sector resource use.	Cutting direct costs, raising labour discipline, limiting compliance costs to business	Need to check resource demands of the public sector, and do more with less.

Source: Hood, C., 'Contemporary Public Management' (1995)

owner-managers are entrepreneurs, nor are all small businesses entrepreneurial and not all large businesses are un-enterprising'

For Bridge et al. (2003)[16] the term 'enterprise' is universally used to describe the small business sector, i.e. small and medium enterprises, shortened to SMEs. The EU notes that 'micro, small and medium-sized enterprises are socially and economically important, since they represent 99% of all **enterprises** in the EU and provide around 65 million jobs and contribute to entrepreneurship and innovation'.[17]

Bridge et al. also note that the term has been attached to a number of policy and SME support schemes and appears in the form of 'Young Enterprise', 'Graduate Enterprise', 'Enterprise Fund' and many more including Ethnic Enterprise.

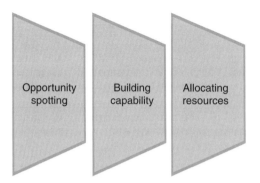

Figure 9.2 **Entrepreneurial mindsets**
Source: Thompson, J., 'A Strategic Perspective of Entrepreneurship'

Clearly 'enterprise' is a term that has become used interchangeably with entrepreneurship, and it appears in a number of guises, especially within policy documents. Enterprise can also be seen as a driver of social mobility through the rewards associated with successful acts of entrepreneurship. For example, there is talk about the 'enterprise culture' as a means of harnessing entrepreneurial firm activity to make an economy stronger. The NCGE Report (2004)[18] notes that enterprise culture and knowledge-based economies are often linked together to provide an ideal state – one in which graduates are seen as the key to unlocking wealth within the economy. The key to success here is the achievement of economic outcomes, namely capital accumulation and wealth creation.

One recent example of the terms being used interchangeably was the DTI's announcement on 'Enterprising Britain' (2007).[19] 'The competition, which launched in 2004, was a key part of the Government's drive to increase entrepreneurship in the UK, and identify areas of enterprise excellence: those places that have created jobs, forged links in communities, and improved the local climate for businesses and residents'. In 2008 it was won by Scarborough and is now the responsibility of the new Department for Business Innovation and Skills (BIS).

The terms 'social enterprise' and 'social entrepreneur', can be contrasted with enterprise and entrepreneurship – and can then be applied to the third sector of the economy that links private and public sector delivery to deliver enterprise excellence.

As Thompson argues:

> Many traits and behaviours of successful social entrepreneurs appear to mirror those of entrepreneurial businessmen and women in the profit-seeking sectors (Leadbeater, 1997). Their leadership and personal qualities are similar, as is their style and approach. They are ambitious and driven. They have been able to clarify and communicate an inspiring mission; around this they have recruited and inspired paid staff (albeit paid less than in the private sector), users and partners as well as an army of volunteers. They have known where they could acquire resources, some of which they have 'begged, stolen or borrowed'. But their vision has been for something which will add value for the underprivileged sections of the community.
>
> (Thompson et al., 2000)[20]

Two questions remain: is it right to use the two terms interchangeably? and which is the more important influence on success in social enterprises?

Enterprising behaviour

The word enterprise may be mixed up with the term entrepreneurship but the term 'enterprising' can mean something different when it refers to an organization. One of the earliest appearances of the term enterprise referring to behaviour is by the OECD (1989)[21] which notes:

> A 'narrow' definition of enterprise which sees it as business entrepreneurialism, the promotion and development of enterprise within education and training systems, is viewed purely as an issue of curriculum development to enable young people to learn, usually experientially, about business start-up and management. A 'broad' definition of enterprise which regards it as a set of qualities and competencies that enable individuals, organizations, communities, societies and cultures to be flexible, creative and adaptable in the face of change This approach is based on the belief that enterprise involves using the imagination, being creative, taking responsibilities, identifying ideas, organising for action, making decisions, managing and communicating with others, assessing performance and the like in a wide range of living and working contexts.

This approach sees enterprise in the form of behaviour and an approach to learning about business. It is a view reinforced by Gibb and Nelson (1996)[22] who make a clear distinction between entrepreneurship, which is seen as a series of attributes, and small business management, seen as a series of tasks. By this definition, entrepreneurship is a set of functional management and leadership skills especially those associated with starting and developing a business.

Enterprising behaviour on the other hand, is a way of learning and approaching business. Unlike other forms of management behaviour it is creative, it is contextualized and it is personalized.

> Enterprising behaviour referred to the development of learning skills to enable learning to be personalised, applied to the workplace and continued beyond the education or training programme, with the participant firmly in control of the process.
>
> Henry (2006)[23]

Enterprising behaviour is still linked with entrepreneurship. Timmons (1994)[24] sees entrepreneurship as being about 'creating and seizing opportunities, often regardless of the resources that are available'. In this model, entrepreneurship is about creating and building something from very little, which implies a steep learning curve. A similar point is raised by Boussouara and Deakins (1998)[25] who suggest that entrepreneurs learn, not through structured teaching, but through experience and trial and error. Being creative is recognized as an entrepreneurial characteristic.

Another dimension to learning is the idea that an entrepreneur is an individual but that businesses, small and large, are successful because of the (entrepreneurial) team. (Casson, 1982).[26] This moves the discussion away from the entrepreneur as an individual hero towards a visionary – someone who creates a 'new world' and whose success depends upon the ability to share that vision with others. In this view the entrepreneur is responsible for creating a framework through which others are able to achieve the vision. Entrepreneurs think in non-conventional ways and challenge existing assumptions. This means that they need to be flexible and adaptable in their problem solving.

Instead of adopting a structured, analytical approach to problem solving, which requires attention to detail, adherence to rules and

systematic investigation, it is believed that they prefer a more intuitive approach that requires more holism and synthesis, lateral rather
than sequential reasoning and random methods of exploration.

(Kirby, 2004)[27]

The same emphasis on creativity is outlined by Piercy (2005)[28] who
notes:

> But the truth is that the winning strategies are smart, innovative and
> original, and break the rules, and most times there is someone some-
> where who has seen through conventions and traditional assump-
> tions to create a new business idea.

These winning strategies refer not to the abilities of a single individual
but to the corporate community that makes up the business.
Enterprising behaviour refers not only to the lead entrepreneur but also
to the rest of the organization who are expected to be creative in
achieving the vision. In this context enterprising behaviour is more
akin to creativity than entrepreneurship: it is the ability to identify and
exploit new opportunities; the rejection of established methods; the
invention of new alternatives; self belief; determination; irrationality as
strategy; unconventional thinking; creative culture as competitive
advantage (Fillis, 2007).[29]

Creativity in organizations

Creativity in organizations focuses on achieving innovation, competitive advantage and social benefits by enhancing the 'level' of creativity
in the organization. This, typically, involves:

- Examining the personality traits and styles of individuals.
- Developing an organizational context in which creativity might be
  fostered (organizational cultures etc.).
- Examining systems (collective-organized efforts coupled with the
  physical environment) to see how the systemic tendencies toward stability might be interrupted ... to stimulate new actions and/or different activities.

This may be why Bridge et al. (2009)[30] note that enterprising people tend
to have more originality than others and are able to produce solutions

that fly in the face of established knowledge. They are also inclined to be more adaptable, and are prepared to consider a range of alternative approaches. They challenge the status quo, which can sometimes cause conflict with their colleagues.

> At the age of six I wanted to be a cook. At seven I wanted to be Napoleon. And my ambition has been growing steadily ever since.
>
> Dali (1942), 'The Secret Life of Salvador Dali'

This discussion has looked at international approaches to entrepreneurship by looking at the European, US and global forms of social enterprise. It has examined the different roles of 'manager' and 'entrepreneur' and it has also looked at what it takes to create an enterprising social organization. The argument is that leadership is more important than good management in times of change. However, social organizations are different from private sector organizations in terms of the leadership that they require. In terms of sustainability creating an enterprising organization is more important than having an entrepreneurial leader whose role within the social enterprise may only be short lived.

Strategies for success

This book looks at what it takes to create an effective social organization – one that can deliver high value added services and still generate the resources it requires to function. The emphasis is on creating an enterprising organization rather than fostering entrepreneurship within individual leaders.

The final chapter will develop the arguments made in Chapter 6 that emphasize the importance of innovation, and look at the recipes for success by taking a more hands-on perspective on creating a successful social enterprise. Before doing this it is necessary to look further into the relationship between structure and strategy. The effective organization can be seen as being a mix of informal and formal structures. In a turbulent environment, one where there is a lot of change in formal structures, building flexibility and shared responsibility will outperform formal and bureaucratic organizations. However, in static environments, highly bureaucratic organizations can prosper as they encourage process efficiency.

How well a firm uses its resources to meet the challenges of its business environment is the key to success in the current changing economic environment.

The effective organization

There is no single ideal organizational structure for an enterprising social organization. What is important is to understand the advantages and disadvantages of different structures, and to be aware of the appropriate model based on an organization's needs. Table 9.3 adapted from Mintzberg, (1983)[31] below describes the strengths and weaknesses of different types of organizational structures.

There is no ideal organizational structure for a business. What is important is to understand the advantages and disadvantages of different structures and to be aware of the appropriate model based on the available resources and the extent to which the business environment is changing. Based on Figure 9.3, there are three basic types of organizational structure.

1. Bureaucratic organizations will tend to have hierarchical policies and procedures. These will act as consistent rules across business. This structure will not support empowerment, and management between business units needs significant co-ordination. Such a format will be cumbersome in an information-based economy but will work well in a stable and unchanging environment. Local authorities and governmental organizations often fulfil this characteristic.

2. Flat structure organizations have few management layers. They tend to have a higher degree of empowerment, trust and participation for staff members. Collaborative decision making will be encouraged to create initiative and innovation. The staff will tend to have a broad base of skills and knowledge. Co-ordination and communication require constant effort to move resources. There are less rigid boundaries between jobs and business units can suffer from unclear policies and procedures.

3. Team-oriented structure seeks to pool the skills and knowledge of key individuals and can result in higher quality output. The theory is that diversity encourages innovation, and this is targeted at staff with a broad base of skills and knowledge. This structure encourages

Table 9.3 *The effective organization*

Bureaucratic and hierarchical	Policies and procedures to guide. Policies consistent rules across business.	Does not support empowerment. Needs significant co-ordination between business units.
Flat structure, few management layers	High degree of empowerment, trust and participation. Collaborative decision making which encourages initiative and innovation. Staff develop a broad base of skills and knowledge.	Co-ordination and communication require constant effort. Less rigid boundaries between jobs and units can result in unclear policies and procedures.
Team-oriented structure	Pooling of skills and knowledge can result in higher quality output. Diversity encourages innovation. Staff with broad base of skills and knowledge Encourages empowerment and participation.	Individual accountability may decrease. Staff must be trained in team process skills. Dominant participants can 'take over' team.
Matrix structure with a combination of vertical and horizontal authority	Project leaders have access to people across organization. Specialists can be brought into projects as needed. Staff develop broad base of skills and knowledge.	Individual accountability may decrease. Staff must be trained in team process skills. Dominant participants can 'take over' team.
Product or service-oriented structures	High degree of focus and expertise on specific products and services. Can lead to increased product/service development. Quick responses to rapidly changing market demands.	Can create internal competition between units. Narrow focus can hamper organization-wide CRM efforts. Specific groups may resist change.

Source: Adapted from Mintzberg, *Structures in Fives* (1983)

empowerment and participation, although individual accountability may decrease and dominant participants can 'take over' the team. Staff must be trained in team process skills. In terms of management, it requires a matrix structure which combines vertical and horizontal authority. Project leaders need to have access to people across the organization, and specialists can be brought into projects if required.

Although the knowledge, skills and the abilities of managers, team leaders, staff and volunteers are important for the implementation of a structure, they should not dictate the ideal design. Rather, the *vision* of

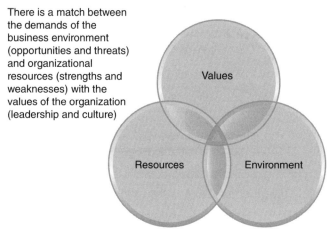

There is a match between the demands of the business environment (opportunities and threats) and organizational resources (strengths and weaknesses) with the values of the organization (leadership and culture)

Figure 9.3   ***EVR congruence***
Source: Thompson, J. and Martin, F., *Strategic Management*, p. 126 (2005)

where the organization is going should be the primary driver of structure. This means that the organization's mission and strategy dictate its structure. Organizational design is part of the strategy to help the enterprise reach its objectives by translating strategy into operations.

The culture and environment of any organization tend to play a large role in determining structure. A more formal bureaucratic organization will tend to have formal structures, while less formal organizations often choose flatter structures with dispersed responsibilities. The formal structure is the one defined by organization charts and in position and process descriptions. As an organization matures through its lifecycle, it will tend to become more formal and less flexible. As it grows it becomes less enterprising.

This is referred to as a 'machine bureaucracy'[32] which might consist of:

- A clearly defined hierarchy driven by procedures and rules for the work that has to be done.
- Exactly defined areas of competence and 'narrow' specializations.
- Impersonal and abstract division of functions and of forming of functions with an emphasis on standardization of the work and narrow specialisms with a high degree of division of labour.
- Trained incapacity with insufficient use of available knowledge and skills.

- Rules and 'standard operating procedures' become a goal, without remembrance to their original service or vision.
- A risk of formalism, ritualism or exaggerated punctuality (negative connotation of the concept bureaucracy).
- De-personalizing the relationships by emphasizing the formal relationships.
- Informal or simple structures are well aligned for social economies where change is endemic. The informal structure consists of the unofficial relationships among individuals and work groups inside and outside the stakeholder constituency.

But social organizations are complex and there will always be a need for a mix of formal and informal communication and workflow.

But if the structure becomes obsolete, social entrepreneurs must revitalize the structure to achieve the social mission. This may include reducing policies, redefining responsibilities, adjusting income streams and revising enterprise training programmes. In this sense internal structure will always follow strategy.

Strategic fit

All businesses, whether they are large or small, private or public, need a business strategy, even if it has never been articulated, and the manager of the business does not know it. It may seem a bold claim that all companies must have a business strategy, that all firms should have an idea of what product or service they want to sell, who they want to sell it to, whether they want to make it themselves or buy it in. A business strategy is like a map, guiding the business towards its goal. A good strategy should never be bogged down in unnecessary detail. Preparing a business strategy involves addressing questions such as:

- Establishing where your business is now.
- Where would you like it to be?
- What resources do you have?
- What resources can you get hold of?
- Modifying goals in the light of the resources available.
- Modifying/changing/scrapping your business strategy in the light of experience.

Too many businesses spend too high a proportion of their time on management tasks and managing internal control systems that do not contribute towards their social mission. They are not making strategic decisions. They are doing what is 'convenient' by working in the business rather than working on the business. Another failure is to spend too much time doing analyses of the market without using the information gathered to make decisions. Thompson (1999)[33] uses a simple strategic tool to outline strategic fit. This model is discussed in the recommended text by Thompson and Martin (2005, pp. 125–30). E-V-R (environment-values-resources) is a strategic decision tool and one that applies especially to the entrepreneurial social organization.

The E-V-R congruence model provides a framework for examining what social organizations must achieve strategically in order to create and sustain organizational effectiveness and success. Success for any business is dependent upon the ability to find a valuable strategic position, whereby the company's resources, competencies and capabilities are deployed and managed to meet and satisfy the demands and expectations of key stakeholders. This invariably involves trade-offs and prioritization, affected by the relative power and influence of the relevant stakeholders. In this way the business adds value in some distinctive way to achieve product or service differences, manage costs effectively and create some form of distinctiveness or competitive advantage. However, sustained success requires that positioning is strengthened constantly in a dynamic and competitive environment, and changed, perhaps dramatically, from time to time. This represents continuous improvement on the one hand, and discontinuous change to a new competitive paradigm on the other (Thompson and Martin, 2005).

E-V-R (Figure 9.3) shows how the environment is a source of opportunities and threats – external key success factors – and that resources constitute strengths and weaknesses, strategic competencies which either match, or fail to match, environmental needs. Sustaining and changing this strategic fit is dependent on leadership, culture and values. Thompson and Martin (2005) go on to show that entrepreneurship is a process which is essential for establishing winning strategic positions and, as such, is relevant and vital for organizations of all types and size.

It is argued that an effective organization has to have a mix of formal and informal structures. Where there is a lot of change, informal structures will perform better than organizations with policies and rules.

Building flexibility is critical to the sustainability of a social enterprise – one that wishes to add real value to its clients and its stakeholders.

It is also argued that strategic fit is important and this means matching the external environment with internal resources. This is where the concept of environment value and resources comes into play as a means of strategically creating and sustaining an effective organization. As indicated, social firms, part of the social enterprise model, seek to provide employment opportunities for people with a range of disabilities, both mental and physical. By employing a majority of their staff with mental disabilities, social firms are at a disadvantage when competing with private sector firms in highly competitive situations.

For example Six Mary's Place (Minicase 8.1) is a social firm that operates as a guest house located in a very prestigious part of Edinburgh close to the city centre. By its very nature, hotel accommodation is a very competitive marketplace especially in a major tourist city. The guest house has managed to succeed through the support of the public (often NHS staff) who value the purpose of the social firm and show this by their continued use of the guest house and the word of mouth the guest house enjoys. This leads to the balancing of the social aspect with the business aspect in terms of the profile of the staff within the guest house and the external credentials of the guest house for example in its support of green tourism and vegetarian food (www.sixmarysplace.co.uk).

The guest house succeeds because its mix of values and resources are such that the social firm can trade successfully in the competitive external environment it finds itself in supported by the internal resources of the social enterprise hub that is Forth Sector who market the guest house to its strong network of referral agents.

Example 9.1 provides a summary of the main points in this chapter.

```
┌──────────────┐     ┌──────────────────────────────┐
│  Examples    ├─────┤ 9.1 Enterprising organizations │
└──────────────┘     └──────────────────────────────┘
```

Example 9.1 Enterprising organizations

Geography or nationality is not the distinguishing factor for social enterprise. It is the management perspective that matters.

In US, the social entrepreneur is closely associated with an individual developing an initiative with social aims. In Europe, 'social enterprise' is applied to businesses engaged in social and occupational integration activities.

In the US, social enterprise is commonly understood to mean the use of non-governmental, market-based approaches to achieving social ends.

The European experience of social enterprise is fragmented despite the Commission's best intentions to co-ordinate it.

US firms operate in a different regulatory environment.

The effective organization can be seen as being a mix of informal and formal structures.

As an organization matures through its lifecycle, it will tend to become more formal and less flexible. As it grows it becomes less enterprising.

The E-V-R (environment-values-resources) congruence model provides a framework for examining what social enterprises must achieve strategically in order to create and sustain organizational effectiveness and success.

Revision questions

1. From within your organization (or one you have an interest in) identify one or more managers that exhibit the characteristics of a leader and critically assess how this leadership is exhibited and its affect on the organization. The person identified does not need to be the top manager. He or she needs to be, in your estimation, the most natural leader.
2. Critically review the statement provided below.

   (a) Can you find an example of such a coordinated community development?
   (b) Who is involved?

Social economy enterprises work because they support a range of community goals. They provide a flexible and sustainable tool that can help communities to achieve their objectives. Whether it is job creation and skills development, the environment, social support systems, or economic growth and neighbourhood revitalization, enterprises can be tailored to the individual needs of the community. These social economy enterprises typically evolve from broad-based community development strategies and involve a range of local partners including local residents, governments, the voluntary sector, private business, learning institutions, and organizations.

References

1. C. Davister, J. Defourney and O. Gregoire, *Work Integration Social Enterprises in the European Union: An Overview of Existing Models*, *EMES* (2004) available at http://www.emes.net/fileadmin/emes/PDF_files/PERSE/PERSE_04_04_Trans-ENG.pdf, accessed May 2008.

2. Harvard Business School, *Social Enterprise Initiative*. Available at http://www.hbs.edu/socialenterprise/whatis.html, accessed June 2008.
3. USINFO. State. Gov, US Charitable Contributions Top $240 Billion in 2003. Available at http://usinfo.state.gov/scv/Archive/2005/May/10-192837. html, accessed May 2008.
4. J. A. Kerlin, *Social Enterprise in the United States and Europe: Understanding and Learning from our Differences* (Washington, DC: The Urban Institute, 2006). .
5. J. Emerson, *Hybrid Spectrum* (2005). Available at http://www.virtueventures. com/setypology/index.php?id=HYBRID_SPECTRUM&lm=1, accessed May 2008.
6. C. W. Hill and G. R. Jones, *Strategic Management: An Integrated Approach* (Boston, MA: Houghton, Mifflin Company, 2004).
7. H. Mintzberg, 'What do Managers Do?' *Harvard Business Review* (July 1975), pp. 49–61. Reprinted in *Harvard Business Review on Leadership* (HBS Press, 1990), pp. 1–36.
8. P. Dunleavy and C. Hood, 'From Old Public Administration to New Public Management', *Journal of Public Money and Management*, July–September, vol. 14, no. 3 (1994), pp. 9–16.
9. K. Isaac-Henry et al., 'Management of Information Technology in the Public Sector', in K. Isaac-Henry et al., *Management in the Public Sector* (London: International Thomson Business Press, 1997).
10. D. McKevitt and A. Lawton (eds), *Public Sector Management: Theory, Critique and Practice* (London: Sage, 1994).
11. C. Hood, 'Contemporary Public Management: A New Global Paradigm?' *Public Policy and Administration*, 10(2) (1995), p. 271.
12. P. Westhead and H. Matlay, 'Critical Issues in Graduate Career Choices', Working Paper No. 23 (Coventry: Global Independent Research, 2004).
13. D. Kirby, 'Entrepreneurship Education: Can Business Schools Meet the Challenge?' *Education Training*, Vol. 46 no. 8/9 (2004), pp. 510–19.
14. J. Thompson, 'A Strategic Perspective of Entrepreneurship', *International Journal of Entrepreneurial Behaviour & Research*, vol. 5, no. 6 (1999), pp. 279–96.
15. A. A. Gibb, 'Entrepreneurship and Small Business Management: Can We Afford to Neglect Them in the Twenty-first Century Business School?' *British Journal of Management*, vol. 7, no. 4 (1996), pp. 309–24.
16. S. Bridge, K. O'Neill and S. Cromie, *Understanding Entrepreneurship and Small Business*, 2nd edn, (Basingstoke: Palgrave Macmillan), p. 25.
17. European Commission, SME Definitions available at http://ec.europa.eu/ enterprise/enterprise_policy/sme_definition/index_en.htm, accessed June 2008.
18. 'Business School Graduates as Nascent Entrepreneurs', National Council for Graduate Entrepreneurship, Policy Paper 06, 2004.
19. 'Enterprising Britain', (2007). See http://www.enterprisingbritain.org/news/ #september2007, accessed September 2007.
20. J. Thompson, G. Alvy and A. Lees, 'Social Entrepreneurs: A New Look at the People and the Potential', *Management Decision* 38/5 (2000), pp. 328–38.
21. Organisation of Economic Cooperation and Development (OECD), *Towards an Enterprising Culture: A Challenge to Education and Training*, OECD Educational monograph No. 4 (Paris, 1989).

22. A. Gibb and D. Nelson, *Personal Competences, Training and Assessment: A Challenge for Small Business Trainers*, Proceedings of the European Small Business Seminar, Finland, 1996, pp. 97–107.
23. C. Henry, F. Hill, and C. Leitch, 'Entrepreneurship Education and Training: Can Entrepreneurship be Taught?, Part II', *Education Training*, vol. 47, no. 3, (2005), pp. 158–69.
24. J. Timmons, *New Venture Creation* (Boston, MA: Irwin, 1994).
25. M. Boussouara and D. Deakins, *Learning, Entrepreneurship and the High Technology Small Firm*, Proceedings of the Enterprise and Learning Conference, Aberdeen, 1998.
26. M. C. Casson, *The Entrepreneur* (Oxford: Martin Robertson & Company, 1982).
27. Kirby, 'Entrepreneurship Education'.
28. N. Piercy, *Market-Led Strategic Change* (London: Elsevier, 2005), p. 269.
29. I. Fillis, Department of Marketing, University of Stirling, (course notes), 2007.
30. S. Bridge, K. O'Neill and F. Martin, *Understanding Enterprise, Entrepreneurship and Small Business*, 3rd edn, (Basingstoke: Palgrave Macmillan, 2009).
31. H. Mintzberg, *Structures in Fives: Designing Effective Organizations* (Englewood Cliffs, Prentice-Hall, 1983).
32. H. Mintzberg , *Mintzberg on Management. Inside Our Strange World Of Organizations* (New York, NY: Free Press, 1989).
33. J. Thompson, 'A Strategic Perspective of Entrepreneurship'.

Additional reading

For an overview of social enterprise in the European Community please refer to the EMES European Network, http://www.emes.net.

Bernanke, B. Chair of Federal Reserve System, 'The Community Reinvestment Act: Its Evolution and New Challenges', speech at the Community Affairs Research Conference, Washington, DC, Federal Reserve System website, 30 March 2007.

Bornstein, D., *How to Change the World: Social Entrepreneurs and the Power of New Ideas* (New York: Oxford University Press Inc, 2007).

Bochee, J. and McClurg, J., *Toward a Better Understand of Social Entrepreneurship: Some Important Distinctions* (Columbus, OH: Social Enterprise Alliance, 2003).

Burns, P., *Entrepreneurship and Small Business* (Basingstoke: Palgrave Macmillan, 2007), Chapter 17.

Confederation of European Social Firms, Employment initiatives and Social Co-operatives. http://www.cefec.de/ourmembers.html.

Emerson, J., 'Hybrid Spectrum', (2005). Available at http://www.virtueventures.com/setypology/.

Spinali, L. and Mortimer, H., 'A Scan of the Not-For-Profit Entrepreneurship: Status of the Field and Recommendations for Action', Kauffman Centre for Entrepreneurial Leadership, January 2001.

Thompson, J. and Martin F., *Strategic Management: Awareness and Change*, 5th edn, (London: Thomson Learning, 2005).

10 recipes for success

Introduction

This chapter summarizes the key learning points covered in Chapters 1 to 9, and it does this from two points of view. Firstly, this book has been written from the perspective of the student who wants to understand the context within which a social enterprise can be successful. It looks at definitions of social enterprises, examined what makes them different and their role in the economy. It has looked at social enterprise networks and models of social firms and how firms seek to achieve a balance between generating revenue and fulfilling their social mission. The question of management theory was looked at in terms of organizational structure and social leadership. This was followed by discussions on social entrepreneurs and the question of ethics. The way in which an organization can be built, especially in terms of managing risk and division, was looked at with special attention paid to the role of stakeholders. Additionally, the ways in which growth can be achieved was also examined in terms of innovation and different funding formats. Marketing of social enterprises was examined as well as the relationship of social enterprises with public sector organizations. Finally, there is a discussion on 'enterprising' social organizations with coverage of the international experience of such organizations and their strategies for success.

This discussion deals with social enterprises as being 'hybrid' organizations that do not lend themselves to convenient definitions. The question now arises: how can the ideas, knowledge and understanding of social enterprises outlined in this book be used, not only by a student who wishes to study social enterprise, but also by the practitioner who wishes to create a successful social enterprise?

In answering this question, we draw on the material contained within Chapters 1 to 9 to look into the 'recipe' for success for a social entrepreneur – someone who is intent on creating a new and successful social enterprise.

In order to focus the discussion, we present a series of questions that the social entrepreneur needs to ask themselves.

1. What makes social enterprises different?

The social enterprise as a business format is an emerging area of study. Definitions are continually being revised. However, we believe that the defining characteristic of a social enterprise is the desire to generate a surplus and the willingness for that surplus to be shared within a community however that is defined. Hence, a social enterprise is a business rather than a charitable venture that brings people and communities together for economic development and social gain. It does not distribute profit to private shareholders but seeks to be self-financing. It generates a surplus but this is not amassed for personal wealth by the directors but to be re-invested back into the community. Consistent with this is the idea of a social enterprise whose guiding principles are based on common ownership and accountability to a community.

When setting up a business, there is a choice:

> If you want the chance to be rich, create an SME. If you want to have an impact, create a social enterprise!

A small and medium-sized enterprise (SME) generates a surplus and that surplus is distributed internally to its founding members and investors. Both social enterprise and SME's aim to be profit generating; it is the distribution of this profit that is the distinguishing characteristic.

A voluntary organization has a social purpose in the same way that a social enterprise has a social purpose. The difference is that a voluntary organization does not seek to be self-sufficient by creating revenue streams. It raises the majority of its funding through trading activities. Voluntary organizations will often create subsidiaries that are social enterprises but they rely more on funding than on revenue generation. Both will ideally seek to create a surplus. A voluntary organization is a 'pure' form of social organization since it does not compromise its social mission by using resources to generate trading income.

> If you want to provide a service create or join a charity and secure one or more funding sources. If you do not want to depend upon external

funding sources create a social enterprise with the opportunity to have diverse forms of funding, and use that to secure your independence.

The evidence would indicate, especially in the current economic climate, that many of the social services previously provided by public bodies will increasingly be contracted out. This represents a major opportunity for the social entrepreneur.

2. Leveraging support

As the number of 'third sector' organizations increase, so this sector becomes a more established part of the business and social community. This means that there is a developing network of contacts and from the practitioner's perspective there is no need to re-invent business ideas and business methods. Two distinct forms of support exist.

1. Formal business support networks at national and regional levels are able to advise on marketing, finance and management skills.
2. Informal networks of social entrepreneurs, trustees and community representatives who have been through the experience of setting up and growing an enterprise can provide a more rounded picture.

If it is management skills you require then accessing the business support network is a good starting point during the start-up stage. If it is an understanding of how to grow a social enterprise then other social entrepreneurs will be better able to provide the insight that is required.

Both forms of support are important but it is informal access to the social 'actors' that will create a sustainable enterprise.

If you are not already a member of a social network then appoint a board that provides ready-made access to an extensive network of formal and informal contacts.

Access to an informal network is important for small firm entrepreneurs, but it is more important for the founders of a social enterprise. There will always be a tension between social goals and a commitment to a self-sustaining commercial operation. The advice of others who already understand how to reconcile these conflicts will be especially important during the early stages of growth. Without access to this advice an organization is unlikely to grow and if it does grow it may not be able to balance its social mission and its commercial activities.

3. The theory and the practice

Social enterprises have more in common with small and fast growing businesses than with larger corporate firms or the public sector. This means that the management thinking on entrepreneurship still applies.

The entrepreneurship link means that most general management textbooks provide a limited insight into the type of leadership and the type of organization best suited to a new social enterprise. This is important because there are business models that range from charitable to social action organizations. It is this model that determines the mix of tangible resources, service delivery, fund raising and revenue streams.

> If you want to grow a social enterprise, read about entrepreneurship and how entrepreneurs build their businesses.

However, the key distinguishing factor of (most) social organizations, like voluntary organizations, is their use of volunteers. While entrepreneurship is well covered in the media, being able to recruit and motivate volunteers is a less developed area.

> If you want control over your workforce then form a small business. If you want access to a diverse set of skills at below-market prices, create a volunteer-based organization.

It is important to note that the ability to recruit and retain volunteers is essential to the business model of most social enterprises. This is an area where it is best to seek the expert advice of others in the social enterprise network that are familiar with this process.

4. The entrepreneurial team

There is no evidence to suggest that social entrepreneurs, in terms of their personal characteristics, are different from any other entrepreneur. Entrepreneurs are usually represented as people who are 'disruptive' and who do not work within the existing institutional frameworks. In terms of their psychology, entrepreneurs tend to be outsiders. They have a high need to achieve and they tend to be seen as risk-taking. They also like to take control. They are often represented as people with a high tolerance for ambiguity and who respond well to uncertainty. This is reflected in their ability to be opportunistic and to be forward looking. It is these characteristics that make a (social) entrepreneur distinct from being a good manager. Being a manager means looking after existing policies and existing practices but being an entrepreneur means developing an enterprising organization.

> If you have management skills then you need to supplement these with entrepreneurial skills. If you have entrepreneurial skills then you need to surround yourself with people who have management skills.

What makes a social entrepreneur different is that they can be expected to behave in a socially responsible manner and their vision and their revenue streams are directly tied into serving specific community needs. In other words a social entrepreneur will use any earned income to pursue a social objective. Arguably, being a social entrepreneur is more challenging than being an entrepreneur!

This distinction refers to the 'double bottom line' argument that combines financial along with social returns. The important difference is not about personality; it is motivation that distinguishes the social entrepreneur. Both are creators of wealth and, through the process of innovation, agents of change.

> If you have the drive, if you have the ambition and if you have the determination you have a choice of creating a for-profit or not-for-profit business. If you do not have these entrepreneurial characteristics, find somebody who has!

An entrepreneurial team, with skills that are complementary will usually outperform an entrepreneurial individual. It is important to remember that being enterprising, which means being creative, flexible and adaptive to change, is a key characteristic for success. Being opportunity-focused means continually spotting new opportunities, building capacity and marshalling resources to take advantages of changes in the business environment.

It is one thing to be a social entrepreneur but the real challenge is to create an enterprising organization. Forming an entrepreneurial team is a starting point. It is also clear that stakeholders, both direct and indirect, need to buy into the vision. This is where the leadership skills of the entrepreneur will be tested.

5. Building an enterprising organization

One of the defining characteristics of the social entrepreneur is being visionary. Social visionaries envision, enact and enable. This usually means embracing change and deliberately developing an organization that is loosely structured and which has a culture that responds positively to change. While the most manageable change may be continuous, most organizations, especially in the public sector, respond with difficulty to punctuated change. For this reason a bureaucracy is the antithesis of an opportunity-seeking enterprising social organization.

The vision provides a sense of direction; it defines goals and objectives and provides a focus. It gives the enterprise its moral and social priorities and forms the basis of leadership. The vision can be expected to evolve and this means that the people, both staff and volunteers along with the income sources, may continue to change. A good social enterprise sells a dream and unlike a public sector body it does not avoid risk.

> If you do not have a dream or the means to make that dream come true, become part of a team that does. If you have a vision of a 'new and better world' use a social enterprise as a means of delivering real change within the community.

Once again the social enterprise shares the same characteristics as a fast growing small business. Voluntary organizations, on the other hand are more likely to be stable and consistent in terms of their management.

> If you like stability, work within the structure of a public sector organization or a larger voluntary organization. If you embrace change create a social enterprise.

6. Growing pains

We would argue that starting a social enterprise is easier than growing a social enterprise. If you can convince others that a need exists, advice and start-up funding is readily available but this, on its own, does not create a sustainable enterprise.

There is a distinct difference between a small growth-orientated business and a social enterprise. The former seeks to achieve commercial success for its founders while the latter looks to create sustainable economic activity that ensures the benefits of its trading activities are redirected back into the local community. Early-stage innovation is the key to creating a sustainable social enterprise. Social enterprises, just like any small business can be fast growing and market led – but only if they choose to be. The culture and the business environment of the organization will play a large part in determining its structure.

For an organization to grow it must be innovative, allowing original thinking and creativity to flourish. At the same time as it innovates, the social firm, unlike a small business, must manage the conflict between being integrated with its community and generating income.

Furthermore, the generation of income becomes all the more important since your social enterprise may not have access to bank-based debt funding. Most social enterprises start off 'boot strapping' but more sustainable income streams are required. Access to finance, whether it is funding through loans and grants or, better still, revenue streams, for products or services supplied, is critical to long-term success.

> If you have access to funding through grants or loans this is useful for the start-up process. If you wish to grow a social enterprise you will need additional diverse revenue streams.

It is important to note that not all social enterprises will wish to grow. A social enterprise is a community-based business that is often set up to serve just the local community so growth opportunities may be limited. Sometimes it is better to be a 'mouse' than a 'gazelle'!

7. Ethics and marketing

There is now general acceptance and desire at government level that public and voluntary sector organizations should behave in a more businesslike manner. This suggests that the third sector needs to be more businesslike and embrace a profit motive. However not all sorts of third sector organizations will embrace 'the free market'. Equally, not all private sector organizations are profit maximizing, with many operating with enlightened self-interest. For example, many Free Trade organizations in the developed world operate in this way creating surpluses to help others in the less developed part of the world.

> Ethical behaviour is not confined to the third sector. Small firms and corporations may share the same social goals and this provides an opportunity for a 'social partnership'.

Small firms and large public corporations can choose to be altruistic and work alongside the third sector in a social partnership.

8. Public enterprise

A social enterprise is one of a number of business formats within the 'third sector' which also includes voluntary, co-operative and mutual organizations. These formats tend to overlap, especially when it comes to the differences between a voluntary organization and a social enterprise. In some cases a social enterprise will be a subsidiary of a voluntary organization.

The legal differences are less important than the fact that third sector organizations, especially within the current economic environment, are being encouraged by policymakers. This encouragement is leading to a change in the relationship between consumers, public sector bodies and social organizations.

As hybrid organizations they are halfway between the private and public sectors. Here a distinction can be made between a social enterprise that works, either partially or fully within a market economy, and a voluntary organization which has a service agreement with public sector agencies.

Compared with SMEs, social and voluntary organizations present a problem – the measurement of their performance. Within the private sector, sales, profits, dividends and share price are key measures. In a social enterprise such measures can be lacking and this can encourage a culture of inefficiency. Social enterprises tend to be more concerned with intangibles such as relationships, often known as social capital. This includes levels of integration within communities and social networks that can be employed to recruit and retain volunteers.

This is not to say that social enterprises are not regulated. The rules governing charitable bodies are being revised and this is likely to have a major impact on the role of governors and on the use of volunteers.

> If you have management training in marketing, finance or HR these have real value in a voluntary or public sector body. If you are a community activist, create a social enterprise but you will need to rethink these traditional skills to encompass social capital.

9. Enterprising organizations

There is no single ideal organizational structure for an enterprising social organization. However, when markets change, an informal and opportunistic organization will be able to outperform a bureaucracy. However, as an organization matures it will tend to become more formal. As it grows it becomes less enterprising.

Being enterprising means being adaptable and challenging the status quo.

The role of the social entrepreneur is to revitalize structures to allow a social enterprise to achieve its mission. This means being innovative and being creative, both of which are classed as being enterprising, unlike management, which is about tasks. Being enterprising is something that is learnt – it is an approach to business. This further reinforces the importance of having trustees who have access to a wide social network – people who are collectively willing to seize opportunities and, through trial and error, create an enterprising organization.

This point is important. It means that the social entrepreneur is less important than the entrepreneurial team. This team, in turn is less important than having an enterprising organization – one that rejects established methods, invents new alternatives, behaves unconventionally and has a high level of self-belief.

Structure follows strategy, which means the vision is more important than the planning processes.

A business strategy is like a map, guiding the social enterprise towards its goal. A good strategy should never be bogged down in the unnecessary detail of a plan.

As a business grows, so the strategy often changes. These changes represent a balance between the environment, the values and the resources available (EVR).

This can mean that the social enterprise must evolve in order to survive. It is this requirement we hope that this text has equipped you for.

index